The 21st Century Army Strategy for Future

THE 21ST CENTURY ARMY STRATEGY FOR FUTURE

Col. M.N. Sodhi (Retd.)

PRASHANT PUBLISHING HOUSE
DELHI-110094

Published by :
Prashant Publishing House
C-34, 28 Foota Road, Gali-3,
West Karwal Nagar, Delhi-110094
Phone : 011-22963970, Mob. : 9810396373
e-mail.: prashantpublishinghouse@gmail.com

The 21st Century Army Strategy for Future

First Published 2015

ISBN 978-93-80565-53-8

PRINTED IN INDIA
Published by Mr. R.K. Jha M/s Prashant Publishing House and Published at H.S. Offset House Press, Delhi.

Preface

The Army Leader Development Strategy (ALDS) builds on our Army's experiences since the end of the Cold War including the past eight years of war in Iraq and Afghanistan and on our assessment that the future operational environment will be even more uncertain, complex, and competitive as hybrid threats challenge us across the full spectrum of operations.

The Indian Army enters the 21st century having just fought a brief conflict with tactics developed in the first half of the 20th century. It has been engaged in operations for much of the last decade giving it both the opportunity to evaluate some tactics but detracting from the time to prepare for other eventualities. It faces the unenviable task of fighting a low cost insurgency fuelled by narcotics trafficking from Pakistan, while preparing for a full scale war, perhaps under NBC conditions, with two countries. How it focuses on both these tasks will determine its success as an institution in the coming decades.

The Indian Army entered the 1990s, wounded by its endeavors in Sri Lanka. Peace enforcement in Sri Lanka exposed many shortcomings in Indian Army. In the heady days of mechanization in the mid-1980s, the Army neglected to reinforce small unit tactics. Exercises were conducted with tanks and armored personnel carriers leaving little thought for infantry operations. Big ticket items like T-72s, BMPs, bridge- laying vehicles, 155mm artillery, Multi-Barrel Rocket Launchers (MBRLs) were purchased, while less glamorous items like better assault rifles, night vision devices, better body armor/helmets were neglected. This resulted in the Army getting into close combat operations with an enemy who was better equipped. Worse, due to the nature of the terrain and the political constraints the heavier equipment was not brought to bear on the enemy. Furthermore, the Army's communication equipment and its communication procedures were outdated. Ultimately, there was a complete underestimation of the enemy. This was a problem repeated again at the end of the century.

The Indian Army modernization and expansion plan had envisaged a dedicated aviation wing for the SF way back in 2001. An internal exercise to examine various proposals from different agencies to get the maximum advantage seemed to have been truncated and shelved. Low cost and low maintenance fixed-wing aircraft operating with ground troops have their advantages. However, operations from the field imply having to be concerned with tactical dispersion, camouflage, enemy situation, assembly area security, ground- to-ground as well as ground-to-air communication issues, and maintaining aircraft in a field environment.

The future prospects for global military interventionism are questionable at best. However much a state or group of states might dominate at the high end of the power spectrum, and however much diplomacy may postpone or alleviate problems, the cost of trying and failing to control a rogue state are likely to rise to points that reward caution, and military leaderships are apt to encourage such prudence. On the other hand, as the experience of the Vietnam War suggests, politicians lacking knowledge of military affairs listen only to the advice they want to hear and even manipulate promotions to ensure that they hear it, and politicians can usually find within the military officers willing to tell them what they want in order to advance or protect their own careers. Thus it is possible that the imperatives of political commitments to, for example, Israel or Taiwan, may override prudence in a crisis.

This book is expected at providing to the fresh and approaching generation of Indian Army leaders, an approaching into the military challenges of the current era and representation them to the articulations of modern military philosophy.

—Editor

Contents

Contents

1

Shaping a 21st-Century Defence Strategy

SHAPING A 21ST-CENTURY DEFENCE STRATEGY: RECONCILING MILITARY ROLES

The principal stimulus driving the need for change is the 2012 Defence Strategic Guidance, which sustains the security strategy shift from deterrence and containment to cooperation through engagement. The emerging consensus suggests the future national security strategy will direct a regionally tailored force for limited engagement. As with any fundamental shift in national policy objectives, strategy, or operational concepts, the initial guidance is seldom the last word. The military must be sized and resourced to adapt to the realities of strategy and policy adjustments as they occur. It is critical that military capabilities are resourced for the national strategy and that they posture the joint force to create and seize opportunities. The objective is a military that protects and advances U.S. interests in times of peace while providing robust and flexible options to confront aggression worldwide.

A SHIFT FROM CONTAINMENT TO ENGAGEMENT

To establish context for the emerging military narratives, it is necessary to trace the trajectory of the national security debate since the end of World War II. The Cold War grand strategy, often attributed to "the father of containment" George Kennan, carried the Nation through the last half of the 20th century. In his famous "X article" published in 1947, Kennan advocated replacing cooperation with the Soviet Union with a strategy of long-term containment of their expansionist philosophies. While the strategy matured during the Cold War, the military's role remained stable. With a few notable exceptions, the Armed Forces provided credible and robust conventional combat capability to defend national interests, exercised legitimate coercive power to maintain international order through containment, and demonstrated a mutually assured destruction capability that discouraged nuclear confrontation.

With the demise of the Soviet Union and the end of the Cold War, a search for a new grand strategy narrative began. President George H.W. Bush presented a vision of a "new world order" to Congress in 1990 that emphasized "cooperation," where "nations of the world can prosper and live in harmony." President Bill Clinton described how the vision could be achieved through a strategy of "engagement and enlargement," thus giving it structure. This particular strategy relied primarily on economic and diplomatic efforts, backed by military force, and was designed to expand the global reach of democracy and economic prosperity. President George W. Bush's National Security Strategy reiterated many of the tenets of the earlier post–Cold War security strategies. Faced with the new reality of terrorist attacks and the emergent demands of two simultaneous wars, Bush emphasized the role of military power and highlighted the U.S. prerogative for preemptive action to counter rogue states or terrorist organizations that might strike without warning. While President Barack Obama's 2010 National Security Strategy acknowledged the role of the military, it reverted to much of the language related to cooperation and burden-sharing reflective of the 1990s.

The national security strategy is in transition again. The strategic environment presents a weak global economy, a struggling U.S. economy, and shrinking defence resources. While the current national security strategy is not fully developed or articulated, it appears to conform to a general trajectory evident since the Cold War, from containment and deterrence to cooperation and engagement, with more limited ambitions than those initially expressed in the 1990s. This emerging narrative is designed to address a security environment that includes a nonhostile but rising rival in Asia (China), international nuclear proliferation (Iran, Pakistan, and North Korea), revolutions against existing world order (the Arab Spring in the African Maghreb and Egypt), continued unrest in the Middle East (the Levant), and growing concern over instability and violence (Mexico and other Central/South American nations) in the Western Hemisphere.

The national security strategy narrative is expected to focus on engagement and cooperative relationships to advance U.S. interests and establish a stable international order. It should appropriately emphasize the use of economic and diplomatic means backed by the limited use of the military as a coercive instrument of national power. In this era of fiscal austerity, emerging consensus emphasizes a regionally tailored military strategy of limited engagement.

The current Defence Strategic Guidance (January 2012) directs the military to adapt to the future strategic environment even as it remains a "global presence emphasizing the Asia-Pacific and the Middle East" and at the same time is "prepared to confront and defeat aggression anywhere in the world," all with a much smaller size and reduced resources. In underwriting this strategy, the Secretary of Defence is expected to develop a joint force that is "smaller and leaner" but "will remain agile, flexible, ready, innovative, and technologically advanced." This is a tall order that requires prioritization and trade-off of risk. The security establishment requires a model for dynamic force adaptation and a framework to develop the narrative that guides prioritization.

The organizational concept of dynamic equilibrium may provide such a model. It draws on an ecological system metaphor to examine an organizational response to a changing environment. The "open system" ecological metaphor is rooted in chaos, complexity, and systems theories. Several elements of the metaphor can be applied to the military's adaptation to the evolving threat, security, and operational environments.

The dynamic equilibrium metaphor captures the interactive and multidimensional nature of systems and the continuous adaptive change imposed by each member of an ecosystem on the other. This interactive adaptation is a dynamic where the norm is constant change in response to multiple simultaneous stimuli from other members and elements of the system. There are two broad mechanisms of change within the theory—iterative evolution and rapid adaptation. The first is more common in nature. The second can produce rapid (transformational or revolutionary) change, but just as often results in the death of many members of the system and the emergence of a new ecosystem. Death occurs when an organism stops adapting and no longer actively influences or is influenced by the system. The remaining sections address several dimensions of the military's environment that must be considered as our leaders adapt the joint force for the future.

Equilibrium in the Military Narrative

Threat versus Opportunity. National security literature tends toward threat-based analysis. Security studies and military planning are likely to focus on approaches that prevent unfavorable order and unacceptable levels of disorder, while identifying and planning for black swan contingencies. Conversely, contemporary organizational and business literatures promote strategies that focus on opportunity identification and exploitation.

Applying this opportunity perspective to security strategy and military implementation concepts can facilitate the identification of alternative approaches to achieving national objectives. Instead of physically "pivoting" to the Asia-Pacific and Middle East, one could envision a strategy that employs military power in various regions to rebalance our global efforts to indirectly influence the regions prioritized by U.S. national leadership. In addition one may develop innovative ways to exploit military relationships and partnerships while employing other instruments of national power.

Time Horizons Equilibrium. The military narrative should include linkages to current policy, strategy, and resources while engaging proactively in actions that adapt the organization to future threats, opportunities, and political perspectives. This results in two time horizons for strategic decisions that affect force development. The near-term horizon is driven by prioritized distribution of available resources, which has to be justified in the context of current national strategy and policy objectives. The long-term horizon is based on estimates of future threats, operational environment opportunities, and the range of potential strategy and policy decisions that may be pursued by future administrations. The long-term horizon requires senior leaders to establish aspirational goals and a vision of the range of military capabilities to achieve them. The Services' primary concern is with the near-term horizon, which requires the distribution of resources to maintain readiness while initiating the evolutionary change and development initiatives that move the force in the direction of the long-term vision.

Military Strategy Equilibrium. Absolute war and peace are archetypal states that are never fully realized. Competition spans a continuum from the civil order of peace through major combat manifested by war. Unattended turmoil and misunderstandings among nonhostile rivals can lead to escalation of hostility and increased incidence of extreme violence. Similarly, managing disorder within the context of combat operations is necessary to nurture the civil order associated with peace.

The U.S. security establishment has acknowledged the vital role of the military in shaping the security environment. In 1997, Chairman of the Joint Chiefs of Staff General John Shalikashvili stated, "The military has an important role in engagement—helping to shape the international environment in appropriate ways to bring about a more peaceful and stable world." In the next sentence he provided a caveat: "The purpose of our Armed Forces, however, is to deter and defeat threats of organized violence to our country and its interests." When faced with austere budgets, reduced force structure, and uncertain futures, senior civilian and military leaders typically revert to a rhetoric dominated by the force sizing and prioritization mantra to "fight and win the Nation's wars," with all other uses of the military being "lesser-included" capabilities.

The military's force-sizing construct since the Cold War has been a two-theaters strategy. While arguably underresourced, the construct was based on an aspiration to fight and win two nearly simultaneous major regional contingencies. In his February 2014 press conference, Secretary Hagel conveyed that the construct was now passé and stated as well that "we are no longer sizing the military to conduct long and large stability operation." He went on to say that the Army will be sized to decisively defeat aggression in one major combat theatre while defending the homeland and supporting a joint force engagement in another theatre.

When not engaged in war, the military structure and its inherent capabilities are available to America's political leaders for other missions. In practice the military does a great deal more than simply preparing for and executing regional contingencies and major combat operations. Especially with regard to landpower, a force capable of fighting two major regional contingencies can accomplish a number of "lesser-included" tasks during periods of relative peace. The deterrent quality of a ready force is intended to provide the Nation with sufficient coercive power to discourage the escalation of national rivalries into major combat operations. Should that deterrence fail, the military's mission has historically been to decisively defeat the enemy.

Realist/Balancer versus Idealist/Engagement Foreign Policy. Air-Sea Battle has occupied a great portion of the public debate regarding the military's strategic narrative since the release of the Defence Strategic Guidance. Air-Sea Battle's key characteristics include military involvement starting at the commencement of hostilities, withstanding an initial attack, executing a blinding and suppression campaign against enemy long-range intelligence, reconnaissance, and surveillance (ISR) and strike systems, and seizing the initiative in the sea, air, space, and cyberspace domains. From this posture, the execution of the concept would create time for "options to resolve a prolonged conventional conflict on favourable terms" through blockades, sustained logistics, and the expansion of military and industrial production.

Considerations of the role landpower plays in this operational concept appeared late in the concept's development. But even as a latecomer, landpower's role was soon recognized in clearing coastal areas of surface-to-ship missiles, providing for land-based air defence, and performing myriad sustainment functions associated with establishing theatre operations and sustaining the joint force. As this joint operational concept is further developed, it is likely that the vital role for landpower will be better understood.

If the United States adopts a realist foreign policy, the approach of balancing rising powers with regional partners and preserving the ability to counter rivals once hostilities commence is a sound strategy. The Air-Sea Battle operational concept facilitates countering a hostile enemy with strategic stand-off and antiaccess/area-denial capabilities.

However, senior national security leaders should reconsider the utility of resourcing an operational concept that limits the range of military options to direct confrontation, especially when countering nonhostile rivals. Such an approach seems unwise, especially in cases where the rival's economic markets may be closely linked to the U.S. economy. This limited approach would leave our leaders with few military options to counter a rival that confronts the Nation directly with economic and diplomatic power, and employs military power through distant or amorphous proxies. One can easily envision the coercive power levers a rival could bring to bear short of hostilities, making military employment options and posturing to deter hostilities moot.

The prioritization of resources to prepare the military for the future must accommodate both the future security environment and the political reality that U.S. policy and international action do not align perfectly with either realist or idealist perspectives of political science theory. Actual policy and international political choice reflect a hybrid approach. The range of military capabilities must accommodate options for dealing with the future environment that are based in both realist and idealist perspectives.

American Landpower: Prevent–Shape–Win

The Army Chief of Staff (CSA) has Title 10 responsibilities to field the Army and sustain America's joint force. General Ray Odierno, in the 2012 Army Posture Statement, presented the Army's primary roles as prevent, shape, and win, with readiness, force structure, and modernization as the principal rheostats to adjust resource prioritization to adapt the Army to the strategic and fiscal environment: Current military force sizing is based on a "fight and win" philosophy. The fight and win imperative encompasses decisive joint combat capabilities for the rapid defeat of enemies and a decisive end to hostilities.

The "win to prevent" paradigm offers two paths to achieving a political objective prior to the onset of combat. A force-in-being's "win" capabilities discourage opportunistic rivals from engaging in hostilities and prevent hostility expansion to other regions after the start of conflict. America must maintain a legitimate military deterrent power by fielding a force-in-being capable of decisively defeating any enemy while demonstrating the political will to use it.

The Air-Sea Battle concept combined with operational concepts for landpower (combined arms maneuver, wide area security, counterinsurgency, and counterterrorism doctrines) provide the basis for decisive combat operations to accomplish the military's "win" mission. Air-Sea Battle facilitates coercive access to contested areas, thereby enabling landpower forces to deploy, stabilize, and exploit successes in the accomplishment of strategic objectives. However, short of resorting to coercive methods and direct hostilities, an emphasis on "win" capabilities offers few military options using cooperation and engagement to address rivals who choose to challenge U.S. interests.

The military's ability to shape the security environment addresses such nonhostile or indirect competition. In addition, shaping provides for the establishment of conditions that support a return to civil order once employment of "win" capabilities manages extant hostilities.

The shaping function is directed toward influencing the focal nation's people and leadership. Influencing segments of a society and their leadership short of conflict is achieved largely through trust relationships and cooperative engagements. For the military these operations are normally landpower-centric. Thus, in addition to traditional fight and win capabilities, the Army needs to develop an ethos that embraces shaping as part of its warrior culture.

"Shape to win" and "shape to prevent" paradigms have their own mechanisms to achieve desired objectives. The "shape to win" model is analogous to flexible deterrent options and has been associated with campaign planning for decades. The "shape to prevent" model manifests itself in several ways, with the common theme of enriching cooperation and partnerships that contribute to favourable order. Shaping contributes to achieving national security objectives in environments that span conditions from civil order to war and back to civil order.

The shaping role contributes to winning and preventing war in a number of ways:

- Forward presence shaping operations provide early warning by means of regional cultural engagement, and opportunities to gather human intelligence and geographic access through established relationships.
- The shaping role develops a cooperation-based capacity and desire for regional partners to confront military challenges in a manner that could not be achieved independently.
- Conducting shaping operations with supportive partners can block rival power ambitions short of hostilities; it is a realist/balancing argument.
- Shaping operations conducted with potentially opportunistic partners offer positive cooperative engagement incentives short of confrontation to modify their behavior.

- Shaping facilitates U.S. force redeployment following hostilities with some assurance of leaving the foundations of sustainable civil order behind.
- Shaping operations permit the military to contribute to the engagement and enlargement objectives associated with promoting liberty under the rule of law, human rights, and the subordination of the military to legitimate civil authority throughout the peace-war continuum.

Unlike combat operations, shaping does not require the threat of hostilities to execute. The military can conduct Building Partner Capacity, Security Cooperation, Stability, and Security Force Assistance missions in the absence of a threat; or it can combine these shaping operations with counterinsurgency and counterterror combat missions to synergistic effect in nonpermissive security environments short of major combat operations.

In 2005, Department of Defence (DOD) Directive 3000.05 established security operations as a core military mission. It directed that stability (shaping) operations "shall be given priority comparable to combat operations." On a national scale, this effort was reinforced when President George W. Bush signed National Security Presidential Directive 44 directing the Department of State to be lead agent, using the Office of the Coordinator of Reconstruction and Stabilization to coordinate and harmonize all strategies and plans associated with reconstruction and stabilization activities for states transitioning from conflict and civil strife.

More recently the 2012 Defence Budget Guidance, which followed the Defence Strategic Guidance, called for "a fresh approach to the traditional 'two war' force-sizing construct that had shaped defence planning since the end of the cold war." Yet, of the military's 10 primary missions outlined in the guidance, only 4 are designated as criteria for force sizing. Three of the four involve building the capacity to win wars. The shaping missions that provide stabilizing presence and support counterinsurgency operations are accompanied by specified caveats limiting their resourcing.

Both 2012 defence guidance documents convey that the U.S. security establishment is more focused on defeating threats than developing military capabilities to manage the security environment. Americans understandably prefer short-duration, decisive conflicts, and they frequently consider wars to be acts of political choice. However, in *The Utility of Force*, Rupert Smith presents a convincing argument that protracted conflicts "among the people" represent the reality of modern warfare. Managing the security environment through shaping offers an attractive alternative to either proposition—decisive large-scale conflict or protracted war "among the people." First, shaping operations provide a feasible and prudent alternative in which U.S. military capabilities advance cooperative behaviors to maintain a stable security environment short of coercive hostility. Second, involvement in wars and deteriorating security environments is not always subject to U.S. preference or choice. History is replete with examples of Washington being compelled to military action to restore order or confront aggression. Forward presence shaping operations can provide early warning and offer noncoercive access, thereby opening a range of military options to prevent war or restore civil order short of major combat operations. Unfortunately, shaping operations associated with forward presence, partnering to build relationships, security cooperation, and stability operations continue to be misunderstood, undervalued, and underresourced in austere economic environments.

The development of shaping operations requires the deliberate resourcing of specific force design, readiness, and modernization initiatives. Embracing shaping does not imply undervaluing the imperative to "fight and win the Nation's wars." Shaping and winning operations are appropriately designed to provide complementary capabilities. One generally accepted lesson has emerged from the last several decades of conflict: the resultant civil order—not the defeat of a specific threat—defines victory in modern warfare. By necessity, if there are insufficient resources to prepare for both missions simultaneously, a portion of the force may temporarily focus on the "win" or "shape" role during a particular operation or deployment. But that does not absolve operational units of the requirement to conduct either decisive combat or shaping operations with a limited amount of predeployment or rotational training.

America's security establishment should acknowledge the vital role of landpower as the force capable of shaping a population-centric security environment, whether through the coercive power of combat operations or the influence generated by shaping operations. "Shape to prevent" and "shape to win" models define the respective conditions necessary to achieve political and military victory in modern warfare.

The arguments against resourcing shaping capabilities and capacities align generally with the following themes. First, it is not the function of DOD or the Army to execute these operations.

The activities associated with shaping operations, primarily Building Partner Capacity, Security Cooperation, and Stability (especially when they involve development or law enforcement) fall outside DOD's roles, missions, and authorities. For this reason, national leaders are reluctant to commit resources to build DOD capabilities to engage in these operations, and security-minded interagency partners are not willing to allow the department to assume responsibility for their execution.

Shaping operations are necessary to prevent conflict, mitigate its impact, and provide the opportunity to transition to some form of a sustainable civil order. In the last decade of war, no Federal agency has marshaled the resources or changed its capability sufficiently to execute these missions as well as the Army.

Some adjustments in roles, missions, and authorities are therefore necessary to enable other agencies to set objectives and provide oversight when developing plans, while requiring the Army to develop and design tailored capabilities to execute these missions. Once U.S. political leadership recognizes the value of military shaping operations as a legitimate foreign policy execution tool during peacetime, the Army will have to embrace the shaping mission within its professional jurisdiction.

A military argument for resisting the prioritization of resources for shaping capabilities is a belief that any reduction in the "fight and win" capability will endanger the military's contract with the American people—to win the Nation's wars. Adherents to this view proffer the opinion that should the military fail at shaping, there are other Federal departments and agencies capable of providing assistance. There is not, however, another agency that can fight and win the Nation's wars.

This argument has merit. DOD and the Services cannot abandon their duty to win wars: The notion of winning in modern warfare (and arguably throughout history) involves a great deal more than simply defeating the enemy's army or planting the U.S. flag in the enemy's capital. It involves encouraging legitimate government and developing indigenous force capabilities that permit U.S. disengagement with some assurance of sustainable security and order.

Conclusion

In summer 2013, DOD's Cost Assessment and Program Evaluation organization released the results of the Strategic Choices and Management Review (SCMR) study directed by Secretary of Defence Chuck Hagel. The SCMR provided resource prioritization guidance to the Quadrennial Defence Review effort within three broad funding bands. It did not alter the regionally prioritized, limited engagement strategy proposed in the 2012 Defence Strategic Guidance.

The continuity of the U.S. post–Cold War security strategy of cooperative engagement, implemented through economic and diplomatic instruments of power reinforced by military power, is appealing. The past two decades suggest that even altruistic aspirations to spread democracy, human rights, and economic prosperity through diplomacy and economic initiatives alone are often foiled by adversaries with different agendas. U.S. military leadership must embrace civilian leaders' expressed desire to reduce the size and economic burden of the force, while at the same time preparing it for the full range of potential confrontations.

The argument that the military must retain the ability to "fight and win the Nation's wars" when shaping operations are resourced as lesser included capabilities is incongruous with current national security strategy aspirations. And it is not realistic to expect the whole-of-government engagement capability to increase given the current fiscal environment. The argument to limit resource expenditures, however, is compelling in light of U.S. fiscal circumstances. Faced with a volatile operating environment, austere resources, and an ambiguous group of adversaries, the Nation must strive for dynamic equilibrium as it adapts the joint force to win conflicts, manage security environments, and shape civil order within constrained resources. The new security culture must embrace the military's "shape" and "win" roles. Shaping operations are primarily landpower centric because they are conducted in the human domain among the people. The Army must and will carry the burden of successfully executing shaping operations in support of America's foreign policy security goals.

Current defence guidance charges the military with defeating future threats and protecting national interests worldwide. To do that in an austere resource environment, the force must improve operational effectiveness and efficiency in both combat and shaping capabilities. The Army's recent addition of a seventh warfighting function, Engagement, is an appropriate and needed addition to its doctrine. The next iteration of defence guidance should prioritize the military's role in shaping operations during peacetime as well as recognize the requirement to conduct combat operations. The future operational environment demands a robust military capability to win conflicts among the people, while improving cooperative engagement shaping capabilities to maintain or restore peace

2

Rebalancing the US Military for 21st Century Threats

INTRODUCTION

First of all the DOD never uses the word pivot. There is a reason for that. If the critics are talking about the rhetoric, they are reading something into it that it is not. We talked about rebalancing to Asia because there was a perception in Asia that we were turning away from Asia. And there were 2 main reasons why people in Asia thought that.

Number one was that in the Rumsfeld-Bush era their vision was that we shouldn't be engaged abroad very much. That was applied to Europe as well. They wanted to retrench from Europe and they wanted to retrench from Asia. They were doing it. When we came in 2009 we said let's take a look at this. This doesn't make sense. The Koreans were as upset about this as the Europeans. Our partners and Allies in Asia were asking what is going on here? We put the breaks on and reversed it in many ways.

The second reason was that for the last 10 years we were massively bogged down in the Middle East. When we say rebalancing to Asia we are not talking necessarily about moving assets and forces from Europe to Asia, but we are sending this message: listen, we've been really focused in the Middle East, we've been bogged down in two wars that are coming to an end and to be responsible national security professionals, responsible shepherds of our defence, responsible managers of the tax payers money, we need to be thinking what comes next in 5,10, 20 years out. And that is what we said: we need to restructure, like you do after every war, we will downsize, back to about the size we were before 9/11. That is what we do in America: when we have a war, we build the military out and then bring it back down. It will be absolutely irresponsible to sustain the level of spending and the size of the military that we have had for the last 8 to 10 years. It just doesn't make sense. What makes sense is to say the following: the world has changed, the threats of the 21st century are different, they require sophisticated multilateral approaches, new technologies, new ways of fighting, new ways of operating with our Allies. Geopolitically, we need to recognize that Asia is as important as Europe. EU is our biggest trading partners and second is Asia. When you think how the trade flows through the Indian Ocean, through the straits of Malacca, we need to secure these global commons. It will be absolutely irresponsible for us as a Pacific Power not to be thinking how our resources should be allocated and reallocated. Secretary Panetta said that the goal is that 60% of our maritime forces will be focused in the Pacific and 40% in Atlantic. Of course we need to keep an eye on what is happening in the Middle East especially on the actions and activities of Iran that continues to be a spoiler in the region.

The vision for Europe is also very clear. NATO is our number one security Alliance, primer security Alliance on the face of Earth and in the history of the world. America has provided leadership for 60 years there. We are going to continue that. But we are going to do that with the focus on the threats of the 21st century not with the focus on the Cold War mindset. Rumsfeld said the same thing, but his attitude was that the Cold War was over so let's come home. Our attitude is that the Cold War is over, the world is a dangerous place but in a very different way. When you think what we did in Libya, America led a pretty broad coalition with NATO, a high-tech military operation, that requires a lot of sophisticated interoperability. That is the kind of example of the things we want to focus on - more intelligence interoperability, more missile defence architecture. These are big investments that indicate our resolve and commitment and it is the exact opposite of abandoning Europe.

The overall idea is that we are not focused any more on the Soviet Union coming crossing the Fulda Gap and the massive amounts of troops that you would need for that. It is not clear to me related to the European based critics to what threats they are looking at. We still have 8 brigades in Europe. We still have more that we have in Korea. We have a lot of airpower and we are enhancing our Special Ops capabilities. Iran is a definitely a threat and that is what the missile defence is all about. One of the biggest threats to Europe is terrorism. It is less military and mostly a law enforcement issue. It is certainly not something for the heavy brigades. Cyber-threats are important so the technological relationships we have with the Europeans partners are huge. The Navy presence is also enhanced because of the missile defence. The overall numbers actually are not going down so much in Europe. It is very much a rebalance to a posture that is much more adequate for meeting what we see as being the 21st century threats.

What does the Obama's shifting away from the Cold War posture of US forces mean for Europe? How could the credibility of the Article 5 commitment of the NATO Treaty be preserved in this context?

I think NATO (and correspondingly, the US's military posture in Europe) has been "shifting away" from the Cold War focus for the last 20 years, and rightly so. NATO has been adapting to the changing geopolitical landscape, starting with the fall of the Berlin Wall. The changes the Obama Administration is making to its NATO posture today are designed specifically with article 5 in mind and with a sense of the changing nature of conflict and the most likely threats facing the alliance in the coming decades. It is future-focused. Gone are the days when massive numbers of ground forces on point for a fight in the Fulda Gap meant "security." NATO needed a qualitative shift in capabilities in order to meet the most likely challenges of the 21st century.

Because the media has focused on the downsizing of two of our four Brigade Combat Teams (BCTs), people have falsely inferred that our presence in Europe is being slashed. On the contrary, while two Brigade Combat Teams, (around 7000 troops) will be part of the U.S. Army's overall downsizing (that is, they will be inactivating entirely, not coming home to the continental US), other more relevant capabilities are being added and the remaining BCTs are being enhanced. Thus, the net changes in numbers to the US presence in Europe are not great.

Remaining in Europe are two modernized BCT's – a Stryker brigade and an airborne brigade, plus seven other enabling brigades. The remaining BCTs will actually grow a bit in size as they are modernized as part of the Army's modularity plan. The Army's new modular structure adds capabilities in intelligence, medical, engineering, etc to each brigade in order to make them more agile and responsive to new sorts of threats. So, to sum it up, the old heavy units will go away and the remaining ones will be larger and optimized for modern war.

But our presence in Europe is not just about numbers of ground troops. Our missile defence infrastructure, air power and airlift projection as well as special forces capabilities are more relevant to current and future threats than large traditional Army maneuver units. Accordingly, the Obama Administration has preserved and enhanced these capabilities in its European posture.

Which are the strategic virtues/roles of the US forward defence and posture in the current strategic landscape? What message would send a radical US retrenchment to the world, its allies and regional opportunistic powers? Which are the dangers of US retrenchment?

A "radical US retrenchment" would be a very bad idea. This is why the Obama Administration is focused on smart forward engagement and partnership. The challenges the world faces in the coming decades require savvy, multilateral responses. From a military perspective, multilateral operations require training and engagement in advance of a crisis. We must train the way we will fight – and that means training as an alliance. This is why our posture in Europe recognizes NATO as the indispensible military alliance and is optimized to enhance the capability of the alliance through forward presence and multilateral training and exercises.

How can the US remain in the business of providing credible strategic reassurance in a time of scarce military resources, rebalanced geographical focus away from the Cold War and the maturation of regional anti-access/area denial capabilities?

The shift in US posture happening today is necessary as we come down from Iraq and Afghanistan. 10 years of war in these regions was costly in terms of blood and treasure. Over 2 million US troops have rotated in and out of these wars. Thus, as the wars wind down, we are faced with have the opportunity to re-orient our military posture and focus on areas of the world that have had less attention, such as Asia.

From a global perspective, maintaining our credibility is about sustained engagement. In fact, as the military gets a bit smaller, it actually makes sense to keep more of our forces abroad. The point is, there are relatively fixed costs for housing and training U.S. soldiers, sailors, airmen and marines, no matter where they are. So posturing forces forward where they can train with allies and partners makes fiscal sense. As I pointed out in a recent Foreign Affairs article: "The United States should position its forces to provide national security in the most efficient and responsible way possible. In the coming years, the U.S. military will likely be operating in a tight budget environment, but Washington can get more for less by positioning a larger percentage of its forces in key regions. Take, for example, the rotation cycles of U.S. naval ships. For every ship out securing sea lanes or deterring aggression, there are three others in various stages of maintenance or in transit. Porting ships closer to their areas of operation in Europe or Asia would save each vessel three to four weeks in transit time and would require keeping one-third fewer ships in U.S. inventories. That alone would save billions of dollars in acquisition, operations, and maintenance costs. Similarly, the strategic forward stationing of U.S. forces, combined with periodic rotations by U.S. forces to train with allies, makes the best use of American resources, enhances cooperation and burden sharing, and ensures that the military is positioned and ready to respond to emerging threats and crises."

You have highlighted in your book "Lifting the Fog of Peace: How Americans Learned to Fight Modern War" in what way did the generation exposed to the operations of the 1990s in Panama, Somalia and the Balkans (Bosnia and Kosovo) change the organizational culture of the US military. In what way do you expect that the post 9/11 generation exposed to the COIN battlefields in Iraq and Afghanistan will change the US military organizational culture?

The 1990's generation was a generation that expected adaptation to be a core competency. This mentality, forged in the post Vietnam era and the rise of the training centers and the lessons learned processes, was what enabled the U.S. military to adapt to the problems in Iraq and Afghanistan. The 1990's generation, like the one that has grown up fighting in Iraq and Afghanistan, has a keen sense of the human elements of modern conflict. I think this focus on the complexity of modern conflict will be reflected as the younger generation moves into leadership positions across the military and national security field.

In a time when there is a huge pressure to rebalance away from the post 9/11 battlefields and mindsets is the US military in danger to purge itself again from the COIN/stability operations know-how?

Of course, as the wars in Iraq and Afghanistan wind down, the overall size of the military will shrink a bit, but the DoD's new strategy clearly directs the US military to sustain its competency in this mission area. The US military has been doing these types of missions for 250 years. They have always been messy and frustrating and they have always been controversial. In each generation there have been those in the military who have falsely assumed that such mission types could be avoided. The worst mistake for the military to make would be to assume that if they avoid planning and organizing for them then they will be able to avoid them in general. The nature of conflict will continue to be human focused. As I said in recent NIC blog post:

"some national security and military leaders may think that now that we are winding down in Afghanistan and Iraq, we will be able to actively avoid anything resembling those population-centric missions in future. But it is a simple fact of military planning – especially in a democracy – that the military does not get to chose where it gets sent, what wars it will fight, what enemies it will face and in which environments. An increasingly urbanized world means the military will find itself in cities, among crowded populations, and fighting savvy enemies who have been paying close attention, learning, and adapting."

What kind of skills should have a contemporary soldier in order to be prepared for winning the peace in today's and tomorrow's battlefields? What kind of soldier do we need in order to be able to respond to "more Mumbai, Mogadishu and Tivoli Gardens" (David Kilcullen) or be prepared for the fact that "any activity a soldier undertakes can rapidly evolve into a combination of combat, governance, and civil support missions" (General Raymond Odierno)? A hybrid/full spectrum one?

We need troops who understand the cultural and legal landscape in which they will find themselves. The line between crime and war is increasingly blurred. Tomorrow's soldiers will need to be fully integrated with law enforcement to meet the complex challenges presented by Mumbai types of events as well as the transnational threats of piracy, trafficking. These bad actors actively exploit our cultural and bureaucratic predispositions to bifurcate police work from military work and they find ways to operate at the edge of the gap between crime and war for which conventional governmental organizations are not well suited.

Why did COIN become a dirty word in Washington? In 2009 during the Afghan surge it was a very trendy notion. And to what extent the DOD decision not to size the future force for large-scale Iraq or Afghanistan-like stability operations signals a larger rejection of pop-centric COIN type of operations?

Military leaders who read the strategic document that was published in January, which said that we are no longer sized for Iraq and Afghanistan and infer that that means giving up all the lessons we learned in Iraq and Afghanistan are massively if not willfully misread the Guidance.

The Guidance from the President and the Secretary of Defence says clear in there, you don't even need to read between the lines, you could read the actual language, that the military is directed to retain the capabilities and the expertise. And there is a reason for that.

The world is going to continue to require, it not may be an insurgency and it might not require an intervention for counterinsurgency but it may, but even if it doesn't, it will definitely require population-focused boots on the grounds types of operations. It is part of the whole COIN thing. I came to it rather reluctantly, because I felt like it is a narrow subset of a bigger issue.

Some thinkers call them small wars, others stability operations, others counterinsurgency operations. I actually felt that COIN is a subset of something that I would call stability operations. It is in the context of a society or of a complex system under stress that is exposed to chronic stresses or to a natural disaster shock like Katrina, when stuff breaks down and spoilers (crime, gang violence or insurgency) take advantage, when law and order breaks down.

At the far end of the spectrum those spoilers become insurgents. It is a simplistic model of thinking about conflict and instability along the spectrum. During the Iraq war we had a lot of smart people who looked back in history and at the military doctrines and research associated with counterinsurgency and determined it was a good place to start. Because you have a doctrine of COIN doesn't mean that you have a policy of invading countries in order to conduct COIN. In America there are a lot people who don't pay attention to the actual intellectual discourse and the actual doctrinal evolution vis-a-vis policy. To the extent that COIN became a dirty word in Washington it is because of this misperception, because they think it is a policy not just a doctrine. We have doctrine for nuclear war but that doesn't mean that I am going now to conduct nuclear war.

What kind of features in the current strategic environment highlight the trend that irregular warfare remains a tactic of first resort in the toolbox of the America's enemies?

I think we have the strongest, most technological advanced military with the largest global reach not only in the world, but in the history of the world. It is still the case that anybody who wants to challenge us would be sort of foolish to do so head on. This is not going to change because of the Republican rhetoric about the hollow force. We are so far advanced and above any other military on the planet that doesn't make any sense to call it a hollow force.

But it also doesn't make sense to any enemy out there who has been paying attention. Any potential enemy who decides that they don't like the US for whatever reason will study what has been happening in the last 10 years in the fight against low-tech, high-impact fighters in Iraq and Afghanistan. They know that we have trouble with this.

Anyone has trouble with this. They would have studied the tactics from IED to suicide bombings to cyber-attacks to leveraging social media, to the way enemies are operating in a densely populated urban environments. These are the things that are challenging for conventional militaries and that present advantages to enemies. That's why I genuinely believe that we need to continue to keep the eye on the ball on these pieces because it doesn't make sense that our next engagement is going to be against someone foolish to take us on conventionally. But we need to maintain our conventional edge, otherwise the whole calculus changes as well. We need capabilities and training along the spectrum. It can be done. One of the last things that I did as DASD for Plans was that I went to visit US forces in Europe. They were conducting one of their exercises at the Combined Training Center: a multilateral exercise with a hybrid scenario. It wasn't only that they were practicing looking at the Afghan experience, but they were leveraging irregular and conventional aspects and they were studying what happened in Lebanon with Hezbollah's hybrid warfare strategy – and they were sharpening their conventional skills as well. They know they have to do it all – because the bad guys will.

NATO was not created for pop-centric counterinsurgency missions. Having in mind a security environment where irregular warfare remains a tactic of first resort, should NATO retain this ability of coordinating complex comprehensive counterinsurgency campaigns? Should NATO retain the COIN know-how that acquired over the past decade in Afghanistan?

Absolutely. Europe faces the same array of threats that the US faces. If the European countries are not going to invest in their militaries and train their militaries across the spectrum of operations, they are going to be in trouble. They need to do that. Our relationship with the European countries and our leadership in the NATO Alliance as a whole is focused on that.

3

Revolution in Military Affairs

INTRODUCTION

Notwithstanding the rapid decline in funding for U.S. armed services in the recent past, it is expected that Congress will authorize the expenditure of substantial sums for defence in the future. In order to make informed judgements on what should be funded, Congress seeks knowledge of the state of military technology and the likely environments American forces might face in future conflict.

The main practical issue for Congress arising from the RMA debate is how to resolve the conflict between expenditures for current and near-term activities and any expenditures needed to deal with an RMA. Funds to support current operations will not be available for future procurement. Other issues involve determining the appropriate detail for congressional oversight, arranging for greater coordination of RMA-related activities in the Department of Defence, and determining how best to foster long-term innovation by the military services.

Following the overwhelming victory of coalition forces in Operation Desert Storm, a good deal of discussion took place whether the world had witnessed a Revolution in Military Affairs (RMA). However, active debate continues over whether in fact there is or will be an RMA, what are the constituent elements of such a revolution, when the revolution is to take place, and what steps would be needed to adapt to the revolution.

This report consists of three parts: 1) A discussion of the debate over the definition and constituent elements of a Revolution in Military Affairs and the possible consequences for the American military; 2) A presentation of the steps that the Department of Defence and the military services are taking now to carry out long-term strategic planning and implementation; and 3) an examination of the major issues raised and what Congress and the Department of Defence might do to understand an RMA, guide U.S. policy, and as much as possible, guide the outcome.

INTERPRETATIONS OF THE CONCEPT

The current term, "Revolution in Military Affairs" has evolved from an earlier term — military technical revolution — used by Soviet military theorists. In the early 1970s the Soviets had identified two periods of fundamental military change in the 20th Century: one driven by the emergence of aircraft, motor vehicles and chemical warfare in World War I, and the second driven by the development of nuclear weapons, missiles and computers in World War II. The next "military-technical revolution" the Soviets thought, would involve advances in microelectronics, sensors, precision-guidance, automated control systems, and directed energy. By 1984, the Chief of the Soviet General Staff was expressing his concern that the emergence of "automated reconnaissance and strike complexes," including new control systems and very accurate long-range precision weapons, would bring the destructive potential of conventional weapons closer to that of weapons of mass destruction. The success of allied forces in Operation Desert Storm convinced the Soviets that the integration of control, communications, electronic combat, and delivery of conventional fires had been realized for the first time.

Based upon an assessment of the outcomes of what have been defined as RMAs in the past, a revolution in military affairs takes place when one of the participants in a conflict incorporates new technology, organization, and doctrine to the extent that victory is attained in the immediate instance, but more importantly, that any other actors who might wish to deal with that participant or that activity must match, or counter the new combination of technology, organization, and doctrine in order to prevail. The accomplishments of the victor become the necessary foundation for any future military activities in that area of conflict. The emphasis on a specific area of conflict is important because it is possible that technologies or organizations proposed as elements of a current RMA — such as the so-called sensor-to-shooter connection — could be countered in a particular conflict by other elements, such as nuclear weapons.

Most true revolutions in military affairs have only been recognized after they have taken place. Except, perhaps, for nuclear weapons, the reality and power of the several revolutions in military affairs which will be briefly discussed below was recognized later, but not during their gestation period. One reason for this is that even in the relatively distant past, warfare itself has been in a constant state of flux. Most of this change was evolutionary, and as such was relatively easily countered. The effects of true revolutions in military affairs went beyond these changes and created a new environment. It should be noted that, from the perspective of the participants in the process, what was seen as evolutionary by the victorious side could have been seen as revolutionary by the losing side — and by history.

PAST REVOLUTIONS

There are several interpretations of the exact number and constituent elements of earlier revolutions in military affairs. One analyst counts as many as ten RMAs since the fourteenth century. The Infantry Revolution and the Artillery Revolution took place during the Hundred Years War. In the first of these, infantry displaced the dominant role of heavy cavalry on the battlefield; in the second, advances in technology led to the development of effective cannons and siege warfare which could quickly degrade the formerly strong defenses of cities.

The outcome of the Battle of Crecy — which marked the end of cavalry supremacy — provides an example of the overwhelming dominance that becomes evident from the completion of an RMA. In that battle the French lost 1,542 knights and lords, and suffered over 10,000 casualties among crossbowmen and other support troops. The victorious English, relying on disciplined formations of infantry with unprecedented use of longbowmen, lost two knights, one squire, forty other men-at-arms and archers, and "a few dozen Welsh."

Other revolutions in military affairs took place at sea where the advent of sail powered warships and cannon changed the nature of Naval Warfare. A Fortress Revolution in the sixteenth resulted from the development of fortifications better able to withstand the siege artillery of the day. The development of muskets and tactics to overcome their weaknesses and exploit their power led to another revolution. The large squares of pikemen and archers which had earlier overcome mounted cavalry, now became targets for artillery and musket fire. The Napoleonic Revolution took place when the French were able to standardize and improve their artillery, greatly increase the size of their armies and greatly improve the organization and command of their military formations.

The development of railroads and telegraphs, and the introduction of rifling for muskets and artillery created another Land Warfare Revolution in the 19th century. The American Civil War was fought by exploiting these developments. A second Naval Revolution took place at the end of the century as the rifled cannon, steel ships, and steam power changed the face of warfare at sea. The end of this period saw the introduction of the submarine and torpedo. The culmination of the tactics, organizations and technology of the two 19th century revolutions was reached in the early stages of World War I with static trench warfare on land and submarine warfare at sea.

The changes in technology and organization which had taken place by the end of World War I set the stage for the Revolutions in Mechanization, Aviation and

Information which took place in the interwar period. These revolutions led to the great military innovations of World War II: Blitzkrieg by the German Army, carrier aviation by Japan and the United States, amphibious warfare by the United States, and strategic bombing by Great Britain and the United States. In the context of the discussion today, it should be noted that all of the elements of the later revolution — motor vehicles and tanks, airplanes and radios — were present in World War I. It was the combination of their technical advancement in the 1920s and 1930s, along with new doctrine and organizations that created revolutions. Finally the Nuclear Revolution took place as a result of the coupling of nuclear weapons with intercontinental bombers and ballistic missiles.

Because a defining characteristic of the last half of the twentieth century has been very rapid, accelerating, unavoidable, technological change, one of the major elements needed for a revolution in military affairs — technological change — is now always present. At the same time, rapid societal change and organizational adaptations by military forces are taking place. The presence of these phenomena has led to continuing discussions as to whether there currently exist, or will exist in the near future, the elements needed to create another revolution in military affairs.

CURRENT PERSPECTIVES ON AN RMA

A difficulty arises in understanding the current debate over the RMA because some participants use the term as referring to the revolutionary technology itself that is driving change, while others use the term as referring to revolutionary adaptations by military organizations that may be necessary to deal with the changes in technology or the geopolitical environment, and still others use the term to refer to the revolutionary impact of geopolitical or technological change on the outcome of military conflicts — regardless of the nature of the particular technology or the reaction of the participants to the technological change. Members of each group use the term "revolution," but in reference to different phenomena. The difference in terms of reference leads to different suggested alternatives.

Although a number of permutations exist, for the purposes of this report, we establish three basic conceptions of a revolution in military affairs. The first focuses primarily upon changes in the nation state and the role of an organized military in using force. This approach highlights the political, social, and economic factors at play worldwide which might lead to the need for completely different types of military force and organizations to apply that force in the future. The second conception — that most commonly assigned the term RMA — highlights the evolution of weapons, weapons technology, and military organization and doctrine among advanced powers. This approach assumes the continuation of the nation-state as it has existed during the past four hundred years, and focuses on the changes made possible by advancing technology. The third conception is that a true revolution in military affairs is unlikely, but rather there will be continuing evolution in equipment, organizations, and tactics to adjust to changes in technology and the international environment.

The End of the Nation State

The views of Carl H. Builder, a senior analyst at the RAND corporation are typical of those whose vision of an RMA highlights the political, social, and economic factors at play worldwide which are likely to lead to the need for completely different types and organizations for the application of military force in the future. According to Builder, in the future, ethnicity, theology, and special interests will dominate the current role of geography, nationalism, and political ideology in producing conflicts. The characteristics of this emerging world are as follows: The relative power of the nation state is declining, while the powers of business, advocacy, criminal, cultural and ethnic special interest groups are increasing. The ability of nations to control the flow of information, commodities and people is declining, while people are becoming more responsive to global events and opportunities. In addition, military weaponry is diffusing beyond the control of governments. The world created will be one in which conflict will be more frequent and more disaggregated. As a result, for the foreseeable future the most challenging situations facing the American military will be lesser conflicts and crises that demand aerial reconnaissance capabilities, rather than capabilities to fight for air supremacy, for constabulary duty rather than armored combat, and for the evacuation by sea of non-combatants rather than control of the high seas.

To deal with this world, Builder would give more emphasis to support forces rather than combat forces. As a result, support responsibilities would transfer from reserve personnel to active duty troops. The capability to undertake what Builder calls constabulary activities to prevent the use of the air, land, or sea would be greatly enhanced. This would be a change in emphasis from the current "big-war" focus of the military. Finally, according to Builder, the size of forces would shrink, but the diversity of capabilities would increase. The number of personnel in activities such as military transport, intelligence, communications, surveillance, military police, civil engineering, and psychological operations would grow while mainstream forces would be reduced.

Another observer, sharing Builder's basic viewpoint on the decline of the nation state, the nature of the emerging international (dis)order, and the different types of forces likely to be needed to deal with that disorder, claims that there is no compelling need today to purchase any additional bombers, submarines, or tanks except to preserve the industrial base. From his perspective, the principal threats that the U.S. military will have to face in the near future will involve dealing with stateless international terrorist and criminal organizations. Dealing with these "wholly unprincipled," non-traditional opponents will involve different doctrines, weapons, and organizations than those presently subsumed under the technology-driven RMA rubric.

The consequences of accepting this view of the RMA are far-reaching. As Builder notes, the structure of the entire U.S. military would be very different. In essence, the focus of attention would change from relatively small, highly sophisticated, technologically advanced forces and organizations, to larger organizations carrying out operations at a generally lower level of sophistication. The concept of "victory" in conflicts involving these larger organizations would most likely be less clear and take more time than a conflict with a smaller, rapid-tempo, advanced technology force.

A System of Systems

The second — and largest — group of analysts dealing with the concept of an RMA focuses on rapidly changing technical capabilities as the major elements of a potential RMA. One of the current difficulties in the debate among members of this group has been the lack of a single definition of the component elements of the RMA and disagreement over the importance of new doctrine and organizations in carrying out the revolution.

Admiral William Owens, Vice Chairman of the Joint Chiefs of Staff, identifies three overlapping areas. These are 1) intelligence, surveillance and reconnaissance, 2) command, control, communications and intelligence processing, and 3) precision force. Owens sets out a number of weapons systems already in or entering U.S. military inventories. These appear on the following page. This approach allows Owens to describe the situation in terms of the creation of "a system of systems." By doing so, he is able to draw attention to the interaction of all of these capabilities. Differing from some participants in the debate, Admiral Owens sees this RMA as coming into existence in the near future.

A variant of this basic position is that there will not be a single RMA, but, because of the rapid pace of technological change, there will be a series of almost continuous revolutions.

Not separately discussed by Owens — but in fact subsumed in the system of systems idea — is another set of categories that have been proposed as the major contributing elements to an RMA. These categories include information warfare, space, stealth, and advanced computer technologies, including more sophisticated sensors and more realistic modeling and simulation.

OTHER PROPOSED MAIN ELEMENTS OF CURRENT RMA

Information Warfare

There are three, interrelated, definitions of information warfare: The first, and clearest, involves either attacking, influencing, or protecting military reconnaissance, surveillance, dedicated communications, command and control, fire control, and intelligence assets. The second definition, involves protecting, influencing, or attacking the basic communications links of a society: voice, video or data transfer, electric power or telephone system control commands, etc. The third involves what formerly were called psychological operations. These involve using television, radio, or print media to attack, influence, or protect the attitudes of soldiers, civilian populations or leaders.

Space

This category focuses on the activities facilitated or made possible by space vehicles: reconnaissance and intelligence gathering, missile defence, navigation, data transmission, communications, and, potentially, force projection.

Stealth

The main contributions of low observability have been to strike and reconnaissance activities. The experiences of U.S. Air Force F-117s in Operation Desert Storm and similar latitude given the B-2 bomber and Tier III (-) Unmanned Aerial Vehicle are claimed to be major contributors to an RMA. Stealth may also be applicable to ships and cruise missiles.

Advanced Computer Technologies

The continuing, rapid, advances in this category are driving all of the other elements in the RMA. The increases in computer speed and reliability, combined with new or more sensitive types of sensors, has made possible dramatic increases in weapons accuracy and lethality, intelligence gathering and dissemination,and communications. The ability to model or simulate processes, activities, or objects has grown exponentially in the recent past. The desire to take advantage of the increasing sophistication of modeling and simulation activities has been one of the major elements in the plans of the U.S. military services to adapt to the future.

A war involving a participant possessing the elements of this vision of an RMA would take place at a very rapid pace, involve synoptic battlefield awareness, the use of very lethal precision guided weapons, control of the entire electromagnetic spectrum, and be highly integrated among all the components and services. This type of warfare would be most effective against "conventional" but less technologically advanced powers, and less effective against unsophisticated opponents or guerrillas.

Some of the consequences of accepting this technology-based view of the RMA would be the obverse of what Builder proposes. Thus, the focus of the Department of Defence would be on *relatively* small, highly sophisticated, technologically advanced weapons and organizations. The word relatively is emphasized because the size of the force would be a consequence of the size of the threat. It is possible to conceptualize a significant, large, technologically competitive adversary in 20 years or less that would require a large, technologically competent U.S. force.

Because a central element of this perception of the RMA is computer technology — which is now highly market-driven — it is unlikely that the pace of change in this area is going to slow. One consequence of this rapid pace could be much shorter production runs for major weapons systems because the systems are likely to become obsolete much sooner. This rapid pace also gives rise to the present tension between those who wish to retain capabilities for some indefinite future and those who believe that the current budgetary environment forces the relinquishment of existing — not necessarily obsolete — capabilities in order to afford future capabilities. Another consequence of the rapid pace of technology is likely to be a continuation of the search for "silver bullets." A notable characteristic of some members of this group is the claim that a single technology — usually the one they are proposing — will create an RMA by itself.

Evolution, Not Revolution

The third sizeable group of individuals in the RMA debate believes that the future will not involve major discontinuities but rather a gradual evolution of existing military organizations and equipment. Most proponents of this viewpoint do not deny that rapid technological change is taking place, and that this change will greatly affect the military, but they argue that a true revolution in military affairs is unlikely in the near future. The basis of this position is the belief that existing organizational ethos and responses will be able to deal with the potential changes caused either by new technology or a new geopolitical environment. A variant of this perspective focuses upon the military advantages that accrue to the United States as a result of the adaptability and flexibility of workers who have participated in the American economy. From this perspective, the U.S. social system produces military personnel better able to adapt to new technology and organizations than any potential adversary.

In addition to the broad differences between the three perspectives concerning the constituent elements and timing of the RMA, other interlinked controversies exist.

Among proponents of the System of Systems, disagreements concern which systems to purchase now, which to postpone, the wisdom of incurring current costs as opposed to future costs in light of technological progress, the feasibility of proposed systems, and assessments of the relative gains for the acquisition of specific technologies when compared with other technologies. Similar conflicts exist over the timing and wisdom of training expenditures and reorganizations.

For proponents of the end of the nation state and evolutionary perspectives, the main concern is assessing the relationship between the requirements of their perspectives and the technological changes inherent in the system of systems.

This is most forcefully expressed as discerning the relationship between future combat and future technology. These concerns are most prominent among Army and Marine Corps leaders, who focus on the requirements for long-term ground presence — anywhere in the conflict spectrum — and how technology will affect these requirements.

LONG-TERM STRATEGIC PLANNING AND IMPLEMENTATION EFFORTS OF THE DEPARTMENT OF DEFENCE AND U.S.MILITARY SERVICES

Many of the changes highlighted by the debate over the Revolution in Military Affairs may take place in the relatively distant future. The purpose of this section is to examine how the Department of Defence and the individual services are attempting to deal with the RMA and concepts and activities that are beyond the end of the present budget cycle five or six years in the future.

Office of Net Assessment

Since the late 1980s, Andrew Marshall, director of the Office of Net Assessment in the Office of the Secretary of Defence has probably been the main catalyst inside the government examining the potential for a RMA. It is Marshall's hypothesis that today we are in a period equivalent to that immediately after the end of World War I in which the technologies, doctrines and organizations which were to win World War II were just being formed. Marshall's office has taken the lead in financing studies on the history of military innovation in the pre-World War II period — innovation which led to such things as carrier strike aviation, amphibious warfare, and *Blitzkrieg* — and in sponsoring its own wargames and other RMA studies today. In addition, each of the services has participated in RMA round tables and war games financed and run by the Office of Net Assessment. For example, from September 1993 through August 1994, the Science Applications International Corporation (SAIC), conducted a series of roundtable discussions with the individual services on the RMA at the behest of the Office of Net Assessment. The report from the series was delivered in October 1994. Among the topics discussed were the impact of declining defence budgets on the ability of the DoD to exploit the RMA; the importance of advances in information technology for future military planning and warfare, the value of space activities for all of the services, the importance of fostering a culture of innovation in the military, and the costs and benefits of increasing jointness.

Marshall has consistently emphasized the importance of developing appropriate concepts of operations, appropriate organizations, and doctrine and practices to take advantage of emerging technology. An emphasis on very long time frames, the development of appropriate doctrine, organization, and practical operations as opposed to a focus on technology alone, distinguishes Marshall's approach to a future RMA. It was the recognition of the importance of these non-hardware issues that led Marshall to emphasize the term Revolution in Military Affairs when earlier efforts in this area, which used the term Military Technical Revolution (MTR), appeared to be too narrow in focus.

DoD Revolution in Military Affairs Initiative

Approved by Secretary of Defence in September 1993, in January 1994, then Deputy Secretary of Defence William Perry established a group to coordinate a DoD-wide project on the Revolution in Military Affairs. In the first phase of the project, the group was to gather data, define the most plausible defence environment for the years 2010-2015 and identify the most promising technologies and operational concepts. In the second phase, war games would be conducted to examine the impact of the findings of the first phase of the project on military operations; the third phase would consist of a report on the results of the war games and the overall findings of the project.

Five separate task forces were set up to examine specific areas of interest. These were: Combined Arms and Maneuver, led by Army and Marine Corps officials; Deep Strike, led by Air Force and Navy officials; Naval Forward Operations, Crisis Prevention and Response, led by Marine Corps and Navy

Officials; Low Intensity Conflict, led by officials from the Office of the Secretary of Defence; and Fostering/Institutionalizing Long Term Innovation, led by officials from the Office of Net Assessment. Based upon the data generated by the first phase of the study, war games were held from June through October 1994 by the Naval Forward Operations, Crisis Prevention and Response, Deep Strike, and Combined Arms and Maneuver task forces.

In its early preparations, the Naval Forward Operations, Crisis Prevention, and Response Task Force set out what it considered the four main threats to be faced along with three projected capabilities to counter these threats.

The threats included the ability for an enemy to covertly deploy mines, coordinated air and undersea assaults on ships; wide area sea denial with remote weapons triggered by satellite control; and advanced weapons technology including tactical ballistic missiles, next generation submarines and very low observable cruise missiles.

To counter these capabilities, the task force recommended that the Department of Defence concentrate on developing organic satellite capabilities, directed energy for ship defence, and what was called the Great Black Fleet — the latter consisting of attack and former ballistic missile submarines.

Typical of the questions the Task Force was given to conduct its wargame were:

What aspects of military operations in 2015 will remain relatively constant?

How would U.S. forward presence be affected by an adversary with 3,000 mile range ballistic missiles and 1250 mile range stealth cruise missiles capable of real-time targeting to 9 feet; with seabed brilliant mines ; and exhibiting a willingness to use weapons of mass destruction?

How would the Marine Corps "Operational Maneuver From the Sea" be conducted in the same environment?

Should a strategic campaign plan include actions to disrupt an opponent's command, control, communications and computer capabilities in advance of hostilities? How important is it to immediately disrupt these capabilities at the outset of hostilities?

The wargame was also given the task of devising operational concepts to exploit such technologies as stealth naval combatants, non-radar tracking, a Universal Global Positioning System and advanced sensor-to-weapon capabilities.

The Deep Strike Task Force was to address emerging weapon technologies and innovative operational and organizational technologies against a battlefield defined in terms of distance and in terms of target importance to the adversary. The task force was also to examine how to deal with the rapidly shortening time available to plan and execute deep strike missions. The Task Force recommended the development of a coherent and transparent theatre command, control, communications, and intelligence system; developing a very low observable, long range, unmanned aerial surveillance system; building cheap, easily disseminated ground sensors; and developing methods to deal with deeply buried weapons of mass destruction or mobile target sets.

According to press accounts, the conclusions of the Combined Arms and Maneuver task force concerning future operations and structure resembled the Army's Force XXI (discussed below). The focus of future operations would be on rapid tempo, including logistics activities; battle space awareness leading to coherent actions; battle space command, relying on high level situational awareness and advanced training; and increased lethality, creating massed effects rather than massed units.

The members of the task force focusing on Fostering/ Institutionalizing Long Term Innovation were attempting to overcome what were viewed as strong incentives for military officers not to innovate. The subgroups in this task force examined innovation and how it takes place, how to encourage innovation through education, war games and simulations, and industry contacts, and the need to create an OSD Strategic Studies Group to report directly to the Secretary of Defence.

Apparently, there was concern among supporters of the RMA initiative that the process would stop after the final sets of reports were briefed to top DoD officials from April to September 1995, and discussions were held about incorporating RMA issues into the Advanced Concept Technology Demonstration process.

Major Organizational Steps

Steps taken by the Department of Defence to institutionalize the examination of long-term change include:

Joint Requirements Oversight Council (JROC). To the U.S. military, the establishment of requirements is the first step in the acquisition process. Formerly, each service essentially defined its requirements. Created in the mid-1980s and consisting of the Vice Chiefs of Staff of the military services and the Vice Chairman of the Joint Chiefs of Staff, the JROC has become a focal point both for furthering jointness in the acquisition process, but more importantly, for assessing future requirements. It is from the work of this forum that Admiral William Owens, Vice Chairman of the Joint Chiefs of Staff, has developed his concept of the "system of systems."

National Defence University. An Information Resources Management College has been created at the National Defence University, and the National War College offers courses on the RMA and on Information Warfare. The Information Resources Management College hosted a conference at NDU in May 1995 on the global information explosion and potential consequences for U.S. national security and for the 1995-96 academic year the School of Information Warfare and Strategy is offering a course on the information component of national security.

The U.S. Army and Force XXI

The United States Army has been the most aggressive of the services in examining the requirements for future warfare and carrying out what Army leadership sees as the necessary steps to deal with this future. General Gordon Sullivan, until recently Army Chief of Staff, was one of the main proponents of carefully examining how the Army should move away from a Cold War orientation and doctrine. Referring to many of the observations concerning Third Wave economics, politics, and warfare in the books of Alvin and Heidi Toffler, Sullivan consistently fostered an approach to the future that deliberately avoided prematurely setting fixed doctrine or acquisition goals until a clearer picture of the future Army was available. Sullivan himself has been a prolific contributor to the written debate over the RMA.

A first step in the transition to a new approach was the publication of Army *Field Manual 100-5, Operations,* in June 1993. This 174 page document incorporated into Army doctrine in some detail the consequences of the end of the Cold War with the lessons learned in Operations Just Cause in Panama, Desert Storm in Kuwait, and the follow-on activities in Iraq. The new Army doctrine emphasized force projection, stronger joint operations with the other U.S. military services and agencies, and combined operations with allies. A new section on Operations Other Than War (OOTW) was added to deal with a number of Army non-combat missions including supporting domestic civil authorities, providing humanitarian assistance, carrying out arms control monitoring, and peacekeeping. The manual also presented an expanded concept of what was now included in the battle space, and more detail on offense and defence at the tactical and operational levels of war.

Force XXI

In March 1994, General Sullivan released a message concerning the development of what he called Force XXI. In the message, Sullivan reviewed the transformation that Army had made in the past four years involving downsizing, new doctrine and training capabilities, the acquisition of "post-industrial" technology, force planning, and the institutionalization of ability to assess change. According to Sullivan, the next step, Force XXI, would encompass the reconceptualization and redesign of the Army at all echelons from combat to the industrial base. Other portions of the message created an Army Digitization Office and assigned responsibilities for implementing various aspects of the Force XXI design. The redesign was to focus on the interconnectivity of each echelon and between echelons. Force XXI was to be organized around the creation and sharing of information followed by unified action by commanders based on that information. It would use information-based battle command that would give the Army ascendancy and freedom of action in 21st century wars and operations other than war. Gen. Sullivan stated that he could not tell what Force XXI would look like, but he could give some of its characteristics. These were:

Battle Command would be based upon real-time situational awareness.

Hierarchical responsibility, but non-hierarchical organization.

Force design would be less fixed, and more flexible in organization; force design would be based on capabilities rather than countering a specific threat.

Force XXI might have smaller building blocks.

Individual units would be resilient and versatile in purpose.

Force XXI would be more strategically deployable, with a full range of early entry capabilities.

Units would rely on electronic connectivity in place of geographic or physical connectivity.

TRADOC Pamphlet 525-5 Force XXI Operations

In August 1994, the Army Training and Doctrine Command (TRADOC) released Pamphlet 525-5, *Force XXI Operations,* which was subtitled "A concept for the Evolution of Full-Dimensional Operations for the Strategic Army of the Early Twenty-First Century."

By its content, the pamphlet could be characterized as encompassing all three of the RMA perspectives set out earlier in this report. In the introduction to the pamphlet, Army Chief of Staff Sullivan placed Pamphlet 525-5 in the line of earlier post-Cold War Army doctrinal changes as preparation to bringing the Army into the 21st century. Elsewhere, Sullivan stated that Pamphlet 525-5 had "established the conceptual foundation for warfighting and for force design." However, in his introduction, the Commanding General of TRADOC indicated that the pamphlet was not doctrine, but "rather a document of ideas...."

The contents of TRADOC Pamphlet 525-5 receive extensive treatment here for two reasons. First, because the ideas which it reflects are driving the future structure of Force XXI. Second, and perhaps more importantly, the operational concepts contained in the pamphlet have, or are becoming, common usage among all of the services. As such, they have to a great extent become standard terms to refer to the structure of the expected future environment for land, sea, and air forces.

The Pamphlet sets out in general terms the overall environment that the Army is expected to operate within in the future and the need for doctrinal changes that would allow the Army to deal with this environment. It then defines *The Future Strategic Environment* with references to geopolitical change due to variations in the balance of power, rising nationalism, rejection of the West, economic competition, population growth, rising ungovernability, rapid improvements in technology, environmental risks, and the impact of increased information interchange on sovereignty.

Another section describes the characteristics of future armies and includes a threat spectrum model that attempts to expand the simple model that existed during the Cold War. On the low-end of the model, the expansion recognizes what Pamphlet 525-5 called "phenomenological threats," which were non-military threats that might require a military response. These phenomena include environmental disasters, health epidemics, famine, and illegal immigration. A second new threat category is "Nonnation forces." These include *sub*national threats involving political, racial, religious, cultural and ethnic conflicts challenging the authority of the nation-state; *a* national threats such as organized crime, piracy, and terrorism which operate outside the authority of the host nation-state; and *meta* national threats such as religious movements and international criminal movements that operate beyond the nation state. On the high end of the model, beyond recognizable internal-security forces, infantry-based armies, and armor-mechanized based armies, are "complex-adaptive armies." These armies will be smaller and extremely expensive to equip, train and maintain. Military operations by these would involve high-technology equipment, multidimensional maneuver, precision munitions, smart weapons platforms, and enhanced situational awareness. For the Army, the importance of the typology is that it had to be prepared to conduct simultaneous operations against foes of various capacities. Faced with preindustrial nations or non-nation groups, the conflict might involve terrorism, insurgency, or partisan warfare.

The section of TRADOC Pamphlet 525-5 on future battlefields deals with the fact that the Army might face conflicts ranging from general war to Operations Other Than War (OOTW). In this overall environment, conventional combat between complex-adaptive armies would exhibit five new aspects: Battle Command, Extended Battle Space, Simultaneity, Spectrum Supremacy, and Changes in Rules of War.

According to the Pamphlet, Battle Command would be much more difficult because the possible range of scenarios faced by commanders would not be nearly as predictable as during the Cold War. Advances in information management and distribution would provide horizontal integration of battlefield functions and help commanders to tailor and arrange their forces. Traditional hierarchical command structures would be replaced by what are called flatter internetted structures. As a result of the increases in weapons accuracy and lethality, individual units, key elements and leaders would be more widely dispersed, leading to a further continuation of the empty battlefield phenomenon. The Extended Battle Space arises because the same technology leads to an increase in the depth, breadth, and height of the battlefield. Because technology will accelerate the ability to detect and attack, commanders will seek to avoid linear actions, close combat, stable fronts and long operational pauses. Attacks against an enemy's follow-on forces will change from a sequenced approach to one involving simultaneous attack. The concept of Simultaneity takes form because the Revolution in Military Affairs would allow advanced forces to achieve multiple operational objectives nearly simultaneously throughout a theatre of operations rather than the familiar form of military operations as a chain of sequentially phased operations. Spectrum Supremacy referred to the fact that information technology advances would insure that future military operations would unfold before a global audience, with significant opportunities to influence national will and popular support. Finally, the authors of the pamphlet stated, recent activities of combatants in using soldiers as hostages, threatening the use of chemical weapons, targeting heads of state, and violating territorial integrity seemed to indicate that observation of the Rules of War was becoming less certain. The chapter concluded by observing that the days of the all-purpose doctrinal threat template and of a single-prescription Army doctrine were gone.

According to the authors, Force XXI must be prepared to face the full spectrum of operational environments described above. The resultant Army would be defined by five characteristics: doctrinal flexibility; strategic mobility; tailorability and modularity; joint, multinational, and interagency connectivity; and versatility in war and Operations Other Than War (OOTW).

Although almost all of the pamphlet dealt with conceptual matters, the section on Materiel went into some detail on the specific types and characteristics of the equipment and technology that Force XXI would require.

Major Organizational Steps

The Army has taken a number of concrete organizational steps to foster and institutionalize long-term change. These include:

Louisiana Maneuvers Task Force. Named after a set of corps-sized Army exercises conducted in 1941 to determine how U.S. troops might fight opponents with armor and attack aircraft, the modern incarnation of the Louisiana Maneuvers Task Force was created by General Sullivan in 1992 to examine the steps needed to be taken by the Army to make the transition to the post Cold-War era. Initially concentrating on working through Army exercises and advanced simulation technology, in April 1994, the Task Force was also made responsible for integrating and synchronizing the creation of the design of Force XXI. One result of their efforts is the Force XXI Campaign Synchronization Matrix below, taken from the Force XXI Internet Site and provided by the Department of the Army.

The Matrix is significant in the context of this paper not so much for its specific content as for two other reasons. First, because it indicates the complexity of the steps that the Army is taking to implement the general ideas behind Force XXI; and second, it indicates the difficulty in integrating these — or any other large scale — changes throughout the Army in a systematic fashion.

The U.S. Air Force, Spacecast 2020, and Air Force 2025

The two most recent Air Force doctrinal White Papers, *Global Reach, Global Power* and *Global Presence*, are not as detailed as Army Field Manual 100-5 or as future oriented as TRADOC Pamphlet 525-5. Each deals with the present and the near future.

On the other hand, Spacecast 2020 was a project undertaken by the Air University at Maxwell Air Force Base to study and report on emerging technologies for space in the year 2020 and beyond. Begun at the behest of Air Force Chief of Staff Gen. Merrill McPeak in September 1993, the final report for Spacecast 2020 was completed in June 1994. The 350 participants in the study included faculty and class members at the Air Command and Staff College and the Air War College, scientists at the Air Force Institute of Technology at Wright Patterson Air Force Base in Ohio, members of the other services, government agencies and laboratories, universities, think tanks, and independent scholars. A majority of the military participants were from the operational line forces of all of the services. The final report consisted of two parts, one classified.

The authors of Spacecast 2020 stated that although they could not know in detail what the future would hold, they could speculate in an informed fashion on the technologies that would be of the most value for space and which were not beyond plausibility.

In the Introduction and Overview, the authors state that the most fundamental characteristic of space from a military perspective is that it possessed unprecedented vantage or view. The Global View given by space is the enabler for the basic Air Force concepts of Global Reach and Global Power. According to the study, implementing the concept of Global View as a reality would depend on three things: creation of an integrated on-demand information system for command users, development of increased and improved sensing capabilities, and availability of relatively inexpensive space lift. Before presenting the papers in the report, the authors of Spacecast 2020 set out four alternative future international environments and the consequences for military and commercial space arising from the characteristics of each. The four possible futures were 1) A Spacefaring World, 2) A Rogue's World, 3) Mad Max Incorporated, and 4) a Space Baron's World.

The seven papers in the Global View section of the report dealt with 1) creation of an on-demand information system (they don't use the term intelligence) for future warfighters, 2) surveillance and reconnaissance in 2020, 3) creation of a Super Global Positioning System, 4) space traffic control, 5) weather information in 2020, 6) deep space based monitors of solar activity, and 7) space monitors to provide warnings of likely disturbances in communications caused by solar activities.

A section of the study on Global Reach addressed the things necessary to reach into space. The four main papers in this section discussed 1) the concept of an aerospace wing which included a squadron of rocket-powered transatmospheric vehicles capable of carrying 5,000 lbs into low-earth orbit, 2) an examination of unconventional methods of getting into space, 3) what would be needed in the way of lift systems and satellite design to allow rapid space force reconstitution in crises, and 4) the idea of using modular units in space to facilitate replacement of failed parts of satellites.

The section on Global Power contained some of the most imaginative papers. Noting that the U.S. and allied forces relied heavily on space-based systems for navigation, weather information, secure communications and surveillance during Operation Desert Storm, the authors of the report indicated that these systems would present attractive targets in the future and that their protection would be critical. The Defensive Counterspace paper examined the idea of developing a series of escort satellites to accompany our high value satellites. The Offensive Counterspace paper described U.S. space based systems that could "influence" enemy satellite capability. The Force Application paper examined concepts to deal with ground and atmospheric targets from space. These included things like hyperkinetic energy, directed energy, and conventional weapons. Other papers in the Global Power section dealt with ways to wage information warfare, the idea of counterforce weather control, and the deflection of potential asteroid collisions.

THE AIR FORCE REVOLUTIONARY PLANNING PROCESS AND AIR FORCE 2025

At the August 1994 Mission Area Plans Review — a process for coordinating Air Force budget proposals — the Chief of Staff of the Air Force asked the Deputy Chief of Staff for Plans and Operations to develop a way to provide revolutionary thinking for Air Force modernization planning. The result was the creation of a three phase Revolutionary Planning Process intended to generate innovative ideas for Air Force institutions, concepts of operations, and technology development programs.

Each phase will conclude with a review and the approval of a panel of four star Air Force generals. The three phases are Generation, Investigation and Integration. The Generation phase will use multiple sources to generate and evaluate ideas that could have a revolutionary impact on the Air Force. The Investigation phase will use analyses, simulations, wargames and exercises to test the merit of the recommended ideas. In the Integration phase the senior officers panel will determine which ideas to fund for basic research, which to fund in Air Force budget planning, or to give to the long term assessment process.

Finally, the planning process is to be institutionalized. Every five years expert panels will be established to review previous ideas and propose new ones. At the present time, the Air Force Studies and Analyses Agency is responsible for coordination of the Revolutionary Planning Process.

The first step in the Generation Phase of the Revolutionary Planning Process was taken in August 1995 by the Air University at Maxwell Air Force Base, Alabama, with the start of project Air Force 2025. Air Force 2025 will be a study of air and space concepts likely to be applicable by the year 2025. The final report of the study is to be delivered to the Air Force Chief of Staff in June 1996, and will consist of a collection of white papers developed from the innovative concepts and technology abstracts obtained from an even wider range of sources than participated in Spacecast 2020. The core research group will consist of volunteer faculty members and students at the Air University and the Air Force Institute of Technology.

At the end of September 1995, Air Force Chief of Staff Gen. Ronald Fogelman announced the appointment of Maj. General John Gordon as his special assistant for long-range planning. Gen. Gordon's position is slated to be abolished at the end of 18 months. At the time of the drafting of this report, General Gordon's exact responsibilities, and his relations to the Air Force Revolutionary Planning Process and to other Air Force planning, budgeting, and acquisition organizations were not clear.

Major Organizational Steps

Air University. As noted above, the constituent elements of the Air University, the Air Command and Staff College and the Air War College and the Air Force Institute of Technology, have been active participants in Air Force long-range planning exercises and Spacecast 2020.

Air Force Information Warfare Center. The Air Force Information Warfare Center is the executive agent for Air Force Command and Control Warfare activities. Located at Kelly Air Force Base, Texas, the Center was activated in September 1993. In addition to its current activities providing support for deployed Air Force Squadrons, Air Force major commands and the Air Staff in the Pentagon, the Center examines future requirements for advancements in command and control warfare. However, the planning horizon of this organization appears to be fairly short.

THE U.S. NAVY, U.S. MARINE CORPS, AND FUTURE WARFARE

The most recent U.S. Navy doctrine or policy statements *From the Sea* and *Forward From the Sea* deal with the transition from the Cold War open-ocean orientation of the Maritime Strategy to a focus on power projection and littoral warfare. As such, they deal primarily with the present and very near future. Institutionally, the Navy is said to be the most resistant to the type of long range strategic planning needed to deal with a potential RMA. Until very recently, virtually no systematic process existed in the Navy for thinking about major innovations in naval warfare or speeding their introduction into the fleet.

Upon becoming Chief of Naval Operations, Admiral Jeremy M. Boorda asked the Chief of Naval Operations Executive Panel to look into the area of future planning. The Executive Panel, composed of current and former U.S. government officials and scientists, convened a Naval Warfare Innovation Task Force from its members. The task force met from June 1994 thorough June 1995. The task force recommended forming small teams to produce ideas for innovations and groundbreaking concepts. One of the first objectives of the teams would be to establish the likely strategic, military, economic and political trends expected by the year 2015. Once this environment was described, the teams could focus on the technologies that could change naval warfare. The task force recommended the extensive use of wargames and modeling and simulation to understand the proposed ideas. In order to surmount limitations in the Navy's current Advanced Concept Technology Demonstration programs, the task force recommended the expenditure of at least $100 million a year for a minimum of three years on ACTD programs to assess the value of innovative concepts.

Responding to these recommendations, Admiral Boorda stated that in September 1995 he was going to revive the Strategic Studies Group based at the Naval War College in Newport, Rhode Island. The small group of Navy and Marine Corps officers, headed by retired Admiral James Hogg, became the first of the teams created to implement the recommendations of the Naval Warfare Innovations Task Force.

As a part of its regular responsibilities for examining operational concepts, the Navy Strategy and Policy Division conducted two Strategic Concepts War Games in 1994. The games were intended to study the nature of war in the year 2013 and examine for future studies innovative operational and doctrinal concepts for employing emerging and future technologies. The postulated conflict involved an adversary capable of challenging the United States politically, militarily, and economically within its own region. The participants in the games examined the requirements for carrying out future forward naval presence, presented a range of potential offensive and defensive technologies needed to establish presence and to fight, and proposed new operational concepts. The Navy which emerged from the games was built around the concept of a sea-based arsenal and logistics exploiting the command, control, communications and intelligence technologies of the Reconnaissance Strike Targeting Architecture, with a Marine Corps Air/Ground Task Force playing a central role in force projection.

From the perspective of this part of this report — the institutionalization of long range planning — one of the significant things about the Strategic Concepts War Games is that they were undertaken by the Strategy and Concepts Branch as part of its "normal" duties. The quality of the conceptualization and results of the wargames indicate that, at least at the initial stages of the process, the current structure of the Navy allows very sophisticated long-term conceptualization. What is unclear, however, is whether the connections between these ideas and any necessary changes in policies, procurement, operations, and doctrine will be made.

Major Organizational Steps

Fleet Information Warfare Center. The Fleet Information Warfare Center was established in Norfolk, VA in August 1994 — and formally dedicated in October 1995 — to apply information-based technologies to warfare. With 500 personnel, the unit combines current Navy activities in the areas of intelligence and command and control. Like the Air Force Information Warfare Center, the planning horizon of this organization appears to be fairly short.

Naval War College. The Naval War College has been very active in conducting wargames and simulations on future warfare both at the behest of the DoD office of Net Assessment and on behalf of the Navy. An elective on the RMA was offered in the Spring of 1995.

Marine Corps Commandant's Warfighting Laboratory. The Marine Corps formally inaugurated a warfighting laboratory at Quantico, Va. October 1, 1995. The lab will undertake activities similar to those of the Army Battle Labs and act as a test bed for integrating new technologies and the development of new operational concepts, tactics, techniques and doctrine.

ISSUES FOR CONGRESS

Congress will strongly influence military change through two constitutionally-basedfunctions: appropriations and oversight. Within this context, the following appear to be the main issues worth consideration.

Setting Overall Priorities

The main practical issue for Congress arising from the RMA debate is how to resolve the tension between current and future expenditures and operations. Funds — and training time — devoted to current readiness and force structure will not be available for future acquisition or training. Skimping on current funding to finance future systems or organizational training may risk unpreparedness, poor performance and high casualties in the short or medium term while preparing for war in the long term. The obverse of this situation is that the cost of maintaining the current high levels of operational tempo might not allow the development of needed future systems, concepts, and organizations. Unlike the period after World War I in which the Navy developed new carrier aviation concepts, the services today are extremely active carrying out current operations.

Guiding Choices of Technologies and Organizational Structures

A second issue is how to oversee and direct the choice of one — or a few — courses of action today among the dozens of possible permutations of militarily significant change. Minor choices can have significant long-term consequences. In their study of military innovation in peacetime, Williamson Murray and Barry Watts note that at the end of World War I, the Royal Navy was by far the leader in carrier-based aviation. However, although British Navy leaders pursued some innovations in the inter-war period, they concluded, among other things, that only a limited number of aircraft could be launched from a carrier at any one time and that on-deck parking was not an appropriate way to store aircraft between missions. As a result of earlier decisions, at the outset of World War II, British carrier aviation was markedly inferior to that of the United States and Japan.

Without attempting to predict a specific future, Congress could authorize seed money for actions likely to foster long-term thinking, such as for the creation of a DoD Future Concept Center.

Providing Focus

Closely related to the issue of choice or choices is the difficulty in maintaining focus. A characteristic of every current vision of an RMA or potential RMA is the multiplicity of potential uses for military forces. If an organization becomes proficient only through practice, how much time is left to develop core competencies when there are so many apparent missions, such as drug interdiction, disaster relief or peacekeeping? Clearly, the requirements for mastery of the new technical skills are not decreasing today. It is possible that the development of additional specialized technical competencies could be done on a cadre basis, with the expectation that later expansion in numbers could take place. On the other hand, it is equally possible that there is some minimum critical size that must be attained before the effectiveness of an organization can be accurately tested and assessed.

Coordination

The question of coordination is important to both the Department of Defence and to Congress. The DoD has several existing mechanisms for coordinating potential RMA activities. The Joint Requirements Oversight Council (JROC), headed by the Vice Chairman of the Joint Chiefs of Staff, is already active at the earliest stage of the acquisition process. In carrying out the transition to Force XXI, the Army has established a colonels/ navy captains group to coordinate with the other services. This group could also be used as a formal resource for inter-service learning and concept exchange. The recent emphasis on joint warfare operations also can act as a coordinating element for the execution of RMA changes.

On the other hand, there are at present, literally hundreds of separate organizations or groups dealing with elements of the RMA. For example, a November 1994 Naval Research Advisory Committee report on Modeling and Simulation listed representatives of at least 40 separate U.S. Government offices, groups or programs as having provided briefings to the committee. The same multiplicity of organizations is actively dealing with things related to "information warfare." While some would encourage this proliferation of organizations as a way to avoid foreclosing the investigation of imaginative avenues of research or operations, at present, there appears little specific oversight or coordination of these operations or their results.

From the perspective of annual congressional oversight, there appears little in the concept or execution of an RMA that distinguishes it from ongoing military activities. Whether the future is seen as evolutionary or revolutionary, the same issues of technological change, and appropriate doctrine and organization will have to be faced. This does not mean that there should be less oversight — only that there do not seem to be any peculiar characteristics of adapting to a potential RMA that would require major changes in the way Congress conducts its oversight activities.

Earlier congressional concerns that led to the passage of the Goldwater-Nichols Act would seem to be even more pertinent in a period of potential or actual RMA. At present, the Army is farthest along in creating institutions to integrate potentially revolutionary technology, assessing the consequences of an RMA, and attempting to incorporate necessary changes into Army doctrine and organization. One issue for Congress is how to assess the slower pace of the other services. On one hand, the overall direction the Army intends to go may be the wrong one. If this is the case, somehow tying the other services to these outcomes could be a mistake. On the other hand, if the Army is correct, the lessons learned could be very helpful to the other services and Congress should encourage high level coordination both to save funds and to build synergies.

Steps to Improve Acquisition

Some commentators have stated that Congress could take specific steps to foster innovation by modifying the Department of Defence acquisition process. Since there already exists a fair amount of latitude either through Advanced Research Projects Agency programs or through the Advanced Concept Technology Demonstrations, what specific, additional, changes would be needed?

Should Criticism Be Institutionalized?

The creation of the functional equivalent of an Office of the Devil's Advocate for RMA issues ought to be given serious attention. As noted above, there is a multiplicity of potential choices involved in various concepts of an RMA. An organization specifically designed to indicate that proposed activities will not work, will cost too much, will take too long to implement, are far beyond near-term technological capabilities, or will result in a much more weakened state if they fail in operation when compared to existing systems — might serve as a necessary counterbalance to the wishes of service leaders and assessments by advocates of the potential benefits arising from the inevitable advances in technology. It is possible that funding limitations might serve to accomplish the same purpose. At the same time, advocates of some perspectives on an RMA propose the suspension of current weapons system acquisitions either as a consequence of the terms of that perspective on an RMA or to allow the situation to clarify with the passage of time. These choices not to spend could have far-reaching consequences.

Assessing the Opportunity Cost of Current Activities

If, as Andrew Marshall of the OSD Office of Net Assessment has asserted, we are in the earliest stages of another RMA, what are the consequences of the Army's commitment today of time and resources to the development of Force XXI? Will the Army's early awareness and adaptations enable a swift and effective response? Or will the opportunity cost of Force XXI be an inability to adjust to the "true" RMA that becomes clearer with the passage of time because of choices in weapons, doctrines and organizations made today? What steps will be needed to assure that the Army will be prepared for 2015 or 2025?

Fostering Intraservice Interchange

Regardless of the actual state of implementation today, one of the "strengths" of the Army's Force XXI Synchronization Matrix is that it shows the connectivity between the general ideas behind force XXI and what is needed to carry them out. While the Air Force and Navy have now undertaken more active long-range planning efforts, there do not now appear to be equivalent efforts to examine what is be necessary to connect the new ideas to concrete Air Force and Navy policies, organizations and equipment. Creating future scenarios is only part of the process; what is also needed is a description of what organizations are needed and what decisions should be made today to create the force needed to function in the future.

THE CONCEPT OF A REVOLUTION IN MILITARY AFFAIRS

According to Andrew Marshall, director of the Office of Net Assessments in the Office of the Secretary of Defence:

"A Revolution in Military Affairs (RMA) is a major change in the nature of warfare brought about by the innovative application of new technologies which, combined with dramatic changes in military doctrine and operational and organisational concepts, fundamentally alters the character and conduct of military operations."

Such revolutions have occurred many times in history for a variety of reasons. The most obvious cause is technological "push". The invention of gunpowder, the steam engine, the submarine, the internal combustion engine, the aeroplane, the aircraft carrier, and the atom bomb are some of the most obvious innovations which led to fundamental changes in the conduct of warfare. Some of these technological changes had origins in the civilian world while other revolutions in military affairs were brought about by "social-military revolutions" such as the development of railways, which enabled military forces to be moved and supplied over great distances.

There is a debate about what exactly constitutes a "revolution in military affairs". Some analysts maintain that there have been only three and that these have been linked to the nature of the societies: agrarian, industrial, and information. Others have identified as many as fourteen. There is agreement, however, that technology alone is insufficient to bring about a true revolution in military affairs. For example, almost five centuries elapsed between the invention of gunpowder and its large-scale employment on the battlefield; and in the early stages of the Second World War, Germany's innovative operational concept that using communications technologies to integrate land and air forces enabled it to defeat French and British forces equipped with very similar technology.

In other words, an appropriate operational concept is just as important as technological invention in bringing about a revolution in military affairs.

THE GULF WAR

The Gulf War in early 1991 gave an indication of some of the key components of the current revolution in military affairs. The Gulf War saw the military use of information technology at its zenith. New technologies enhanced Coalition forces' ability to exchange and use information, and highlighted the imperative of denying the adversary the ability to communicate with his forces.

But the most obvious capability was that of precision strike. New guidance technologies have led to the development of munitions that can be delivered with remarkable precision. These include munitions delivered by aircraft, cruise missiles, and artillery. What is often forgotten is the impact that such munitions have on logistics and operations. The ability to destroy certain targets using one or two precision-guided munitions instead of by large-scale bombing cuts the logistic "tail" dramatically.

For instance, during the Gulf War, 6,250 tons of precision-guided munitions were used compared with 81,980 tons of "dumb" bombs. Between 80 and 90 per cent of the precision-guided munitions (PGMs) hit their targets compared with about 25 per cent of dumb bombs. As well as yielding logistic benefits, precision-guided munitions enabled the Coalition forces to minimise collateral damage. It should also be noted that the use of systems such as stealth aircraft and cruise missiles enabled certain attacks to take place against highly defended targets virtually without warning.

Equally important but less obvious was the role played by sophisticated surveillance, reconnaissance, and intelligence gathering systems. These included proven land, air and space systems as well as some prototypes that were pressed into service. Systems included the E-3 Sentry airborne warning and control system (AWACS) aircraft that provides all-weather surveillance, command, control and communications; the RC-135 Rivet Joint electronic intelligence-gathering aircraft; the prototype Joint Surveillance Target Attack Radar System (JSTARS), as well as a wide variety of photo-reconnaissance aircraft.

Extensive use was also made of space assets, both military and commercial, belonging to the United States, the United Kingdom, France, and Russia. These provided the Coalition forces with communication, navigation, surveillance, intelligence, and early warning. Using some 60 satellites, Coalition forces had secure strategic and tactical communications enabling time-sensitive information to be exchanged between ground, naval, and air units spread throughout the theatre. Furthermore Coalition forces were able to locate and designate targets with remarkable precision, navigate through the Iraqi desert better than the Iraqis themselves, and find troops in distress faster than ever before thanks to the Global Positioning System (GPS).

Another feature of the Gulf War was, of course, the use of Patriot missiles to intercept Iraqi Scud missiles.

Much has been written about whether actual performance of precision-guided systems and the Patriot missile interceptor was as impressive as it seemed at the time. Rather less has been made of other shortcomings that were identified such as the presence of many incompatible communications and information systems. Whatever the shortcomings, however, the Gulf War illustrated trends in military technology and provided many lessons for future conflicts.

TECHNOLOGY TRENDS AND NEW AREAS OF WARFARE

Current trends in military technology can be categorised in a variety of ways but all present a broadly similar assessment. The following categories were developed by General Gordon Sullivan, former Chief of Staff of the United States Army and co-author Lt.Col. James M. Dubik:

- Greater lethality

- Increased volume and precision of fire
- Better integrative technology leading to increased efficiency and effectiveness
- Increasing ability of smaller units to create decisive results
- Greater invisibility and increased detectability.

These need little elaboration. Essentially, the trend is towards smaller, more lethal forces, able to deliver a high volume of precise fire through the integration of delivery systems with effective sensor and information distribution systems. At the same time, forces are becoming better able to conceal themselves while their ability to detect hostile forces is increasing.

As with previous revolutions in military affairs, the current revolution is leading to the emergence of new warfare areas. A warfare area is a form of warfare with unique military objectives and is characterised by association with particular forces or systems. Past examples include air warfare, armoured warfare, and strategic bombing, to mention but a few.

As with trends in technology, different categorisations have been developed and all suffer from some degree of overlap. One particularly useful formulation was produced by a team from Science Applications International Corporation (SAIC).The team identified four potential new warfare areas - long-range precision strike, information warfare, dominating manoeuvre, and space warfare.

Precision strike systems have been developed since the 1970s and rapid progress continues to be made. Current systems include long-range cruise missiles, and precision-guided munitions delivered by aircraft and artillery. Provided that adequate targeting information is available and can be distributed efficiently, such systems can be used to mount a co-ordinated attack on hostile targets while minimising collateral damage, friendly-fire casualties, and enemy counterstrikes.

According to the SAIC team, "Precision strike, in the context of the ongoing RMA, is the ability to locate high-value, time-sensitive fixed and mobile targets; to destroy them with a high degree of confidence; and to accomplish this within operationally and strategically significant time lines while minimising collateral damage, friendly fire casualties, and enemy counterstrikes."

The team cites a vivid example to illustrate this area of warfare.

"In 1943, the United States 8th Air Force prosecuted only 50 strategic targets during the course of the entire year. In the first 24 hours of Desert Storm, the combined air forces prosecuted 150 strategic targets - a thousand-fold increase over 1943 capabilities. By the year 2020, it is not out of the realm of possibility that as many as 500 strategically important targets could be struck in the first minute of the campaign - representing a five thousand-fold increase over Desert Storm capabilities."

Information warfare is identified as another new warfare area. Although the critical value of information in warfare has been acknowledged since ancient times, warfare nowadays relies on information systems to an unprecedented degree. Information-gathering systems such as reconnaissance and early-warning satellites, a wide variety of manned and unmanned air-based systems, etc. provide huge amounts of data which can be sorted and channelled through advanced information distribution and communications.

Highly capable information systems are a critical force multiplier and at the same time a potential vulnerability. The goal therefore in this area of warfare is to retain effective use of one's own information assets while destroying or disabling the opponent's. Last year's General Report [AP 237 STC (97) 7] examined the potential for using information systems alone as a means of disrupting both civil and military information infrastructure. In open warfare, however, information warfare is taken to include the use of physically destructive means - such as missile attacks and bombing - to knock out key information assets.

Some analysts have gone so far as to add information warfare as a fourth dimension of warfare to the traditional three of air, land, and sea. "As first wave wars were fought over land, and second wave wars were fought over physical resources and productive capacity, the emerging third wave wars will be for the access to and control of knowledge."

Dominating manoeuvre is also seen as a new warfare area. Manoeuvre has always been a key element in military operations, but the revolution in military affairs envisages manoeuvre on a global scale, on a much-compressed time scale, and with greatly reduced forces.

Dominating manoeuvre is defined as the positioning of forces - integrated with precision strike, space warfare, and information war operations - to attack decisive points, defeat the enemy's "centres of gravity", and accomplish campaign or war objectives. These centres of gravity are key points in command, organisation, resources, transport, etc., whose loss would severely erode an opponent's ability to wage war.

Dominating manoeuvre is distinct from traditional concepts of manoeuvre in several ways. Manoeuvre refers to the "employment of forces on the battlefield through movement in combination with fires, to achieve a position of advantage in order to accomplish the mission." Dominating manoeuvre refers to the positioning of all the forces that could be brought to bear on a theatre of operations, and the integration of precision strike, space warfare, and information warfare. The goal would be to employ these various assets against the enemy's critical points simultaneously rather than sequentially, and to re-engage those targets whenever necessary.

Ideally, this would entail the employment of new means of movement such as sea transportation systems capable of 100 knots, supersonic air transport, advanced logistic support and perhaps smaller, more self-sufficient field units.

Space warfare is viewed as another new area of warfare. The military importance of space has been clear for over 40 years but only recently has it become possible to envisage an almost seamless integration of space systems into military operations. The utility of space systems for communications is well established but their use for global, real-time surveillance, reconnaissance and targeting is a more recent phenomenon.

Space systems also provide precise navigation and meteorological data.

Further into the future, space transportation systems, anti-satellite weapons, missile defences, and even space-based ground attack systems might play important roles in the conduct of military operations although some of these capabilities would raise complex arms control issues that would have to be addressed.

Certainly, the achievement of superiority in space assets would be a critical advantage and its denial to an opponent would be an important war goal.

NEW OPERATIONAL CONCEPTS

Although most analysts are persuaded that some sort of revolution in military affairs is indeed taking place, others maintain that the changes now occurring are significant but essentially incremental, that there is a need to deal with the growing complexity of modern warfare but that wholesale changes in operational concepts are unwarranted. The main focus of debate, however, is on what the revolution in military affairs will mean, and how best to develop operational concepts to take full advantage of it.

Joint Vision 2010

Many of the concepts that have been discussed in the context of the revolution in military affairs have clearly been absorbed by the United States military leadership. In May 1996, the then Chairman of the Joint Chiefs of Staff, General John Shalikashvili published a document entitled "Joint Vision 2010" (JV 2010) which is a conceptual template describing how United States armed forces should expect to conduct warfare in the early 21st century. This makes clear that technology is only one dimension, and that military effectiveness also depends upon leadership, personnel, training, organizational structure, and operational concepts.

JV 2010 acknowledges that technologically superior equipment has been critical to the success of United States forces in combat. The report also identifies four key technological trends that will greatly enhance capabilities. These are as follows:

- Long-range precision capability, combined with a wide range of delivery systems
- The ability to produce a broader range of potential weapons effects, from less-lethal to hard-target kill
- Low observable technologies and the ability to mask friendly forces
- Information systems and systems integration.

JV 2010 asserts that the combination of these technologies will provide an order of magnitude improvement in lethality. Underpinning future operations will be information technology that will provide the ability to see, prioritize, assign, and assess information so that American forces will achieve "dominant battlespace awareness". This is described as "an interactive 'picture' which will yield much more accurate assessments of friendly and enemy operations within the area of interest." A key goal, therefore, will be "information superiority", the capability to collect, process, and disseminate an uninterrupted flow of information while exploiting or denying an adversary's ability to do the same.

Another key aspect of warfare described in JV 2010 is - as the name implies - the conduct of joint operations.

"By 2010, we should be able to change how we conduct the most intense joint operations. Instead of relying on massed forces and sequential operations, we will achieve massed effects in other ways. Information superiority and advances in technology will enable us to achieve the desired effects through the tailored application of joint combat power."

JV 2010 introduces four new operational concepts: dominant manoeuvre, precision engagement, full-dimensional protection, and focused logistics.

Dominant Manoeuvre

This concept calls for the co-ordinated employment of forces that might be extremely dispersed. It also calls for simultaneous rather than sequential operations. According to JV 2010: "Dominant manoeuvre will be the multidimensional application of information, engagement, and mobility capabilities to position and employ widely dispersed joint air, land, sea, and space forces to accomplish the assigned operational tasks.

Dominant maneuvre will allow our forces to gain a decisive advantage by controlling the breadth, depth, and height of the battlespace. Through a combination of asymmetric leverage, achieved by our positional advantages, as well as decisive speed and tempo, dominant manoeuvre allows us to apply decisive force to attack enemy centres of gravity at all levels and compels an adversary to either react from a position of disadvantage or quit.

Dominant manoeuvre will require forces that are adept at conducting sustained and synchronized operations from dispersed locations. They must be able to apply overwhelming force in the same medium and create asymmetric advantages by attacking cross-dimensionally, such as air or sea against ground or ground and sea against air defences.

These forces must have the ability to outpace and outmanoeuvre the enemy. Current systems, enhanced by information superiority, will provide a clearer picture of enemy and friendly locations.

Information superiority also will allow joint commanders to co-ordinate widely dispersed units, receive accurate feedback, and execute more demanding, higher precision requirements. Increasingly lethal direct and indirect fire systems, with longer ranges and more accurate targeting, will increase the punch of these forces as they manoeuvre."

Dominant manoeuvre is also seen as providing additional self-protection since force elements would be more dispersed, and force build-up times more rapid, because missions would be conducted with less manpower and equipment in the actual theatre of operations. "Altogether...dominant manoeuvre is a prescription for more agile, faster moving joint operations, which will combine air, land, and maritime forces more effectively to deliver decisive combat power."

Precision Engagement

Precision engagement envisages the employment of precision delivery systems by widely dispersed forces co-ordinated through highly capable information distribution systems.

"Precision engagement will consist of a system of systems that enables our forces to locate the objective or target, provide responsive command and control, generate the desired effect, assess our level of success, and retain the flexibility to re-engage with precision when required. Even from extended ranges, precision engagement will allow us to shape the battlespace, enhancing the protection of our forces. Information operations will tie together high fidelity target acquisition, prioritized requirements, and command and control of joint forces within the battlespace. This combination will provide a greater assurance of delivering the desired effect, lessen the risk to our forces, and minimize collateral damage."

It is important to stress that precision engagement means more than just striking targets more accurately. It is a broader concept that brings together the many means of achieving precision strikes so they form a means of conducting a precisely co-ordinated attack involving subsequent damage assessment and re-engagement if necessary.

Full-Dimensional Protection

Full-dimensional protection essentially entails protecting friendly forces from the full spectrum of potential threats. Again, information systems would lie at the heart of this capability.

"The primary prerequisite for full-dimensional protection will be control of the battlespace to ensure our forces can maintain freedom of action during deployment, maneuver and engagement, while providing multi-layered defenses for our forces and facilities at all levels. Full-dimensional protection will enable the effective employment of our forces while degrading opportunities for the enemy. It will be essential, in most cases, for gaining and maintaining the initiative required to execute decisive operations. The concept will be proactive, incorporating both offensive and defensive actions that may extend well into areas of enemy operations. Full-dimensional protection will be built upon information superiority which will provide multidimensional awareness and assessment, as well as identification of all forces in the battlespace. Information warfare will support this effort by protecting our information systems and processes, while denying an adversary the similar capabilities."

Full-dimensional protection will incorporate techniques ranging from information warfare and concealment to passive defences and layered missile and air defences. Again, the employment of widely dispersed forces also limits the ability particularly of hostile regional powers to disable or disrupt operations. Emphasis is also placed on the employment of new sensors to detect chemical and biological attacks at great ranges.

Focused Logistics

The importance of logistics in warfare cannot be overstated. The delivery of appropriate supplies to the right place at the right time is vital. Although much has been made of the tempo of operations in the Gulf War, this tempo could only be achieved after months of building up supplies in the region. JV 2010 envisages future operations being conducted with fewer resources in the actual theatre, but the logistic challenge will be no less severe given the intention to achieve an even more rapid tempo and intensity of operations with force elements that are more widely dispersed.

JV 2010 introduces the concept of "focused logistics" to meet the demands of operations in the early 21st century. Logistics will be "responsive, flexible, and precise" through the fusion of information, logistics, and transportation technologies. The goal is to be able to track and redirect assets even while en route, and to provide support in hours or days rather than weeks. Modular supplies, specifically tailored "combat service support packages", and pre-positioning will be used extensively, and lessons, techniques and assets from the business sector will be incorporated as appropriate.

THE CONCEPT FOR FUTURE JOINT OPERATIONS (CFJO)

The Concept for Future Joint Operations (CFJO) expands the new operational concepts contained in JV 2010 to provide a more detailed foundation for follow-on capabilities assessments. It also represents an important step toward the objective of achieving the right capabilities for the challenges to be faced in the 21st century.

The CFJO aims at thinking about the future joint operations in the context of the broad range of challenges anticipated; it also aims at identifying shortcomings in order to develop better and faster processes for evaluating and adapting emerging warfighting capabilities. The CFJO amplifies JV 2010's four operational concepts - dominant manoeuvre, precision engagement, full-dimensional protection, and focused logistics - each enabled by information superiority and technological innovation. The idea is to transform key JV 2010 ideas into actual joint force capabilities. The CFJO is intended to be a living document that will provide the initial basis for a variety of assessment activities.

In sum, the JV 2010 constituted an intellectual work defining concepts, whereas the CFJO document is moving to the next step: the actual experimentation so as to turn the concepts into capabilities. The CFJO looks at doctrine, implications of future organisations, how to train the future force, the leadership required for the future force, the materiel aspects and people. The CFJO intends to assess whether the four concepts are relevant and correct. The experimental process consists in war games, command post exercises, field exercises to experiment with the concepts and prove their accuracy for the future force.

"The CFJO is the first step toward implementing JV 2010. It is intended to be a marketplace of ideas - a tool to help think about future operations. It is a starting point which allows to explore the effects of different combinations of technological and operational variables in seminars, materiel, simulations, exercises, and other experiments to find the combination that best facilitates JV 2010 Full Spectrum Dominance. This exploration will generate ideas for making timely and relevant changes in six critical areas: personnel, leadership, doctrine, education and training, organisation, and materiel."

Army Vision 2010 and Army After Next

Army Vision 2010, released in November 1996, identified the patterns of operations, concepts, enablers and technologies the Army needed in the 21st century to convert its vision into reality. It represented a conceptual template of how the Army would achieve new levels of effectiveness as the land component member of the joint warfighting team.

Army Vision 2010 focused on a coherent view of the future and on the Army's unique ability to conduct prompt and sustained operations on land across the full spectrum of crisis. It also identified the operational imperatives and enabling technologies that the Army needed in order to remain a full spectrum force in the Information Age.

Army Vision 2010 visualises developing concepts and technologies to improve capabilities through 2010, while the Army After Next (AAN) project is working on conceptualising the geostrategic environment 30 years into the future. The AAN was established in February 1996 to provide the Army leadership with a long-term view of the Army's future from about 2010 to 2025. This programme would help the Army adapt to the demands of future warfare. The AAN project includes a series of wargames, workshops, and conferences that provide a venue for development of a long-term vision for the Army. There are four major areas of research: geopolitics, military art, human and organisational theory, and technology.

The AAN is a theoretical construct for the Army senior leaders to gain insights about the likely nature of future warfare, the requirements for land power in those years and the issues which must be addressed in order to exploit future opportunities.

The Full Spectrum Dominance (FSD)

The main purpose of all those documents is to attain the Full Spectrum Dominance (FSD), which is the ability to dominate an adversary and control any situation across the whole range of military operations. The capability to acquire battlespace situational awareness - i.e. the capability to maintain real-time, all-weather awareness of what is occurring in and above a wide geographical area of operations - and information dominance is the cornerstone for obtaining full spectrum dominance in the battlespace. The warfighter must be able to see, hear, disrupt, deny, out-communicate and out-think any adversary.

Full spectrum dominance and the ability to conduct prompt and sustained operations throughout the entire spectrum of crisis will be achieved through the US Army Vision 2010, which, with its set of operational imperatives - Project the force, Decisive operations, Shape the battlespace, Protect the force, and Sustain the force - serves as the linchpin to the concept of future warfighting capabilities in Joint Vision 2010. It also serves as the foundation for the Army After Next, which represents a long-term vision.

IMPLICATIONS FOR THE ALLIANCE

The debate about the revolution in military affairs has been conducted almost exclusively in the United States. While several of the United States allies have in recent years conducted defence reviews, no other nation has had such a public debate about the future conduct of warfare, nor does any other nation seem to be undertaking such a wholesale reappraisal of operational concepts.

In some respects this is not surprising. The United States maintains a defence research and development effort that dwarfs those of all other nations.

In 1996, the United States government spent about $37 billion on defence research and development, while France, the United Kingdom, Germany, and Italy together spent less than $10 billion. Furthermore, European defence R&D efforts are predominantly national in nature and not part of a co-ordinated programme.

Given this disparity, the existing technology gap can only widen so that there is an increasing risk that the United States will continue to develop technologies and concepts that dramatically outpace those of the European allies. Already the United States is unique in NATO in possessing substantial long-range heavy-lift capabilities, the full spectrum of military space-based assets, stealth fighters and bombers, and tactical missile defences.

Its capabilities in many other areas such as amphibious operations, electronic intelligence gathering, electronic warfare, and precision strike are also far more substantial than those of its allies.

While disparities in equipment numbers are inevitable, provided that equipment technology levels and operational concepts are similar, the Alliance can successfully operate as an integrated force.

However, if technologies and concepts of operations are markedly different, it will become increasingly difficult to truly integrate Alliance forces into a cohesive whole.

Certainly, today's compatibility problems in areas such as tank munitions and communications would seem trivial by comparison.

The United States has already shown its concerns for this "technology gap". The Department of Defence has recently asked the Defence Science Board to conduct a study to determine how to make the revolution in military affairs work in the context of coalition operations. As the DoD exploits this revolution, "it must ensure" - it is declared in the terms of reference for the study - "that the emerging US military capabilities are compatible with potential future coalition partners". More specifically, the task force overseeing the study, which is due by the end of this year, is gathering information on issues such as:

- experiences of recent coalition operations (e.g. Bosnia)
- plausible future coalition scenarios
- the role of advanced concept technology demonstrations and simulation techniques in fostering coalition compatibility

- development of command, control, communications, computers, intelligence, surveillance and reconnaissance systems (C4ISR)
- balancing interoperability with security needs
- strategies and tactics that make complementary use of US and coalition partners' strengths.

Of course, the revolution in military affairs might turn out to be more of an evolution than a revolution. Changes in operational concepts might actually be slower in arriving than expected.

A certain "cultural" resistance, as well as contrasts among the different military services, US Army, Air Force and Navy, should be taken into account. Even if that is the case, the United States' allies cannot afford to be complacent.

There is no doubt that the transatlantic defence technology gap exists and is widening. Without remedial action by the United States' allies, sooner or later - and probably sooner - the gap will become a rift. And how could an equitable partnership be preserved where one party had undergone a revolution in military affairs and the other had not?

Joint Vision 2010 states that United States' "history, strategy, and recent experience" suggest that it will usually work in concert with its friends and allies in almost all operations.

While this is certainly true, the revolution in military affairs begs important questions about how the allies can ensure that they will be able to work in concert with the United States.

The answers to those questions are, understandably, political as much as economic.

While all European members of the Alliance are facing stable, or slightly declining, defence budgets, defence equipment costs, according to recent estimates, are rising at an average of 10 per cent each year in Europe. In this environment, it becomes impractical for individual nations to develop and produce independently the technologies and the weapon systems needed to keep pace with the revolution in military affairs. And since coalition warfare is the most likely future scenario, the only viable option is co-operation in the development and production of defence systems.

This co-operation will have to involve the geopolitical, military and industrial arenas on both sides of the Atlantic. It will also be facilitated by the ongoing efforts to increase the efficiency of the defence industrial structures in the United States and Europe and to improve transatlantic industrial ties.

On the European side, moreover, a consolidation of defence industries is a prerequisite for reducing the transatlantic gap. In the last ten years, a dramatic consolidation process has taken place in the United States: today's top five defence firms then numbered more than 50 independent businesses.

Similar opportunities certainly exist among European NATO partners, as we have begun to see.

In the next few years, consolidation will eventually increase the competitiveness and the capacity for developing autonomous initiatives of the European industry. Of course, this process has its limits, and many weapons programmes must, and will, remain national. However, consolidation and co-operation is the only option for all systems that require interoperability in coalition conflicts: air defence, communications, intelligence, chemical and biological defence, information warfare and security.

Since it is clear that the European defence industry will have to co-operate with the United States in many sectors, this strategy, as a German industrialist has indicated, needs to be clearly defined:

"It is, however, necessary that the European industry agrees on the way how to consolidate and to define those sectors, on which a cooperation on an equal basis - and this is important - with the United States of America is wished and possible. From a European point of view a coordination between Great Britain, France and Germany which is to be expanded soon to Italy, Sweden and others is a prerequisite. (...) Out of a German point of view this cooperation is unavoidable taking political security into consideration and this cooperation is most desirable for Europe. It is, however, at the same time necessary to determine the fields in which Europe should further compete with the United States."

In conclusion, even if the European NATO nations develop their own revolutions in military affairs - and it is desirable that they do so - and they succeed in achieving a certain form of integration in the European defence industry, they will always have to rely on US high technologies, especially in the field of "information dominance". Obviously, it is in the interest of the United States themselves to share part of these defence systems and technologies in order to fill the gap with their allies and maintain the problems of interoperability at a manageable level.

4

War and Strategy in the 21st Century

Current debates over America's place in the world often move uneasily between military and diplomatic factors. It is misleading, however, to abstract security issues from the wider context of foreign policy. Events in the twenty-first century will test the limits to American strength but not its fundamentals. These tests will underscore, however, the inability of technology to overcome all challenges and the risk that excess militarization of foreign policy would discourage what America needs most: acute and ongoing assessments of its capability and limitations.

To emphasize the limitations of military power may be surprising given the current conventional wisdom that the United States is the sole superpower. According to the generally established view, the so-called Revolution in Military Affairs based on information warfare capability and other factors will enable the most technologically advanced powers, especially the United States, to overcome both distance and resistance to secure victory with minimal casualties. In many respects, this is another version of the mechanization of the military imagination that has been so potent ever since the advent of the airplane and tank.

It is obviously important to seize and develop every advantage new weaponry can bring, but it is mistaken to imagine that a technological edge guarantees victory at low cost. To be sure, advantages in weaponry are valuable in symmetrical warfare between opposing forces that operate in a similar fashion, but even then a host of other factors intrude, including strategy, tactics, leadership, unit cohesion, morale, and contextual issues such as the respective determination of the powers engaged. In asymmetrical warfare, by contrast, the advantages conferred by superior weaponry are severely curtailed. Compare, for instance, the frustration of American forces in the asymmetrical Vietnam War with Israeli success in the Six-Day War. Finally, technological advantage in both types of conflict inevitably inspire the development of countermeasures involving weapons, tactics, or strategy. Thus the impact of air power has been lessened by the development of antiaircraft weapons whose cost-benefit payoff is immense compared to that of a state-of-the-art bomber.

There is no reason to imagine that this process will cease. Thus, there will remain military limits to effective force projection, and skillful policymaking will continue to require a shrewd understanding of capability and limits.

This process is not new. Former great powers also struggled to learn and adjust to their capabilities and limits. Spain, the first state whose empire spanned the world, reached its limits in the late sixteenth century in Chile, northern Mexico, and the rebellious Netherlands. In the mid- seventeenth century, the Dutch proved unable to hold coastal Brazil against Portuguese reconquest and bases on Taiwan against the Chinese. Between 1775 and 1842, the British lost hold of their thirteen North American colonies, intervened unsuccessfully in Argentina and Egypt, and suffered defeat in Afghanistan. In historical terms, therefore, it is perfectly logical to suppose that while American power will dominate the twenty-first century, it will also encounter its limits. The understanding of this apparent contradiction is important if the American public and policymakers are to be brought to appreciate what the United States can and cannot reasonably do in the world.

Yet such an assessment flies in the face of the natural tendency, especially prevalent in "can-do" America, to formulate goals and then assume that they can and ought to be implemented. Two philosophies are at issue. The first is the optimistic Whiggish tradition of interventionism and the creation of systems to solve problems and prevent their recurrence.

The other tradition is the realistic, or conservative, emphasis on the mutability and uncertainty of human affairs and the risks of a system-based approach, a tradition that in Britain looks back to the more cautious approach to foreign policy taken by Tories in the eighteenth century. This entails a pragmatic and prudential approach to foreign commitments. As Samuel Johnson pointed out in his Thoughts on the Late Transactions Respecting Falklands Islands (1771), a pamphlet written to urge caution in the great- power confrontation with France and Spain:

> It seems to be almost the universal error of historians to suppose it politically, as it is physically true, that every effort has a proportionate cause. In the inanimate action of matter upon matter, the motion produced can but be equal to the force of the moving power; but the operations of life, whether private or public, admit no such laws. The caprices of voluntary agents laugh at calculation.

The military dimension of this tension can be discussed generally with regard to grand strategy and more narrowly in terms of force structure. A Whiggish tendency will encourage intervention, or, in military terms, forward commitment and force projection. Aside from the problems that this poses in foreign policy —taking on commitments, narrowing options, risking relationships with allies, and threatening domestic consensus— it also has serious military implications that the shrinking size of modern militaries only exacerbates. While the decrease in size has not lessened the capability of a high-tech military to deliver a hard punch in symmetrical conflict, it has definitely affected its ability to follow through by occupying territory. Indeed, America's ability to mount more than one large-force projection exercise involving a significant ground presence can now be questioned. It would certainly place undue strain on existing commitments.

Again, this is not a new phenomenon. The Boer War in South Africa (1899–1902) entailed a heavy burden for Britain and led to a dangerous draw down of military resources in the British Isles. The army would have been hard pressed had those years also brought major agitation in Ireland or Russian pressure on the northwest frontier of India.

Men, Machines, and Missions

Resource limitations encourage short-term commitments of overseas forces. Technology can help, not least with air deployment and resupply, but it cannot eliminate the problems of dealing with intractable local opposition, whether the mission is defined as a conflict, peace-keeping, or police action. Major-General John "Boney" Fuller, a leading thinker on military affairs, wrote to an American correspondent in July 1965: "Today your government and its military advisors appear to have accepted the concept that the way to defeat Communism in Vietnam is by bombing when clearly the precepts garnered from World War Two should have told them that ideas cannot be dislodged by TNT."

The future prospects for global military interventionism are questionable at best. However much a state or group of states might dominate at the high end of the power spectrum, and however much diplomacy may postpone or alleviate problems, the cost of trying and failing to control a rogue state are likely to rise to points that reward caution, and military leaderships are apt to encourage such prudence. On the other hand, as the experience of the Vietnam War suggests, politicians lacking knowledge of military affairs listen only to the advice they want to hear and even manipulate promotions to ensure that they hear it, and politicians can usually find within the military officers willing to tell them what they want in order to advance or protect their own careers. Thus it is possible that the imperatives of political commitments to, for example, Israel or Taiwan, may override prudence in a crisis.

Force structure is a related issue that is particularly serious for the United States. An emphasis on preparation for great power symmetrical warfare, first with the Soviet Union and now with China, has led to a stress on air power and long-range missiles. In the 1950s, jet aircraft carrying nuclear bombs appeared to be the best challenge to overwhelming Soviet conventional superiority. The shift to submarine and land-based intercontinental ballistic missiles took the approach further, and it continues with the interest shown in space-based weapons.

This emphasis led to a relative shift of resources away from conventional forces, especially the army, and downplayed the multiple tasking of forces and preparation demanded by the range of commitments the United States might face. The result became clear in Vietnam, where courage and can-do spirit could not compensate for the lack of adequate training and doctrine in counterinsurgency warfare on the ground and in close-support air operations.

Coordinating air and ground forces effectively has always been a problem since the air force became an independent service. The doctrine and structure of air power have emphasized its capacity to deliver decisive victory independently, rather than through support of land and sea operations. This remains an issue for the United States, since the joint structures and doctrines that have been developed still focus on symmetrical conflict rather than supporting forces in asymmetrical roles such as counterinsurgency or peace-keeping.

Indeed the challenge of counterinsurgency warfare touches on the relationship between the United States and its allies. The specific linkage comes from the idea that "policing" roles can be left to allies while Americans focus on high-tempo warfare and the weapons, training, and doctrine it requires. This argument clearly suits particular interest groups within the American military, but it neglects the realities of alliance warfare and the U.S. need to maintain the capability to control allied operations.

Alliances and (Mis)perceptions

Tension exists between the military "reading" of alliances and its diplomatic counterpart. The military emphasizes instrumentality, the question of whether allies will do as they are told in what is a clear hierarchy of roles and decision making. From the perspective of this question, the debate over alliances revolves around two points: the U.S. sense of its allies' ingratitude, as reflected in their policies and lack of preparedness, and the allies' resentment of being expected to meet goals that they had little or no role in setting.

While both perspectives are valid, they reflect a weakness in perception and an overly rigid sense of the character of alliances. Regarding ingratitude, there is often a fundamental failure in understanding the perceptions, interests, and problems of allies. The United States at times has been the recipient of this sort of misunderstanding. After the War of American Independence, the French resented American political and economic actions that seemed to ignore their recent assistance. Conversely, it can be argued that American sentiment from the late 1930s through 1941 was misunderstood by those who were surprised at the American failure to confront and fight Germany, not least because this view overlooked concerns about Japan.

Policymakers and the informed public in the United States have expressed in recent years their own anger about the failings of allies. These resentments have related to specifics, such as Britain's failure to take the same role in Vietnam that it had taken earlier in Korea, and also to more general concerns over general attitudes policies. A frequently expressed view is that both European countries and Japan refuse to invest adequately in advanced weaponry. Consequently, they rely on American protection and fail to pull their weight.

While understandable from a certain perspective, this analysis involves major flaws. First and foremost is the characteristic tendency of the American public to treat the world as an isotropic surface, everywhere equal. Militarily, that leads to the conclusion that all powers should strive to match American forces and that Europeans in particular must "mind the gap."

Of course, this argument ignores the role played by military forces in different societies and the tasks they are assigned.

Because Americans are not used to the idea that their army might be deployed for policing duties within the United States, they tend to underplay the army's role as the ultimate arm of state, as typified by the British army's deployment in Northern Ireland. Indeed, many states view counterinsurgency efforts and other domestic responsibilities as more important than preparation for warfare against other states. This is particularly true in Latin America.

Other European countries, notably France and Italy, have used conscription to teach citizenship as much as to promote military effectiveness. Governments that have felt threatened by the professional military also welcome the added political benefit of diluting the power of the officer corps. Such policies seem clearly anachronistic if military forces are ranked by their technological proficiency and capacity for high-tempo operations. But that perspective neglects the multiple contexts within which military power must be considered and the role of choice. Political contexts always override abstract considerations about optimal doctrine and structure.

Resentment among the European members of NATO arises from the perceived lack of American consultation with them with regard to delivering the alliance's goals. It is difficult for many Americans to appreciate the fundamental differences between American views on, for instance, the Middle East, East Asia, or Cuba, and those of their allies. But those differences impose one of the most severe limits on American power and underline the important role foreign policy expertise will play in preserving America's superpower status. Understanding the parameters within which allies can be expected to operate demands knowledge, deftness, and expertise that have not always been the U.S. government's strong suit.

Unilateralism vs. Multilateralism

Even without allies, the United States will remain the world's leading power and continue to achieve most of its own goals so long as it keeps those goals limited. Again, it remains unclear how public opinion would accept the concept of limits in defence and foreign policy since the American people, hence their politicians, have a low tolerance of vulnerability and fear. This leads to demands for an invulnerable and comprehensive defence system, but in practice no military establishment is likely to be both. A powerful clue can be found in popular culture, such as Clive Cussler's adventure novels or Hollywood westerns and action films. In both cases, allies generally appear to be unreliable, if not dishonest, and the lone hero is transposed into an image of American power.

Such an image might work for an isolationist state with few links to the global economy and international finance, but it is difficult to see the United States adopting this role in coming decades. Were it to do so, Americans would face the same risks that obtained in the 1930s: the consolidation of power blocs that can be threatening no matter how economically inefficient they are in the long run. American disengagement would encourage the alignment among France, Russia, and Germany, an alignment that is already too powerful within Europe, and encourage Japan to accommodate Chinese power, possibly at Taiwan's and even South Korea's expense. Most threatening would be an accentuation of Russo- Chinese links that have been forged in recent years and are among the most unwelcome legacies of the Clinton era.

Given these scenarios, it is easy to understand why missile defence systems and greater American self-reliance appear to be the correct military and political responses. This is particularly true given that the United States faces few challenges near its borders, with the possible exception of instability in post-Castro Cuba. But such a grand strategy will leave America with a force structure and a military doctrine that provide scant preparation for other commitments. The United States can still exploit advances in military doctrine and weapons in order to retain its lead, but aggregate military capability is not the same as capability or success in any particular scenario. The specific danger the United States faces is the conviction that the technological edge known by the shorthand of the Revolution in Military Affairs can substitute for the political willingness to commit troops and shed blood.

To be sure, it is better to be prepared for the wrong war than not to be prepared at all— but only marginally so.

September 11 and After

It might legitimately be asked how far the appalling attacks of September 11 have led to a need for revision since this paper was originally presented at the Foreign Policy Research Institute in spring 2001. Such a brutal assault on civil society and Western power is exactly what could have been expected in a struggle with terrorism that knows no boundaries. A historian and friend to America can point out that nothing makes the success of terrorism any more inevitable than the victory of policies against it. The United States and other Western governments cannot avoid aggressive measures against terrorism. Aside from the obvious analogy with law enforcement, namely that the continuation of crime does not lead us to dispense with policing, there is also the concern that failing to act against terrorists simply will lead to more terrorism and discourage its domestic and international opponents. There is a particular need to act when guerillas terrorize civilian populations and undermine justice and authority by destroying those they term collaborators.

Specific circumstances dictate the success or failure of particular military strategies. Napoleonic France suppressed popular resistance in Calabrese, but not in Spain. Counterinsurgency operations after World War II succeeded in Greece, Lithuania, Ukraine, and Malaysia, but not in Vietnam. Political circumstances, particularly the degree of domestic support for insurgents and their access to foreign support, have been the decisive factor in each case. Tito's decision to stop aiding Greek Communists after he had broken with the Soviets in 1948 played an important part in ending the conflict in Greece. Similarly, anticommunist guerilla movements in Eastern Europe were gravely weakened by the lack of adequate foreign support in the 1940s and 1950s.

Thus, alongside the need to strike back militarily after September 11, a comparable political response is also required. America's military is highly capable of conducting effective in-

and-out operations, and there is no political call for the sort of lengthy occupation in which the attacker becomes the defender. However, it must be noted that political strategies can create problems as difficult as those raised by the ill-adapted military doctrines and force structures discussed above. Here there is room for debate that takes a hard look at aspects of American society and public culture that increase vulnerability to terrorism as well as foreign policies and commitments that are inopportune. The troubling persistence of anti-Americanism in parts of the Islamic world requires a thoughtful political response that will contribute to the defence of America and, with it, the free world.

A COOPERATIVE STRATEGY FOR 21ST CENTURY SEAPOWER

A Cooperative Strategy for 21st Century Seapower is the United States' newest maritime strategy. It was presented by the U.S. Chief of Naval Operations and the Commandants of the U.S. Marine Corps and U.S. Coast Guard at the International Seapower Symposium at the U.S.Naval War College in Newport, Rhode Island on October 17, 2007. The new maritime strategy explains the comprehensive role of the sea services in an era marked by globalization and uncertainty.

The development of a new strategy began in June 2006 at the direction of former Chief of Naval Operations and Chairman of the Joint Chiefs of Staff, Admiral Mike Mullen. The last maritime strategy was published at the height of the Cold War in 1986 and needed to be updated to reflect the challenges of the 21st century. This was the first maritime strategy to be signed by the leaders of all three U.S. sea services, the Navy, Marines, and Coast Guard.

A Cooperative Strategy for 21st Century Seapower is not infused with typical military-focused language. The strategy makes a case for the value of seapower in preserving the American way of life by maintaining safe, global commerce operations across the seas. It acknowledges that there is a global system of connected economies which depends on the freedom of movement across the maritime commons; the principal means for the transit of 90% of the world's commerce by weight and volume. With such a global interconnection of economies, shocks to the system caused by regional conflicts, terrorist attacks, natural disasters, and war all have potential global impact.

The strategy states that U.S. vital interests are best served by having forward positioned maritime forces around the globe, postured in a way to prevent, deter, limit, and localize conflicts, wars, and disruptions to the global system that all rely upon. International from beginning to end, the strategy describes the necessity to forge global partnerships to establish a resilient peace.

During testimony before the House Armed Services Committee on December 13, 2007, General James T. Conway, Commandant of the U.S. Marine Corps said:

The basic premise of our newly published maritime strategy is that the United States is a force for good in the world-that while we are capable of launching a clenched fist when we must- offering the hand of friendship is also an essential and prominent tool in our kit. That premise flows from the belief that preventing wars is as important as winning wars.

Expanding naval core capabilities

A Cooperative Strategy for 21st Century Seapower articulates that U.S. maritime forces be able to operate across the full spectrum of operations, raising the prevention of war to a level equal to the conduct of war. The strategy delineates the following six expanded core capabilities for U.S. Seapower to achieve a balance of peacetime engagement and major combat operations capabilities:

1. Forward presence
2. Deterrence
3. Sea control
4. Power projection
5. Maritime security
6. Humanitarian assistance/disaster response

The first four core elements listed have always been fundamental to U.S. maritime forces and were essential elements to the United States and its allies and partners during theCold War. The last two, Maritime Security and Humanitarian Assistance/Disaster Response, were elevated to core elements by the new maritime strategy. The U.S. sea services have traditionally done these types of missions but they will seek to be more proactive and purposeful in training, missions, and resourcing the missions and capabilities associated with them.

The new maritime strategy reaffirms the need for regionally concentrated, forward deployed combat power; but also places emphasis on globally distributed, mission-tailored maritime forces. Specifically the new maritime strategy states that:

1. Regionally concentrated, credible combat power: The U.S.sea services will maintain credible combat power forward "in the Western Pacific and the Persian Gulf[sic]/Indian Ocean to protect vital interests, assure friends and allies of the continuing U.S. commitment to regional security, and deter and dissuade potential adversaries and peer competitors." The maritime strategy states that the U.S. does not seek adversaries, nor single out any one nation, but will be best postured to maintain security and freedom of movement across the maritime domain.
2. Globally distributed, mission-tailored maritime forces: The U.S. sea services will establish a persistent global presence using distributed forces that are organized by mission, comprising integrated U.S. Navy, Marine Corps, and Coast Guard capabilities. Aircraft carrier and Expeditionary Strike Groups will continue to deploy much as they do now, but they will also use smaller groups or units to provide this presence across the globe, such as the Global Fleet Station.

In signing a cooperative strategy, the U.S. sea services also raise the importance of cooperative relationships as the basis for global maritime security – a common goal of all maritime nations regardless of political differences. Maritime nations have always shared common interests on the sea and even land-locked nations rely on the safety of those seas to maintain and enhance their way of life. The challenge for the United States is how to apply seapower in a manner that protects U.S. vital and domestic interests, even as it promotes greater collective security, stability, and trust across the globe.

During the presentation of the new strategy to nearly 100 chiefs of navies and coast guards from around the world at the Naval War College on October 17, 2007, Chief of Naval Operations, Admiral Gary Roughead, the Navy's top uniformed officer, said humanitarian and disaster aid is built on, "peace-time relationships to help mitigate human suffering by working together with other agencies and other nations responding to crises."

While presenting the U.S. Coast Guard perspective on the new U.S. maritime strategy at the same symposium, Admiral Thad Allen, Commandant of the U.S. Coast Guard, said the new maritime strategy reinforced the time-honored missions his service carried out in this U.S. since 1790. He said:

It reinforces the Coast Guard maritime strategy of safety, security and stewardship, and it reflects not only the global reach of our maritime services but the need to integrate and synchronize and act with our coalition and international partners to not only win wars... but to prevent wars.

The new strategy is viewed as a welcome makeover from the Soviet-centric document developed in 1986, but has drawn some criticism from military analysts who say it is too broad-based and lacked a fourth, "implementation" stage. Former Secretary of the Navy John Lehman hailed its tenets but pointed out it was lacking information on the actual hardware needed to carry out the policy. In the November 2007 issue of Proceedings magazine, he explained, "we (need) a clear and well-articulated statement of what we need to implement that strategy – tightly bound to the strategy itself." He concedes however, that the most important attribute of the updated strategy is, "that it exists at all ... and that its development was taken so seriously."

Development of the new maritime strategy

The new maritime strategy included many voices during its development. Input was sought from individuals and organizations such as the United States Department of Defence, the Joint Staff, Unified Combatant Commands, business and academia and other U.S. interagency partners.

During development of the new strategy, military planners sought to address the changing 21st century world and anticipate key uncertainties such as what the United States' grand military strategy and foreign policy will be in the next few decades. Planners considered a range of maritime strategy options: primacy, cooperative security, selective engagement and offshore balance.

These paradigms commonly are used by military planners to measure the quality of strategic components against hypothetical challenges. A series of war games conducted by the Naval War College helped determine which options were the best to focus upon.

From six hypothetical paradigms, planners drafted five possible maritime strategies, which were later whittled down to three. With three strategies in hand, teams of senior leaders and military planners from the U.S. Navy, Marine Corps and Coast Guard traveled to locations around the United States to present the strategy options to American citizens as part of a program called the "Conversation with the Country" to elicit their feedback and input on potential strategies.

The Conversation with the Country program is discussed in the preface of the new strategy:

Our citizens were deeply involved in development of this strategy through a series of public forums known as the "Conversations with the Country." Three themes dominated these discussions: our people want us to remain strong; they want us to protect them and our homeland; and they want us to work with partners around the world to prevent war. This message, coupled with rigorous academic research, analysis and debate, led to a comprehensive strategy designed to meet the expectations and needs of the American people.

The sea services hosted "Conversations with the Country" in the following cities during the development of the maritime strategy:

1. Phoenix – January 24, 2007
2. Atlanta – February 9, 2007
3. Seattle – March 9, 2007
4. San Francisco – March 12, 2007
5. Chicago – April 9, 2007
6. New York – April 16, 2007

Feedback from the participants in the first round of the Conversations with the Country program helped shape the final maritime strategy, which was unveiled October 17, 2007. Another round of Conversations began following the launch of the new maritime strategy that brought senior officers from the Navy, Marine Corps and Coast Guard to more U.S. cities, where they presented the new strategy to business and civic leaders and discussed future roles of the three sea services in protecting the homeland and working with global partners to prevent war. American cities visited since the new strategy was unveiled were:

1. Miami – November 15, 2007
2. Houston – January 24, 2008
3. Portland – February 21. 2008
4. Denver – March 27, 2008
5. Los Angeles – April 17, 2008

In addition to the city symposia, Navy, Marine Corps, and Coast Guard leaders met with local universities and faculty in a program called "Campus Conversations." Sea service leadership felt it was important to present the strategy to future leaders and listen to feedback. Campus Conversations took place at the following universities:

1. University of Miami – November 16, 2007
2. Rice University – January 23, 2008
3. Oregon State University – February 20, 2008
4. Denver University – March 26, 2008
5. University of Southern California – April 15, 2008

Humanitarian and disaster relief operations and seapower strategy

A Cooperative Strategy for 21st Century Seapower calls for a diplomacy-building approach echoing the mantra that "preventing wars is as important as winning wars" and "focuses on opportunities versus threats; on optimism over fear and on confidence instead of doubt." It recognizes the challenges imposed by the uncertain conditions in a time of rapid change and makes pro-active assistance and disaster response crucial elements to building relationships across nations. By working with the U.S. State Department,U.S. Agency for International Development (USAID) and non-governmental organizations, maritime forces provide unique capabilities to bear in times of crisis as set forth in the strategy.

While humanitarian missions are generally not traditionally thought of as major sea service missions, military leaders say these tasks are crucial for promoting maritime security. Admiral Gary Roughead said this strategy takes homeland defence, "a step further." He says that "through globally persistent, maritime forces, U.S. seapower will always exist primarily to fight and help win our nation's wars but... we can do more."

When Tropical Cyclone Sidr struck the southern coast of Bangladesh on November 15, 2007, U.S. Navy Sailors and Marines offered almost immediate assistance. Within days, the 11th Marine Expeditionary Unit (MEU), embarked on the amphibious ship *Tarawa*, was in the devastated country providing crucial care to wounded and displaced citizens. Military corpsmen and doctors bandaged the wounded and worked in concert with the U.S. State Department and the U.S. Agency for International Development (USAID) helping the neediest from a storm that left several hundred thousand Bangladeshis homeless. After the storm, U.S. service members also provided maritime security patrols around the coast of Bangladesh.

The military sea services also responded swiftly to the tsunami that struck Indonesia and Southeast Asia in December 2004. Marines from Naval Environmental and

Preventive Medicine Unit Six (NEPMU-6) left their home base of Pearl Harbor a few days later deploying to Indonesia. Once there, dozens of NEPMU members provided humanitarian support including medical help and conducted water quality testing and insect collection for disease examination. Less than a week after the storm hit, Navy helicopters from the aircraft carrier, *Abraham Lincoln* were flying over the Indian Ocean transporting supplies, bringing in disaster relief teams and supporting humanitarian airlifts to tsunami-stricken coastal regions.

The U.S. Coast Guard provided relief to the tsunami-affected regions of Southeast Asia, delivering over 40,000 pounds of food January 21, 2005 in the form of emergency high energy biscuits, to Medan, Indonesia and over 21,000 pounds of medical supplies, and temporary shelters to Utaphao, Thailand via two Coast Guard C130 airplanes. Additionally, the U.S. Coast Guard cutter *Munro* shuttled more than 80 tons of humanitarian relief supplies from Singapore to the Navy amphibious assault ship *Bonhomme Richard* for distribution to tsunami victims in northern Indonesia.

Admiral Gary Roughead said the U.S. response to the 2004 tsunami in Southeast Asia was, "a demonstration to ourselves and to others of the value of being able to render humanitarian assistance and disaster response from the sea." He added, "There is no way we could have done it without the sea-based capabilities of an aircraft carrier and expeditionary forces."

The U.S. sea services also respond to domestic emergencies when needed. When Hurricane Katrina flooded large portions of New Orleans and the Gulf Coast in 2005, maritime forces responded. Following the late-summer storm, *Harry S. Truman*, *Iwo Jima* and other Virginia-based Navy ships headed to the Gulf Coast to help with relief efforts. Thousands of military members were dispatched including Naval Mobile Construction Battalions and six Disaster Relief Teams (DRTs) providing amphibious construction equipment, medical personnel and supplies to the flooded areas.

Global partnerships

Speaking to the San Diego Military Advisory Council (SDMAC) October 17, 2007, Vice Chief of Naval Operations, Admiral Patrick M. Walsh spoke of a "global system in transition...unsettled, unbalanced and potentially dangerous for the U.S. and the global community, means we need to seek a balanced and stable world, one where we can be best postured and trained to promote stability." He discussed the importance of partnering with allies, relief organizations and maritime forces of other nations for a long-term approach and doing so, "before a contingency situation arises."

According to U.S. military leaders, a key ingredient to carrying out a successful maritime strategy is building relationships with other countries before an emergency strikes. Admiral Walsh told the group that the maritime strategy's long-term goal was for a "sustained approach (so that) when we train, organize, equip and recruit, it's with that goal of building strong global partnerships in mind." Admiral Walsh added that developing relationships with other countries during peace-time promotes global security. "What's important today is what we build in peace. What comes next is generosity, humanity, recognition of other positions without compromise of national interests."

Africa Partnership Station

Bilateral relationship development is happening currently with operations such as the Navy's Africa Partnership Station, (APS). This sea service focused program has U.S. and European troops working alongside non-governmental organizations and governmental organizations to promote better maritime security and stability in the waters off West Africa. During a seven-month deployment that began October 30, 2007, crews of two U.S. Navy ships conducted exercises and port visits with their counterparts throughout West and Central Africa and the Gulf of Guinea.

The team, made up of representatives of multiple U.S. federal agencies, was embarked on the amphibious dock landing ship *Fort McHenry* and the High Speed Vessel *Swift*, where they conducted training exercises with their African partners to help build their capacity to increase maritime security in their regional waters. The training focused on building critical "at sea" skills that included boarding, search and seizure, search and rescue, damage control and other critical skills.

In March 2008, the Navy partnered with the private non-governmental organization, Project Hope delivering half a billion dollars worth of medical supplies and equipment to nations throughout West Africa as part of the Africa Partnership Station program. On March 27, 2008, Liberia's president, Ellen Johnson Sirleaf, visited Liberian Army members on board the *Fort McHenry* who were taking leadership courses with their U.S. military counterparts. She lauded the Africa Partnership Station for coming to Liberia to provide humanitarian and military services to the people of Liberia as well as personnel of the Armed Forces of Liberia. Speaking at program marking the donation of medical supplies and equipment, as well as, postal boxes to the government of Liberia by the U.S. Navy in collaboration with the U.S. Embassy in Liberia, Johnson-Sirleaf said "it was amazing to see people from different countries volunteering their services to help others who were in need."

Maritime cooperation

A Cooperative Strategy for 21st Century Seapower highlights cooperation by the U.S. sea services with maritime counterparts around the world. It calls for U.S. maritime forces and their international partners to be vigilant about keeping the sea lanes free and open for commerce, ensuring pirates and smugglers are thwarted and sea borne terrorist events are prevented.

The "Thousand Ship Navy" concept, later renamed the "Global Maritime Partnership," calls for the voluntary development of networked and self-organizing partnerships to guard the martitime commons. Such coalitions have taken shape over the last decade in response to piracy off the coast of Somalia and in the Strait of Malacca.

Speaking at the International Seapower Symposium held at the Naval War College October 17, 2007, U.S. Navy Admiral Gary Roughead said the key to maritime security is being aware of that which is, "moving above, on and under the ocean, or "maritime domain awareness". Roughead told the international audience that trust among nations is critical to carrying out the strategy and that "trust cannot be surged... it is something that must be built over time, through discussions, activities and through exercises (and) initiatives that each of us may undertake and bring others into."

5

Strategy and Tactics in Military

STRATEGY AND TACTICS, MILITARY

Military strategy and tactics are essential to the conduct of warfare. Broadly stated, strategy is the planning, coordination, and general direction of military operations to meet overall political and military objectives.

Tactics implement strategy by short-term decisions on the movement of troops and employment of weapons on the field of battle. The great military theorist Carl von Clausewitz put it another way: "Tactics is the art of using troops in battle; strategy is the art of using battles to win the war." Strategy and tactics, however, have been viewed differently in almost every era of history.

The change in the meaning of these terms over time has been basically one of scope as the nature of war and the shape of society have changed and as technology has developed. Strategy, for example, literally means "the art of the general" (from the Greek *strategos*) and originally signified the purely military planning of a campaign.

Thus until the 17th and 18th centuries strategy included to varying degrees such problems as fortification, maneuver, and supply. In the 19th and 20th centuries, however, with the rise of mass ideologies, vast conscript armies, global alliances, and rapid technological change, military strategy became difficult to distinguish from "grand strategy," that is, the proper planning and utilization of the entire resources of a society military, technological, economic, and political. The change in the scope and meaning of tactics over time has been largely due to enormous changes in technology. Tactics have always been difficult and have become increasingly difficult to distinguish in reality from strategy because the two are so interdependent. (Indeed, in the 20th century, tactics have been termed *operational strategy*.) Strategy is limited by what tactics are possible; given the size, training, and morale of forces, type and number of weapons available, terrain, weather, and quality and location of enemy forces, the tactics to be used are dependent on strategic considerations.

Strategic and Tactical Principles of Warfare

Military commanders and theorists throughout history have formulated what they considered to be the most important strategic and tactical principles of war. Napoleon I, for example, had 115 such principles. The Confederate general Nathan Bedford Forrest had but one: "Get there first with the most men." Some of the most commonly cited principles are the objective, the offensive, surprise, security, unity of command, economy of force, mass, and maneuver. Most are interdependent.

Military forces, whether large-scale or small-scale, must have a clear objective that is followed despite possible distractions. Only offensive operations seizing and exploiting the initiative however, will allow the choice of objectives; the offense also greatly increases the possibility of surprise (stealth and deception) and security (protection against being surprised or losing the possibility of surprising the enemy). Unity of command, or cooperation, is essential to the pursuit of objectives, the ability to use all forces effectively (economy of force), and the concentration of superior force at a critical point (mass). Maneuver consists of the various ways in which troops can be deployed and moved to obtain offensive, mass, and surprise. A famous example that illustrates most of these principles occurred during World War II when the Allied forces eventually agreed on the objective of defeating Germany first with a direct offensive against the European continent. Under a combined command headed by Gen. Dwight D. Eisenhower, they effectively massed their forces in England, deceived Germany regarding the point of invasion, collected intelligence on the disposition of German forces, and set the vast maneuver called Operation Overlord into motion.

Unthinking rigid attention to a principle of war, however, can be unfortunate. In the face of two Japanese naval forces, Adm. William Halsey's decision at the Battle of Leyte Gulf not to divide the fleet (the principle of mass) led to the pitting of the entire enormous American naval force against a decoy Japanese fleet. Division of the fleet (maneuver) would still have left Halsey superior to both Japanese forces.

Strategic and Tactical Maneuvers

Classification of actual military types of maneuvers and their variations have long been a part of military science. New technology and weapons have not drastically altered some of the classical types of offensive maneuver: penetration, envelopment, defensive-offensive maneuvers, and turning movements.

The penetration one of the oldest maneuvers is a main attack that attempts to pierce the enemy line while secondary attacks up and down the enemy line prevent the freeing of the enemy reserves. A favorite maneuver of the Duke of Marlborough (early 18th century), it was also used by Gen. Bernard Montgomery at El Alamein (1942).

The envelopment is a maneuver in which a secondary attack attempts to hold the enemy's center while one (single envelopment) or both flanks (double envelopment) of the enemy are attacked or overlapped in a push to the enemy's rear in order to threaten the enemy's communications and line of retreat. This forces the enemy to fight in several directions and possibly be destroyed in position. New variations include vertical envelopments (airborne troops or airmobile troops) and amphibious envelopments. Noted single envelopments were accomplished by Alexander the Great at Arbela (or Gaugamela, 331 BC), Robert E. Lee at the Battle of Chancellorsville (1863), and Erwin Rommel at Gazala (1942; leading to the capture of Tobruk); famous double envelopments include those of Hannibal at the Battle of Cannae (216 BC), the American Revolution War Battle of Cowpens (1781), and the destruction of the 7th German Army at the Falaise Gap (1944).

Defensive-offensive maneuvers include attack from a strong defensive position after the attacking enemy has been sapped in strength, as in two battles of the Hundred Years' War, the Battle of Crécy (1346) and the Battle of Agincourt (1415), or feigned withdrawals that attempt to lure the enemy out of position as performed by William the Conqueror at the Battle of Hastings (1066) and by Napoleon at the Battle of Austerlitz (1805).

Turning maneuvers are indirect approaches that attempt to swing wide around an enemy's flank to so threaten an enemy's supply and communication lines that the enemy is forced to abandon a strong position or be cut off and encircled. Napoleon was a master of the turning movement, using it many times between 1796 and 1812. Robert E. Lee used the maneuver at the Second Battle of Bull Run (1862); the German drive to the French coast in 1940 was another example.

THE HISTORICAL AND THEORETICAL DEVELOPMENT OF STRATEGY AND TACTICS

The historical roots of strategy and tactics date back to the origins of human warfare and the development of large-scale government and empire. The dense tactical infantry formation of overlapping shields called the phalanx, for example, existed in an early form in ancient Sumer (*c*.3000 BC). The development of strategy and tactics parallels to some extent the growth, spread, and clash of civilizations; technological discoveries and refinements; and the evolution of modern state power, ideology, and nationalism.

Early Strategy and Tactics. The Mediterranean basin saw the dawn of modern military strategy and tactics. It was under such leaders as Philip II (382336 BC) and Alexander the Great (356323 BC) of Macedonia and Hannibal (247183 BC) of

Carthage that the first great strides were made in military science. Philip combined infantry, cavalry, and primitive artillery into a trained, organized, and maneuverable fighting force backed up by engineers and a rudimentary signaling system. His son Alexander became an accomplished strategist and tactician with his concern for planning, keeping open lines of communication and supply, security, relentless pursuit of foes, and the use of surprise. Hannibal was a supreme tactician whose crushing victories taught the Romans that the flexible attack tactics of their legions needed to be supplemented by unity of command and an improved cavalry. The Romans eventually replaced their citizen-soldiers with a paid professional army whose training, equipment, skill at fortification, road building, and siege warfare became legendary. The Byzantine emperors studied Roman strategy and tactics and wrote some of the first essays on the subject.

The Middle Ages saw a decline in the study and application of strategy with the exception of the great Mongol conqueror Genghis Khan. Medieval tactics began with an emphasis on defensive fortifications, siegecraft, and armored cavalry. The introduction, however, of such new developments as the crossbow, longbow, halberd, pike, and, above all, gunpowder began to revolutionize the conduct of war.

The Emergence of Modern Warfare. Gustav II Adolf, king of Sweden (r. 1611-32), has been called the father of modern tactics because he reintroduced maneuver into military science. His disciplined national standing army differing from the common use of mercenaries was organized into small, mobile units armed with highly superior, maneuverable firepower and supplemented by mounted dragoons (his creation) armed with carbine and saber. Frederick II (the Great) of Prussia (r. 1740-86), the master of initiative and mass, conducted war in an age of limited warfare armies were small and expensive; road and supply systems were inadequate. In the Seven Years' War (1756-63), Frederick faced a coalition whose various forces almost surrounded Prussia. Using a strategy of interior lines, Frederick supported by a highly disciplined army and horse artillery (his creation) would quickly maneuver, assemble a superior force at some decisive point along the line of encirclement, and, with massed howitzer fire, strike hard against an enemy flank before moving to another point.

With Napoleon I, however, the age of modern warfare was born. The French Revolution had produced a mass patriot army organized into loose divisional formations. Napoleon carefully planned his campaigns and quickly maneuvered his troops by forced marches to a selected field of battle. His battles began with skirmishing and cannonading, followed by an overwhelming concentration of forces in shock bayonet attacks against enemy flanks in turning and enveloping movements designed to utterly destroy opposing forces. Because of the greater complexities of warfare, a rudimentary general staff began to emerge under Napoleon.

The 19th Century: Theory and Technological Change. Napoleonic strategy and tactics were closely studied by the first great theorists of war, the Prussian general Carl von Clausewitz (17801831) and the French general Antoine Jomini (17791869). Clausewitz's *On War* (183234; Eng. trans., 1908) emphasized the close relationship between war and national policy and the importance of the principles of mass, economy of force, and the destruction of enemy forces. Jomini, on the other hand, emphasized occupying enemy territory through carefully planned, rapid, and precise geometric maneuvers. Whereas Jomini's theories had influence in France and North America, Clausewitz's teachings in particular were influential on the great Prussian military strategists of the 19th century, Helmuth von Moltke architect of victory in the Franco-Prussian War (1870) and Alfred von Schlieffen creator of the Schlieffen plan (defence against Russia and envelopment of France), which Germany applied in a modified form at the beginning of World War I.

The 19th century was an era of far-reaching technological change that vastly altered the scope of tactics and strategy, an alteration seen in what has been called the first total war, the U.S. Civil War. Railroads and steamships increased the volume, reach, and speed of mobilization and of conscription. The consistent support of war industry became critical. The growth in range and accuracy of rifle firepower created new tactical problems: artillery had to be placed farther behind the lines, massed charges became ineffective if not disastrous, cavalry became limited to reconnaissance and skirmish, and troops began to fight from trenches and use grenades and land mines. Telegraph communications linked widening theaters of war and made large-scale strategy and tactics possible. During the U.S. Civil War the large-scale strategy of the North (blockade, division of the Confederacy, destruction of the Confederate armies and supplies) backed by superior industry and manpower were the key factors in its victory. The development of the machine gun late in the 19th century would have its most telling effect in World War I.

World Wars: Trench Tactics to Nuclear Strategy. World War I began with immense, rapid, national mobilizations and classical offensive maneuvers, but after mutual attempts at envelopment at and after the Battle of the Marne, stationary trench warfare ensued across a wide battlefront. A war of attrition set in that called for total national involvement in the war effort. Two key technological developments in the war were to fashion the strategic and tactical debates of the 1920s and 1930s. The use of airpower was advocated by such theorists as Giulio Douhet (18691930), Billy Mitchell, Henry ("Hap") Arnold, and Hugh Trenchard (18731956). They insisted that airpower alone could win wars, not only by striking at enemy forces but by strategic bombing the massive attack on cities, industries, and lines of communication and supply that characterized part of Allied strategy during World War II. The other World War I development was that of motorized armored vehicles such as the tank. The use of the tank as the new cavalry of the modern age was advocated by B. H. Liddell Hart, Charles de Gaulle, and J. F. C. Fuller (18781966) in the interwar period. The Germans were the first to effectively use the tactical offensive combination of air and tank power in the field of battle in the blitzkriegs, under such commanders as Heinz Guderian and Erwin Rommel, which conquered much of Europe in World War II.

The primary tactical advance in World War II may have been that of amphibious warfare. The principal significance of that war, however, was in the first application of truly global strategies wielded by massive coalitions dedicated once again to the offensive. The development of nuclear weapons, which continued after the war, introduced the new science of nuclear strategy and tactics. The immense destructive nature of these weapons, however, meant that warfare of limited strategic goals, using conventional tactics and conventional but technologically advanced weapons, would predominate in the "limited" wars that followed World War II. The very need to keep wars limited has produced a new strategic form: the small, mobile special forces, armed with light but sophisticated weapons and trained in guerrilla tactics, that can be rapidly deployed and as rapidly withdrawn from hostile territory.

MILITARY STRATEGY AND OTHER DEFINITIONAL BURDENS

Before proceeding there are three terms which should be addressed: strategy, national security strategy, and national military strategy.

Strategy. Strategy is an easy word to use but is difficult to define. Most standard dictionaries are more confusing than enlightening on that particular entry because a strategy refers to a holistic system and process. Our interest in the word strategy will focus on its component parts because of their utility in analyzing the whole. The U.S. Army War College utilizes a simple but powerful formula to express what a strategy is and what its critical component parts consist of: *Strategy = Ends + Ways + Means*. In this equation "ends" are our objectives or goals, "ways" are the courses of action we choose to achieve those goals, and "means" are the resources either at hand or which must be developed to enable the courses of action. There are three important aspects of this model to keep in mind. The first is that the three components of a strategy—ends, ways and means—are interdependent. All of the components must be appropriate to the whole and in proper balance with the others if the strategy is to be successful. The second point to keep in mind is that when we attempt to study someone else's strategy, such as the PLA's, focusing on only one component of the strategy without an understanding of the other two may lead to incorrect or incomplete conclusions. The third point is the utility of this model as an analytic tool. It is almost universal in its applicability and is not limited to military affairs. One can easily use this equation to craft, describe or analyze political or economic strategies. Also, in the realm of military planning it is applicable across the three levels of warfare—the strategic, operational and tactical levels.

National Security Strategy. American analysts often use the term "national security strategy" or "security strategy" in the context of a nation's military concerns or military-related issues. This chapter adopts a variant of the much broader definition used by the U.S. Joint Chiefs of Staff. A National Security Strategy (NSS) will refer to the development, application and coordination of all the elements of national power (political/diplomatic, economic, informational, military, sociological/cultural) to achieve a nation's objectives in domestic and international affairs in peace as well as in war. In pursuing the national objectives set forth in a NSS, multiple strategies co-exist: an economic strategy, a political strategy, a diplomatic strategy, a social strategy, and a military strategy, at the very least. There are two points to make about this definition. First, Lykke's equation is still a valid construct. A national security strategy will have to articulate ends (objectives), ways (courses of action), and means (resources). Also, it should be noted that the military element of national power is a subset within the broader national security strategy. This brings us to a description of a national military strategy.

National Military Strategy. A National Military Strategy (NMS) is the military component of a nation's overall National Security Strategy. Its objectives are derived from those within the overarching NSS. It is the role of the national military leadership to ensure that the military element of national power will be available to contribute to the NSS in both peace and war, in the here and now and in the future. The NMS is the vehicle through which the national military leadership articulates, revalidates, and adjusts the ends, ways, and means of the armed forces to comport with changing NSS objectives, a changing security environment, or changes in the availability of national resources to be applied to the armed forces. A national military strategy is usually influenced by civil political and economic decisions. Consequently, national military strategies are dynamic and require constant review, revision and updating. At the national level of military planning—the level at which a NMS is generated—direction, guidance and policies are articulated in broad terms to steer the armed forces in the correct direction. Specific decisions, programs and detailed planning follow in due course.

Once again, the equation is still valid. A NMS must articulate ends, ways and means. In the case of a NMS, the equation is rewritten to reflect the national level of military strategy: *National Military Strategy = National Military Objectives + National Military Strategic Concepts + National Military Resources*. National Military Objectives (NMOs) will be derived from the NSS. The National Military Strategic Concepts (NMSC) will articulate the courses of action that will be undertaken to achieve the ends. The National Military Resources (NMRs) describe the types of capabilities that will be required to be on hand or be developed to enable the NMSCs.

The starting point for crafting a NMS is the articulation of NMOs. From these are developed NMSCs and NMRs. But before articulating NMSCs strategic planners first must use a critical "strategic filter" that identifies the imperatives of conflict and the possible constraints planners may have to consider. At minimum, the strategic filter: (1) considers political decisions handed down to military planners or brokered between military and civilian leaders; (2) assesses the current and projected security environments (conflict with whom? when?); and (3) performs an analysis of the operational environment (what kinds of conflicts?).

The synergistic relationship between the three elements of a NMS is readily apparent. If the resources are not available to enable the NMSCs, then weighty political-military decisions are in order: either adjust the NMOs and NMSCs or commit the resources (usually funding) to develop the NMRs. But such a zero-sum set of decisions is usually unacceptable for political reasons and impractical for reasons of national security. Consequently, at the national level of military planning, the NMS often encompasses multiple substrategies for different time frames. At a minimum, one strategy must be focused on current capabilities and near-term contingencies. Another should consider the requirements of coping with future potential security problems. Crafting military strategies for the here and now while accounting for over-the-horizon problems is a conundrum that is encountered almost exclusively at the national level of military planning and, save success in war, is probably the ultimate test of a nation's generalship.

With the preceding discussion behind us we can now move on to consider the case of China. To do so we will take the iterative and dynamic process that is used to *craft* an NMS, which is a cyclical process, and artificially stretch it out in linear fashion in order to be *descriptive* of its components.

THE STRATEGIC FILTER FOR MILITARY PLANNERS

At a minimum, the "strategic filter" for military planners at the national level must address three issues. First, they must account for political decisions that have been handed down to them or that have been brokered with civilian counterparts. These decisions usually encompass fiscal decisions and affect allocation of resources. Political decisions can also dictate or constrain military courses of action. Second, military planners must survey the security environment and assess what threats, current and future, must be addressed. Third, the nature of warfare must be examined to determine what kinds of engagements on the spectrum of military conflicts are most likely to occur. We attempt to use a "strategic filter" to look through Chinese eyes and attempt to see their strategic planning environment as they do. In some cases, we have definitive Chinese statements on these issues. In others, we can only try to transform ourselves into a PLA staff officer (*canmouguan*) sitting in the General Staff Department and speculate in an informed manner.

Political Decisions. Three key political decisions made by the top Chinese leadership affect what strategic military concepts are acceptable or possible for the PLA's national planners. These political decisions are not recent developments but long-standing policies.

The first is that China does not participate in formal military alliances. This means the PLA must plan on being a "go-it-alone force" when it does go to war or when the military element of national power is employed. It also means that PLA planners do not have to concern themselves with questions of interoperability with potential allies or even temporary coalition partners. This goes for doctrinal issues as well as hardware and combat systems which, in any case, the Chinese would prefer to produce indigenously. It explains as well the deep reluctance of the PLA to accept invitations from foreign militaries to participate in combined training exercises even when these events are couched in terms of serving as confidence-building measures.

A second political decision in effect is that the PLA will not station combat forces abroad (trans., stationed on foreign soil). The reasons for this are a combination of geopolitical reality (who would invite the PLA to permanently station combat troops on its soil?) and budgetary considerations (it is expensive to station troops abroad). Moreover, since China does not engage in formal military alliances, such an eventuality is difficult to imagine. Of greater significance, this policy also dictates that the defense of China must take place close in, on, or near China's actual land borders or off the Chinese littoral. These decisions make "forward presence" for the Chinese a relative concept. It also dictates that the PLA must maintain a certain scale or size, especially in its ground forces, to compensate for vast borders and the need to fight close to them.

The third political decision with which PLA planners must grapple has already been mentioned—that the funding the

PLA requires to operate, train, maintain and especially to modernize the armed forces will be subordinated to other national priorities. We will not enter the great PLA budget debate here. The jury is still out on the real value of investments China makes in national defense, especially given the opaque nature of their system, the multifurcated streams of funding that find their way to the armed forces, the obviously low official figures, and the issues surrounding the "hidden budget" that is the result of PLA domestic and global enterprises. The numerical spread in foreign estimates of the real value of the Chinese defense budget continues to inspire an awe of its own. For 1994, the range of estimates ran from about $10 billion U.S. to $149 billion U.S. For our purposes the trend is what matters. The recent "official" defense budget increase the PLA received during the 9th NPC (12.8 percent, for an official budget of 90.9 billion Yuan) indicates that while defense spending is going up yearly, no fundamental political decision has been made to reverse national priorities and provide the armed forces with a massive infusion of state funds. The PLA leadership undoubtedly does not receive the funding it would like (in this regard they have much in common with their brothers-in-arms across the globe). The question that we still have difficulty answering is: Are they getting what they need to fund their key current programs and underwrite their future requirements?

The PLA Analysis of the Security Environment. The basic and oft-repeated Chinese articulation of the nature of the world security environment is well known. Beijing sees the next two or three decades as a period in which the possibility of world war is negligible. The basic trend is toward "peace and development." China faces no immediate major direct military threats and the world is generally at peace. It is this assessment, originally made by Deng Xiaoping, that has impelled China to concentrate on economic reform as its primary national security objective. China continues to have, and continues to need, a window of relative peace to experiment and move forward in this endeavour. Jiang Zemin revalidated this assessment at the 15th Party Congress:

The international situation at present as a whole continues to move toward relaxation, and peace and development are the main themes of the present era.... For a fairly long period of time to come, it is possible to avert a new world war and secure a favourable, peaceful international environment and maintain good relations with the surrounding countries.

At the same time, Jiang also pointed out that there are serious security problems that require China's attention: However, the Cold War mentality still exists, and hegemonism and power politics continue to be the main source of threat to world peace and stability. Strengthening military alliance between various military blocs is not conducive to safeguarding peace and ensuring security. The unjust and irrational old international economic order is still infringing upon the interests of the developing countries, and the gap in wealth is widening. It is still serious that human rights and other issues are used to interfere in the internal affairs of other countries. Local conflicts due to ethnic, religious and territorial factors crop up from time to time. The world is not yet tranquil.

Jiang's "caveat" is a relatively subdued echo of PLA concerns. For their part, Chinese military strategists seem to view the world as a place basically hostile to Beijing's national interests, especially China's sovereignty. It is a world where dangers to national security lurk everywhere. The strategists view competition between nations for advantage as the norm and as a zero-sum equation. Change in the global and regional security environment is viewed as constant and usually dangerous. The absence of war does not mean the absence of hostility toward China. And, over the horizon, today's much-needed trade partners can slowly transform into serious economic, political, and military rivals. China's Defense Minister General Chi Haotian is Beijing's top military spokesman on these issues and he continues to be quite straightforward and frank in publicly highlighting the dangers that PLA planners see bubbling beneath the surface of a relatively peaceful world. As recently as March 1998, he underscored that pockets of antipathy toward China continue to require military vigilance:

Hostile international forces have never abandoned their strategic plot to westernize and split China, and the great cause of the motherland's ultimate reunification has yet to be accomplished. Under the long, peaceful environment and the situation centering on economic construction, we must be prepared for danger in times of peace and enhance our awareness of hardship. We must not become intoxicated by songs and dances in celebration of peace.

Fair enough. It is the job of defense ministers around the world to remind the troops that preparedness is why they are paid. What is interesting is that in this particular talk to PLA delegates at the 9th NPC Chi couches the need for preparedness not just as a matter of general professional responsibility but as a result of clearly identified security challenges.

In April 1996, General Chi spoke of the competitive nature of world relations when he wrote that "Major countries successively take contending for economic and technological superiority and enhancing comprehensive national strength as their development strategies and try by every possible means to gain the strategic initiative in the 21st century." These types of official statements set the analytic tone for PLA strategic planners. But what are the specific concerns these planners see that might affect the formulation of national military strategic concepts, especially those that must be incorporated into their national military strategy? We will now survey them briefly. What we will find is that if one were a Chinese military planner contemplating the various possible contingencies for which military force might be required now or in the future, there would be very little reason to feel complacent. What does the PLA planner see when he looks around the map? What are the major near-term, mid-term, and long-term concerns and shaping factors?

Geography. Geography continues to be a critical factor for Chinese military planners. China shares land borders with fourteen other nations. All told, the Chinese claim more than 20,000 kilometers of land boundaries and 18,000 kilometers of coastline that must be defended. Moreover, these borders encompass almost every major type of climate and terrain known in the habitable world. Just being able to secure its land borders is an almost staggering proposition for the PLA. It should be pointed out that since 1949 all of China's wars or military campaigns (Korea, India, Indochina-Vietnam, Soviet Union) have been fought either to secure control over disputed portions of those borders (India, Soviet Union) or to preempt a potential threat to those borders (Korea, Indochina-Vietnam). But the new international security environment and proactive diplomacy by Beijing have guaranteed that threats to China's land borders remain minimal. Rapprochement with Russia has alleviated a tremendous pressure on the PLA. Moreover, the dissolution of the USSR broke up what was previously the longest land border in the world. Cautious but steadily improving relations with Hanoi continue to keep the Sino-Vietnamese border pacific. The 1996 five-nation agreement between China, Russia, Kazakhstan, Tajikistan, and Kyrgyzstan is addressing problems in the northwest. If China still has a major potential border security problem it is with North Korea, which we shall come to shortly. But for the most part, China's land borders have never been more secure than they are today.

Defense of the Economic Centre of Gravity and the New Maritime Imperative. The same cannot be said of China's coast. In the last twenty years there have been two significant changes in China's security environment. The first is rapprochement with Russia. The second, ironically, is the result of two decades of successful Chinese economic modernization. China's economic centre of gravity has shifted from deep in the interior, where strategic industries were sequestered in the 1960s to protect them from a possible Soviet invasion, to its current location on China's eastern coast, where Beijing's new market economy is strongest. This "gold coast," from Dalian in the north to Hainan in the south, defines the current economic *schwerpunkt* of China and its likely future location as well. And, arguably, Beijing's ongoing and future potential success in developing this coastal economy will be a major factor in defining China's importance in the future international order.

This shift has resulted in a profound change in the PLA's security calculus. Previously a large land force was required to protect the Chinese interior and its industries against a protracted land war with invading Soviets. Today, however, this pronounced shift in the economic centre of gravity presents China with a littoral and maritime defense requirement that it probably has not had since the mid-Ch'ing Dynasty. For the PLA today (and more than likely tomorrow) *the essence of defending China will be defined by the PLA's ability to defend seaward from the coast in the surface, subsurface and aerospace battle-space dimensions*. This is precisely the type of warfare that the PLA is currently least well postured to conduct. Hence, the emphasis in military modernization over the past few years has been on naval forces, air forces, and missile forces—the three services whose force projection capabilities are required for and best suited to defend the new economic centre of gravity. Because of this shift it could be argued that even if the PLA did not have a Taiwan "problem" to consider, it would still emphasize force projection capabilities with a maritime (and maritime airspace) control and denial focus.

Defense of Maritime Sovereignty. In line with China's new coastal defense requirements, it is clear that the PLA has other maritime issues to contend with. Besides their 18,000 km of coast, the Chinese claim to have "more than 6,000 islands, and three million square km of territorial waters..." to defend. The PLA must develop the capability to enforce Beijing's claims over disputed areas in the South China Sea and other maritime claims. While the waters have been relatively calm since the "Mischief Reef" incident, China could decide to employ the military element of national power once again if, from its perspective, it feels provoked by the other claimants in the region. Besides the Spratly Islands, China has competing claims with Vietnam over the demarcation of the Gulf of Tonkin and with Japan over the Diaoyu/Senkaku Islands. The issue of the South China Sea also highlights the importance China places on maritime resources (oil, fishing, and minerals) as it proceeds with economic modernization. And it is worth highlighting again that in his articulation of China's national military objectives earlier in this chapter Defense Minister Chi Haotian specifically cites the need of the PLA to safeguard China's "waters and maritime rights and interests." These two requirements—defending China's maritime territorial claims and defending its maritime resources—are specifically included in the articulation of the objectives of the PLA Navy by its commander, Lieutenant General Shi Yunsheng.

Close to Home: The Prospect of Instability. PLA and PAP military planners cannot discount the possibility that their classic internal defense mission will become more important in the next decade. As mentioned earlier, the social dislocations attendant to China's economic modernization are becoming greater and greater. Over the past few years worker protests, sit-ins, and physical attacks on local party officials and headquarters have been reported in the press with increasing frequency. As the social safety net continues to erode, by political mandate or by virtue of poor management, the possibility of increasing social instability cannot be discounted. China already has a "floating population" of some several millions which the state security apparati blame for increasing crime. If Jiang Zemin and Zhu Rongji actually implement the reforms of the state-owned enterprises as they have promised at the 15 Party Congress and 9th NPC, then over the next three years some three to five million additional Chinese could become unemployed and be without any social benefits at all. The "Great Amway Riots" of April 1998, as I like to call them, could be a harbinger of worse situations to come. And should the Asian financial crisis eventually hit China hard, the social chaos could be totally unmanageable.

But beyond the social unrest that could take place, China has other internal problems that must certainly keep PLA planners alert. In Xinjiang, the Uighur separatist movement has not been crushed. It is difficult to determine just how large or minuscule the problem is in fact. Last year several "terrorist" attacks in Beijing and other parts of Han China were reportedly tied to the East Turkistan freedom movement. We do not know if that linkage is true. But for the first time that one can remember (or that has been reported outside of the mainland)

China now has a terrorist problem and the Chinese certainly believe the Pan-Turkic problem is potentially serious. This means that the PLA will need to have contingency plans on file if the PAP and other state security forces cannot handle future unrest in Xinjiang Province.

And always there is Tibet. The on-again, off-again unrest in that region is certainly a part of the PLA planning calculus. The issues of Xinjiang and Tibet directly attack Beijing's national security objectives of sovereignty and stability. Consequently, there is no reason to think that Beijing would not employ the PLA in either combat or military operations other than war (MOOTW) in either of these locations if its capabilities were needed to quell serious unrest.

Taiwan. Taiwan represents both a near-term contingency and a long-term readiness problem for PLA planners. Beijing will not renounce the right to use military force against Taiwan. Consequently, the PLA must develop a serious conventional deterrent capability vis-à-vis Taipei. The problem, of course, is that the only credible military deterrent is real conventional capabilities (we assume the political will is there). The next question must be, capability to do what? Whether the March-April 1996 mini-crisis in the Strait was a success or failure for Beijing is still being debated abroad. But one thing is certain; if one were a Chinese military planner, it should be painfully obvious that the PLA needs to develop a more diversified set of conventional military capabilities to employ as flexible deterrent options (FDOs). Relying heavily on missiles as a FDO runs the risk of being too provocative (witness the U.S. reaction). This is true whether the PLA must act against Taiwan or in defense of its claims in the South China Sea. In the 1996 affair, the PLA quickly escalated from "forward presence" (large military exercises on the coast) to "demonstration of force" (missile launches). It appears that either the PLA did not have many other options in between with which to *slowly* escalate or they totally miscalculated the external response. My own inclination is that it was both.

Russia. Russia should probably be viewed as a long-term potential problem for the PLA. In spite of increasingly friendly relations and their new "cooperative strategic partnership," there is no dearth of mutual distrust between Russia and China, especially in Siberia and the Russian Far East. China is still viewed by the Russians as a threat and these views have their political champions on the far right in Moscow. Beijing's economic strength at a time when Moscow is relatively supine is felt most sharply in Russian Asia, and the Maritime Provinces recoil at what they see as Moscow's kowtowing to Beijing at their expense. For their part, Chinese military planners likely view Russia as a possible "over the horizon" problem. They may worry about the day when the Russians recover their national strength and the imperatives of geography and the legacies of historical animosity act to unleash rivalries anew, not just on their common border but perhaps in Central Asia. These rivalries will probably be driven by competition for natural resources: lumber, oil, minerals, and food from the sea.

Korea. Chinese military planners discount the possibility of an all-out war in Korea á la 1950. Nevertheless, they should be worried about the security problems China could face if the economic and political situation in North Korea deteriorates to the point of a total meltdown. An implosion in the north has the potential to send tens of thousands of North Korean refugees streaming over the border into China's ethnically Korean provinces. This type of chaos on China's border is precisely the type of situation for which the PLA is historically deployed. But in this sort of scenario the PLA would not be fighting a classic war. China's armed forces would be engaged in MOOTW. They would have to secure their borders, deal with thousands of refugees, and possibly keep the Korean People's Army at bay simultaneously. The scenarios are endless. The point is, the PLA must be prepared to intervene unilaterally to secure China's own interests in the event of total chaos on its border with the Democratic People's Republic of Korea (DPRK).

Japan. The Chinese view Japan as the only Asian nation that has the political, economic, technological, and (potential) military strength to challenge Beijing for regional dominance in the next century. Japan is likely viewed by the PLA as the primary mid-term strategic concern. While it may seem irrational from an American perspective, Beijing believes that under the veneer of a generally pacifist Japan lurks an undercurrent of unrepentant Japanese militarism and a strong desire on the part of the Japan Self-Defense Forces to overturn constitutional limits on their roles and missions. Tokyo's reluctance to directly confront its role in World War II and Japanese military participation in United Nations Peace-Keeping Operations (PKOs) in Africa and the Middle East fuel these Chinese suspicions. However, *the* most worrisome development from the perspective of the PLA is the recent promulgation of the revised U.S-Japan Guidelines for Defense Cooperation. This instrument is viewed as a codicil under which the Japanese armed forces, especially the navy, will justify operating even further out from Japan proper while still claiming to be a force purely for the defense of the Japanese home islands. Even more damning, China considers Tokyo the "other black hand" behind Taiwan's drift toward independence. This is because of a variety of reasons that go back to Taiwan's status as an Imperial Colony (1895–1945) and Lee Teng-hui's ties to Japan. These two factors (Chinese suspicions of Japanese military expansion and the Taiwan factor), when combined with maritime territorial disputes, makes for an imposing set of military planning requirements for PLA staff officers.

India. Up until the May 1998 nuclear detonations by India and their accompanying barrage of anti-China rhetoric, relations between Beijing and New Delhi seemed to be on the road to mending. The fact that the nuclear detonations occurred shortly after the visit to India of GSD Chief General Fu Quanyou was a double slap in the face. It is still too early to say what impact these events will have on overall Sino-Indian relations or what impact the Indian detonations will have on China's nuclear policies. These questions notwithstanding, the Indians have handed PLA planners a set of potential problems that encompass both a readiness issue on land in the disputed border areas and possibly a mid- to long-term maritime-aerospace planning problem in the Indian Ocean. At a minimum, India will continue to be viewed as an enduring security concern.

The United States. The United States poses a special conundrum for the PLA. China needs good relations with the U.S. to achieve its overarching national security objective of modernization. But this should not be confused with a shared vision of how the post–Cold War security regime in Asia should unfold. For one thing, the Chinese do not subscribe to the U.S. argument that Washington's bilateral military alliances in the region are necessarily stabilizing. Moreover, from the viewpoint of PLA planners, the forward presence of the American armed forces throughout the Pacific and Asia on land, sea and air cannot be a happy fact of life. The Pacific Ocean is still an American lake and the looming shadow of the U.S. Navy casts a pall over all others. It is in the interests of China and the PLA to see the U.S. military presence in Asia reduced at some point in the future. There is probably little debate in Beijing on this basic point. Where there may be significant debate is on the timing of a U.S. force withdrawal.

Some Chinese security analysts could argue that the American military presence has some utility for China by acting as a guarantor of the regional stability Beijing must have. They might argue that a quick drawdown by the U.S. would result in Tokyo filling the military vacuum quicker than the PLA could be prepared to credibly face down the Japanese. Others might see utility in the continued U.S. military presence in Korea as a check on instability close to home, although that argument will disappear after Korean unification or reconciliation.

Yet, there is a residual distrust and apprehension in some circles in the PLA about the true intentions of the United States in Asia and the role of its armed forces in the Pacific. The United States, through its forward military presence, has the *potential* to act as the great spoiler to two of Beijing's *core* security concerns: Taiwan and Japan. Because the United States underwrites the security of Taiwan, some Chinese security analysts argue that Taipei can continue to be recalcitrant in negotiating cross-Strait political issues and reckless to the point of provocation in its foreign and domestic policies. Moreover, it is the United States, some PLA planners would argue, that is goading the Japanese to rearm and pressuring Tokyo to expand its military role in the region under the false flag of increased host-nation burden sharing. Moreover, the "China Threat" theory that was in vogue in the U.S. a couple of years ago had its Chinese analogue. Some PLA analysts seriously believe that the U.S. is attempting to contain China militarily using Japan as the "northern anchor" and Australia as the "southern anchor." And Chinese opposition to NATO expansion is borne of a fear that the Partnership for Peace might spread to Central Asia and exponentially enhance U.S. influence on China's western doorstep.

Consequently, PLA views of the U.S. are highly dichotomous. On the benign side, the U.S. is probably viewed by PLA strategists not so much as a *direct* military threat to Beijing, but as a lumbering but lethal giant that can wreak havoc on China's various national security interests because of (as viewed through Chinese lenses) vacillating American domestic political tacts and ignorance of the greater strategic implications of Washington's ever-changing policies. On the more cynical side, the U.S. is seen as capable of undermining core interests concerning Japan and especially Taiwan. More than likely, the PLA must constantly factor the potential reaction of the U.S. into almost every military contingency plan it may have. Assuming there are a variety of PLA contingency plans targeted against Taiwan, the "U.S. factor" is a significant unknown variable for the PLA. Beijing's suspicions about Tokyo's future path and the vagueness of the phrase "areas surrounding Japan" in the U.S.-Japan Guidelines for Defense Cooperation have probably only heightened concern about the U.S. role.

Nuclear Threats. Beijing's decision to develop nuclear weapons decades ago was in part a function of the desired status that capability conferred upon the PRC in the world order. However, Chinese security analysts are also quick to point out that China had no choice but to possess atomic weapons because China had been subjected to "nuclear blackmail" in the past—first by the United States during the Korean War and later on by the Soviets.

For the past thirty years, Beijing has adhered to a nuclear strategy of minimum deterrence and has publicly declared a no-first-use policy. It would appear that China's leadership has been satisfied with this approach.

But whether this will remain the case indefinitely may be open to debate, certainly within China. One reason is the recent nuclear detonations by India. Second, over the past few years there has been growing concern among China's nuclear scientists and Beijing's security policy establishment over the possibility that the U.S. might in fact develop a national ballistic missile defense system and concerns about what China views as U.S. pressure on Russia to amend the Anti-Ballistic Missile Treaty to allow high-capability Theatre Ballistic Missile Defense systems. The prospect of India having offensive nuclear capabilities, and the U.S. possessing highly capable high-altitude ballistic missile defences cannot be a comforting combination for those charged with responsibility for China's nuclear strategy.

China's Security Environment: A Recapitulation of the View From Beijing. In reviewing a PLA planner's view of China's security environment, we can come to the following generalizations:

- The PLA must be prepared to deal with internal unrest every day.
- The PLA must be prepared with military options for China's leaders to consider in dealing with Taiwan should the national leadership decide to employ the military element of national power to achieve its political ends. This is a current requirement and will endure.
- The PLA must develop a credible defense of its economic centre of gravity: the coast. It must also be prepared to enforce Beijing's maritime claims.
- Any bilateral security concern that involves China with another country on its land border (India, Korea, Vietnam, Russia, etc.) should be considered an enduring security concern regardless of how pacific the situation is at the moment or promises to remain in the future.

- Russia is a long-term and enduring security concern for Beijing due to proximity, historical mistrust, and its potential to regain its great power status.
- For the foreseeable future, the United States remains an enduring security concern not because it is perceived as a direct military threat to China but because of its unpredictability, its power, the proximity of its military forces, its web of bilateral military alliances, and its potential role as "spoiler" for core Chinese security interests (Taiwan, Japan).
- Japan is probably the one country in the region which in the mid-term Beijing views with the most suspicion as a potential challenger in the military as well as political and economic realms.
- As for force structure and mix of arms, the PLA must enhance its maritime and aerospace capabilities. At the same time, because of the continuing possibility of internal unrest and current (India, Korea) and potential (Russia, Vietnam) security concerns along China's long borders, the PLA cannot totally neglect its ground forces.
- Finally, China must continue to field a credible nuclear deterrent, especially in light of India's recent actions and Chinese concerns about the potential for the

U.S. or Russia to acquire credible ballistic missile defense systems.

Analysis of the Operational Environment. The final element we will consider in the strategic filter is the PLA's assessment of the nature of warfare—what kinds of conflicts or wars PLA planners believe they have to be able to fight. This question is about the "what" of warfare, not necessarily the "who." For PLA planners—indeed, for all military planners around the world—this is a critical question because it affects the dedication of scarce resources, force structures, manning levels, equipment priorities and training methods. In most militaries, this is as much an internal and bureaucratic issue as it is a "warfighting" issue. Among PLA defense intellectuals, the question of what kinds of wars the armed forces will have to fight and when generates a tremendous amount of study, research and publication. This question also generates a modicum of debate. As we know, "contending schools" on military issues is not new to the PLA. Different visions of what kind of wars the PLA must prepare for and how they will be fought have been going on since the days of the Red Army and the Long March, through the "Red versus Expert" debates of the 1950s and 1960s, and even through the 1980s when there was resistance to abandoning Mao's classic prescriptions for People's War (hence such politically correct but contradictory doctrines such as "People's War Under Modern Conditions"). In these previous debates the professional and personal stakes were extremely high, with losers often purged.

These days, however, the internal debates in the PLA about which kind of war(s) to prepare for are no longer live or die issues. Indeed, a benchmark of the level of professionalism that the PLA has achieved is that there are so many voices in the military journals and military press on this subject. Today the debates do not centre about the political orthodoxy or heterodoxy of a point of view but around the questions of how much the PLA can accomplish, what it must accomplish, how quickly it can accomplish it, how much the PLA can afford, and whether one possible path should be funded at the expense of another.

Today in the PLA there appears to be two major schools of thought on this question which live side by side. The first school of thought is that the PLA must prepare to fight "local wars under modern, high-tech conditions." The second school of thought looks out over the horizon and argues that the PLA must prepare to deal with the international "Revolution in Military Affairs" (RMA) of the 21st Century.

While the PLA's top leadership is cognizant of both types of warfare and, presumably, would aspire to be able to deal with both, there is a profound difference between them. First, PLA strategists see local wars under modern, high-tech conditions as a form of warfare with which they must grapple now and well into the next century. This is because it is a form of warfare that many highly developed nations can conduct now, albeit with differing degrees of proficiency, while the PLA still cannot. Second, it is a form of warfare that is relatively well defined in both theory and practice. It has been seen in action in its incipient form (the Gulf War), and is intellectually digestible to a large portion of the top warfighting PLA leadership.

Third, there are discrete and finite measures the PLA can take in incremental steps to achieve some degree of ability to engage in this type of warfare. Put differently, there are metrics that can be used to peg achievable benchmarks of proficiency. And last but not least, Jiang Zemin, in his capacity as Chairman of the Central Military Commission "officially" coined this terminology in 1993 and instructed the PLA to use it as the guiding principle for military reform in the "new historical period."

This is not to say that the PLA leadership is not interested in the RMA or thinking about it or even experimenting with some of its concepts. The problem for the PLA is that the RMA is still a moving target. The concepts behind it are still evolving. Even in the United States, where it generates a great deal of thought among military futurists, it continues to be a subject hotly debated in various circles. This is precisely why the PLA's best military scholars and thinkers are paying close attention to the RMA debates in the U.S. and why they are even developing their own concepts of an "RMA with Chinese characteristics." In some circles of military theorists in China there are even some who argue that it might be possible for the PLA to "leap-frog" the local wars stage of development and exploit technologies to become a mid-to late-21st century military. These are appealing ideas to a military organization such as the PLA that currently is so vast, so unevenly modernized, relatively underfunded, and, from their perspective, so perpetually threatened. Theoretical work on the RMA will continue.

The RMA, however, will not be the fundamental basis of PLA planning, training, professionalization, restructuring, or equipping for the first decades of the next century. Preparing for local wars under modern, high-tech conditions will serve as the foundation and focal point upon which and around which China will build a PLA capable of coping with the challenges of warfare in the first half of the next century. PLA views of local wars under modern, high-tech conditions is a subject too vast to do justice to in this chapter. Nevertheless, a brief overview is in order.

As mentioned earlier, the decision to have the PLA focus on "local wars under modern, high-tech conditions" (hereafter LWUMHTC) as the basis for its future operational planning is officially credited to Jiang Zemin in a directive to the CMC in 1993. The fact that this directive is credited to Jiang was but one of many moves he was making at the time to establish his *bona fides* as Chairman of the CMC (no doubt with Deng's approval). Jiang, as we know, had little to do with the military prior to his remarkable rise to national power in the wake of Tiananmen in June 1989.

The concept of LWUMHTC was the natural outgrowth of a previous major 1985 decision that revised the PLA's assessment of the kind of warfare they would have to conduct as major changes to the security environment unfolded. This was, of course,

Deng Xiaoping's "strategic decision," which declared that "early, major and nuclear war" (with either of the two superpowers) was unlikely and that the PLA now faced "local, limited war (*youxian jubu zhanzheng*)." By the late 1980s the concept had a qualifier added to it, "under modern conditions" which began to take new technologies into account to a certain degree. But it was Jiang Zemin's iteration in 1993 that added "high-tech (*gao jishu*) conditions" to the formulation. So in fact, the PLA's concept of "local war" has been evolving for over ten years. It will undoubtedly continue to evolve, especially as PLA researchers continue to track and digest the "Military Technological Revolution."

When the PLA speaks of LWUMHTC they are describing two aspects of warfare. The first aspect, "local," means that this kind of war will be limited in geographic scope. It will be confined to one particular theatre of operations and not a general war on all fronts. The second qualifier, "under modern, high-tech conditions," means that the weaponry the PLA expects a notional advanced enemy to employ against it will be of the most sophisticated technological types. Over the past five years there has been an explosion of PLA writing on the nature of LWUMHTC, and the list of the operational characteristics that define it gets longer all the time. For the sake of brevity, the list below captures the essence of the new operational environment PLA strategic theorists believe China now faces and will continue to face through the turn of the century.

6

Chinese Strategic Thinking: People's War in the 21st Century

People's war is not a static or dead theory. As the People's Liberation Army (PLA) modernizes through the processes of mechanization and informationization, "China is striving to make innovations in the content and forms of people's war" (2008 China's Defence White Paper).

Contrary to the perception that people's war relies "on 'rifles and millet' and overwhelming numbers (e.g. human wave attacks) with an emphasis on guerrilla warfare and protracted conflict," according to The Science of Military Strategy people's war "is a form of organization of war, and its role has nothing to do with the level of military technology".

In part to compensate for its technological shortfalls, mobilization of the Chinese population is key to supporting the country's war effort "by political, economic, technical, cultural and moral means".

The recently concluded annual meeting for the Standing Committee of the National People's Congress (NPC)—China's legislature—signed the National Defence Mobilization Law, which provides a legal basis for integration of civilian resources into military operations when "the sovereignty, unity, territorial integrity or security of the nation are threatened." The law "sets out principles and organizational mechanisms for national defence mobilization, personnel and strategic material storage" and will go into effect July 1 (Xinhua News Agency, February

26). Its text is widely available, in Chinese, on the internet (ChinaNews.com, February 26).

The passage of the mobilization law underscores the continued relevance of people's war in Chinese strategic thinking. In order to understand how the Chinese armed forces will fight Local Wars under Informationized Conditions, people's war in its modern permutation must be considered.

PEOPLE'S WAR

From 1998 on, every White Paper on China's National Defence has declared that the PLA adheres to the "strategic concept" of people's war as part of China's "military strategy" of active defence. Even after an updated war fighting doctrine was issued in 1999, people's war has remained a basic tenet of Chinese military thought. The concept is prominent in authoritative works like The Science of Campaigns and The Science of Military Strategy where people's war is described as "a fundamental strategy ... still a way to win modern war".

At its essence, people's war is a strategy to maximize China's strengths (its size and people) to defend the mainland from attack by either foreign or domestic enemies. For many decades, China's military strategy concentrated on continental defence. By the mid-1980s, the PLA began to push its defensive envelope farther out and adopted an "offshore defence strategy." Though no specific distances were defined in official documents, "offshore defence" often overlapped with discussions of protecting China's EEZ out to 200 nautical miles. In a noteworthy revelation, the 2006 White Paper stated: "The Navy is ... exploring the strategy and tactics of maritime people's war under modern conditions."

Just weeks after a series of incidents at sea between Chinese military and civilian vessels and the USNS Impeccable and Victorious in the spring of 2009, which arguably is an example of "maritime people's war," the official-Xinhua News Agency reported, "China will not build an offensive navy cruising the globe, but concentrate on its offshore area. Even if in [the] future the navy is modernized, the defensive nature of the naval strategy will not change." Geographic limits were set by traditional claims of Chinese sovereignty: "In order to defend China's territory and sovereignty, and secure its maritime rights and interests, the navy decided to set its defence range as the Yellow Sea, the East China Sea, and the South China Sea. This range covered the maritime territory that should be governed by China, according to the UN Convention on the Law of the Sea, as well as the islands in the South China Sea, which have been its territory since ancient times".

Strategically Defensive, But the Offense is Decisive

Though people's war starts from a strategically defensive posture, like Clausewitz and American and Russian/Soviet strategists, Chinese military planners understand the decisive nature of the offense. Chinese doctrine seeks to gain the initiative and take the offensive after the enemy strikes the first blow; however, it also allows for preemptive action at the tactical and operational levels: "if any country or organization violates the other country's sovereignty and territorial integrity, the other side will have the right to 'fire the first shot' on the plane of tactics". After conflict has been initiated, Chinese forces will seek to shift to the offensive whenever possible.

The Science of Military Strategy outlines 10 principles of people's war, describing a framework that seeks to integrate all types of forces (military, paramilitary, and civilian) in flexible, aggressive operations appropriate to the situation. While the PLA strives for early victory, it also acknowledges "a large-scale war cannot be won by a single decisive battle" and urges caution before initiating conflict. In combat, "five combinations" of regular and irregular forces will mix:

1. Regular troops with the masses
2. Regular warfare with guerrilla warfare on the sea
3. "Trump weapons" with flexible strategy and tactics
4. High-tech weapons with common weapons
5. Military warfare with political and economic warfare.

Fighting methods emphasize close quarters engagement, night fighting, and surprise attacks. The reference to "guerrilla warfare on the sea" foreshadowed the tactics demonstrated in the spring of 2009, but as can be seen from all "five combinations," people's war is not just guerrilla war.

Today, people's war principles are seen in many training events practiced by the Chinese armed forces and civilian populace, especially in anti-terrorist, nuclear and chemical defence, and air raid drills. People's war is also revealed in the extensive "socialization" or "outsourcing" of many logistics functions to the civilian sector. Civilian support is especially necessary for air and sea transport of personnel and equipment over long distances.

PEOPLE'S WAR AND FORCE STRUCTURE

Most recent foreign analysis of PLA modernization focuses on important improvements in main force units equipped with advanced missiles and electronics, ships and submarines, and modern aircraft and force projection capabilities. Little has been written about the 200,000 or more total personnel assigned to PLA ground force coastal and border defence units. The PLA Navy (PLAN) commands six shore-to-ship missile and antiaircraft artillery (AAA) regiments and independent battalions in its coastal defence force. The Navy also maintains some 253 patrol and coastal combatants (including over 80 surface-to-surface missile boats) in five division-level units. The PLA Air Force (PLAAF) has three surface-to-air missile (SAM) divisions, one mixed (SAM and AAA) air defence division, and nine SAM and two AAA brigades. Of its total of over 1,600 combat capable aircraft, over 800 are J-7- and J-8-series fighters dedicated to local air defence. A full one-third of the PLA reserve force's roughly 40 divisions and 25 brigades is dedicated to local air defence. Approximately another 100,000 People's Armed Police (PAP) troops are assigned land and sea frontier defence missions throughout China.

Since 1998, PLA reserve units and the militia have been reorganized and modernized in parallel to the active duty PLA. Much of their work focuses on providing rear area security, especially air defence, for PLA active duty units as well as the civilian population; logistics support; and repair of infrastructure damaged from long-range strikes on China. Some militia units likely will be included in China's prosecution of information war (IW).

The aforementioned forces make up a significant portion of the Chinese armed forces. Yet they will be integrated into PLA war plans for mainland and coastal defence, and the majority of them do not add to the PLA's power projection capabilities, except as they protect the rear areas of main force deployments and, for a small fraction, in the conduct of information operations.

People's War and Information War

Chinese strategists see information operations as a particularly useful vehicle to employ their traditional war fighting methods of stratagem, surprise and deception. A common conceit is that "The idea of winning victory by stratagem has always been the main idea of traditional Chinese strategic thinking .... U.S. strategic thinking has not shaken off its traditional model of attaching importance to strength and technology".

Shen Weiguang, sometimes referred to as the "Chinese father" of information warfare, calls IW "a people's war in the true sense of the term". Major General Dai Qingmin, a former director of the General Staff Department's Fourth Department (for electronic warfare), notes attaining information superiority is crucial to the use of stratagem and deception in people's war.

While some elements of information operations are considered "trump card" weapons (as are many other weapons and tactics), The Science of Campaigns recognizes "information warfare is a means, not a goal". Thus, the PLA aims to integrate information operations with firepower, maneuver and special operations as it conducts campaigns.

Active duty PLA forces have a variety of electronic warfare and intelligence units that are capable of both offensive and defensive information operations, including cyber operations. In recent years, training in complex electromagnetic environments has been a key task for all PLA units. Exercises frequently begin with enemy electronic jamming and cyber attacks on friendly units. Over the past decade, militia information warfare units, including both offensive and defensive electronic and cyber capabilities, have been created.

Yet, due to the difficulty in controlling non-military hackers and the potential for their actions to interfere with China's strategy and political signaling, it is unlikely that the Chinese government would employ an army of civilians in a "people's cyberwar." As a recent U.S. study concludes, "Western media reports that claim that the PRC government has recruited an 'internet army' from among the millions of Chinese hackers, are spurious at best". PLA and militia information warfare units, on the other hand, can expect to be very busy in future campaigns.

Conclusions

The principles of people's war remain an important foundation of China's military thinking about both peace and war. People's war is also an important element of China's multi-layered, integrated deterrence posture. As described in The Science of Military Strategy:

"China currently has a limited but effective nuclear deterrence and a relatively powerful capability of conventional deterrence and a massive capacity of deterrence of people's war. By combining these means of deterrence, an integrated strategic deterrence is formed, with comprehensive national power as the basis, conventional force as the mainstay, nuclear force as the backup power and reserve force as the support".

As an element of deterrence, people's war is also a means for Beijing to "subdue the enemy without fighting" and attain strategic objectives: "Warfighting is generally used only when deterrence fails and there is no alternative .... Strategic deterrence is also a means for attaining the political objective". Yet, as demonstrated off the Chinese coast in 2009, people's war tactics may not always lead to success.

One hypothesis that could be drawn from those maritime incidents is that for people's war to be successful, it must be conducted on a large scale for it to adequately incorporate the advantages of China's size. A multitude of military and civilian forces allows China to "flood the zone" with activity, confusing and complicating opponents' intelligence collection and targeting capacity. Massive deployments may also divert attention from the main effort, perhaps permitting certain movements to occur undetected. Could the harassment of the USNS Impeccable and USNS Victorious been conceived to mask other activity happening at the same time? Indeed, these events took place as the People's Liberation Army (PLA) Navy's South Sea Fleet was conducting exercises involving destroyers, submarines, and helicopters in the South China Sea (exact location not specified) (Jiefangjun Bao Online, March 9, 2009).

By its nature, people's war has a greater chance for success on or near the Chinese mainland. It becomes much less effective the further PLA forces operate from mainland. A few new weapons hold promise to extend the PLA's operating and striking range, but the longest reach currently available to the Chinese armed forces is its information and cyber war potential. These newest capabilities still need to be exercised and tested in peacetime to work out kinks as well as determine how they would be best integrated with other forces and combat methods.

The emphasis of people's war on some types of mobilization, such as economic and technological mobilization may not be as viable as political mobilization except in extended war scenarios. An undue reliance on the "latent capacities" of the Chinese industry likely overestimates the ability of civilian support to provide the specialized equipment necessary for modern military operations in anything but a very long war. Political mobilization and internal and external propaganda efforts to prove the "just" and defensive nature of any military activity, the Chinese armed forces are certain to be conducted.

Skeptics of the continuing relevance of people's war to PLA doctrine may argue it is a pathetic example of political correctness run amok—simply making a virtue out of necessity. They may be correct to a degree. Yet such commentary misses the fundamental precept that the Chinese armed forces pledge their absolute loyalty to the Chinese Communist Party. The political system within the forces is tasked to ensure that its allegiance to the Party is secure. As long as "the Party controls the gun," people's war will remain the basis of Chinese strategic thinking.

SECOND ARTILLERY'S PLACE IN CHINA'S STRATEGY

As the CMC drastically reduces personnel strength while continuously increasing the military budget, is it possible for an outsider to perceive any implications for the role of nuclear weapons in the grand strategy? The answer to this question would be found in the repository of Chinese nuclear weapons, the PLA's Second Artillery Corps (Second Artillery), also known as the Strategic Missile Force. Second Artillery operates China's land-based and tactical ballistic missiles, strategic nuclear weapons and conventionally armed SRBMs. It is composed of 100,000 officers, NCOs and conscripts and is the smallest of the various branches and services in the PLA's order of battle. Its nuclear inventory is approximately 400 warheads—280 strategic and 120 tactical.

It should be noted that being the smallest branch of the PLA, Second Artillery actually increased in numbers despite the troop reductions cited above. Second Artillery controls its own budget. Additionally, the budget for its nuclear weapons has reportedly been constantly maintained at five percent of the overall defence expenditure, which is a not a paltry sum considering that the defence spending was estimated to be between $50-80 billion this year.

What do these well-funded forces contribute to China's defence? According to the *White Paper,* "Second Artillery Force organizes and commands its own troops in case of launching nuclear counterattacks with strategic missiles and conducting operations with conventional missiles. Under it are missile and training bases, and... support troops."

Evan S. Medeiros noted in *Evolving Nuclear Doctrine*: "Indeed, the nuclear counterstrike campaign is the only nuclear contingency that the PLA leaders has identified for the Second Artillery." China's entire nuclear arsenal is estimated at approximately 400 warheads. Presently, it is assumed that virtually all operational and deployable warheads in their nuclear arsenal are in Second Artillery's hands. Why? The airborne leg of their proto-triad is composed of 100 B6 BADGER (1965 vintage) and 30 A-5 FANTAN (1970 vintage) aircraft. It is unclear if these platforms are still assigned to strategic strike missions. Additionally, the problem-plagued, 1980s-vintage, XIA-class, (Type 092) SSBN (nuclear-powered ballistic missile submarine) never successfully performed one patrol and, therefore, still does not pose a credible threat. However, the *White Paper* stated that the "Navy aims at gradual extension of the strategic depth for offshore defensive operations and enhancing its capabilities in integrated maritime operations and nuclear counterattacks." Supporting the *White Paper*, Lt. Gen Mi Zhenyu, senior strategist at China's Academy of Military Science wrote: "China's political and economic focus lies on the coastal areas [and] for the present and a fairly long period to come, strategic focus will be in the direction of the sea." In 2006, the PLAN launched two new JIN-class (Type 094) SSBNs that are expected to be deployment-ready by the end of the decade.

"Improve the Survivability of the Strategic Nuclear Weapons"

There are other dramatic changes occurring within the Chinese nuclear forces, changes that have been on-going for decades at a modest pace. Have the Chinese told outsiders what their strategy would be regarding the upgrade of their forces? In 1989, then-deputy commander of the Second Artillery, Major General Yang Huan, published a paper on the Defence Industry of China informing the world of China's intentions:... we should improve current weapons to raise the quality and the comprehensive fighting capability. Science and technology should be our guideposts... strengthening the study of single-item high technology weapons. We should work hard on the survival, fast reaction, accuracy, and break-through and high-command technologies for weapons systems. These should be the direction for the development of our strategic nuclear weapons.

- Improve the survivability of the strategic nuclear weapons... We should strengthen research on small, solid fuel and highly automated mobile missiles and on the technology of invisibility, for reinforcing defence work against nuclear or nonnuclear strike; and improve the survivability of missiles before launch and in flight...
- Improve the striking ability of strategic nuclear weapons...
- Improve the penetration technology of strategic weapons.

There is seemingly no deception intended in General Yang Huan's words. In fact, he actually provided a litany of items on Second Artillery's things to do list. Since his article appeared 18 years ago, China has been able to introduce road-mobile, strategic, nuclear-tipped ICBMs, the DF-31 and the extended-range DF-31A, which may target of most the world, including the continental United States. These missiles are solid-propellant—a major improvement over the previous liquid-fuelled missiles. Another significance of that upgrade is that China's ICBMs are no longer confined to silos. Additionally, launch times have been reduced from several hours to minutes, since there is no requirement to fuel the missiles immediately prior to launch with highly-corrosive, liquid rocket fuel. It is obvious that making nuclear ICBMs solid fuelled and road-mobile tremendously increased their survivability. Another open source document in the Liberation Army Daily from 30 May 2001 praised the then-new Russian road-mobile ICBM calling it an assassin's mace weapon: ""... that could ensure "the most reliable" nuclear retaliation.""

The sea-based leg of their triad has also been upgraded with the addition of the JIN-class SSBNs, which will carry the naval version of the DF-31—the JL-2 SLBM. The XIA SSBN was designed to carry 12 JL-1 SLBMs and the JIN was designed to carry 16 JL-2 missiles. The addition of the nuclear-powered JINs armed with nuclear-tipped SLBMs will provide the CMC with an additional, survivable nuclear option in its grand strategy. A review of the items on General Yang Huan's, that many of those items have been acquired: they have improved current weapons to raise the quality and the comprehensive fighting capability, they have improved the survivability of strategic nuclear weapons, and they have obtained small, solid fuel and highly automated mobile missiles. One hears on TV commercials: Yang Huan also called for improving the striking ability of strategic nuclear weapons as well as improving the penetration technology of strategic weapons. In this case, the Chinese are waiting to see how effective the U.S. national missile defence (NMD) system will be. The Chinese will not be able to design countermeasures for the NMD system until they (and the United States as well) know if it will really work. According to Saunders:

Chinese responses to BMD could consist of three categories of programs: expansion of China's current BM forces, technical countermeasures to penetrate and defeat U.S. BMD system, and the possible use of asymmetric measures such as the development of ASAT weapons to attack key components of the U.S. system.

The Chinese have proven themselves to be capable of creating and deploying military technology without the advanced knowledge of foreign intelligence services. For example, Bill Gertz wrote about China's Yuan-class submarine that was built secretly and completely underground.

China also fired a warning shot across the bow of countries possessing space-based intelligence satellites by successfully destroying an old Chinese weather satellite with an ASAT. If the Chinese can successfully hide the construction of a submarine, successfully launch its ASAT, and deploy road-mobile ICBMs with miniaturized warheads, can they develop other assassin's mace weapons without their adversaries' knowledge? An affirmative answer would suggest that hedging will also continue on all sides, since no side can be certain of what the other side is doing and, therefore, cannot base its security on the belief that it knows everything that the other side might do to improve its relative position.

The Inferior Defeats the Superior

Chinese leaders know that they cannot defeat the United States in a face-to-face encounter. They have studied the results of the Gulf Wars. They also know that the United States, whose forces would confront theirs in a face off over Taiwan, would somehow have to be neutralized in a short-term conflict to achieve the desired results, or face defeat in a long-term conflict. The CMC knows that the U.S supply lines are long, that U.S. forces require enormous amounts of fuel and ammunition, and that they require intricate communications paths—both terrestrial and space-borne. This issue received detailed attention in *The Science of Military Strategy*: In regard to information systems, we should firmly destroy their surface facilities, jam and cut the enemy's information feedback transmission circuits first, and then try our best to knock off his awareness platforms and damage his information flow which can form capabilities, so as to achieve the effect of "decapitation."

Chinese military planners would have to devise a means of interrupting U.S. supplies and communications for just as long as it would take for them to seize and occupy Taiwan. The Chinese do not want a protracted war, but would like a *fait accompli*. According to *Military Power,* in order to successfully accomplish their military strategy: China's leaders have placed a near-term emphasis on asymmetric programs and systems to leverage China's advantages while exploiting the perceived vulnerabilities of potential opponents—so-called Assassin's Mace (*sha shou jian*) programs.

The Chinese have adapted Sun Tzu's ancient stratagems to today's strategic requirements. In this particular case, the doctrine is called "The Inferior Defeats the Superior." Michael Pillsbury has culled Chinese open source writings and described the process by which the Chinese will implement this assassin's mace program.

In order to be successful at the doctrine of "The Inferior Defeats the Superior," China assumes it can initially lull the opponent into complacency, or deceive him to take steps that will help China win. The premises here are quite elaborate...

These concepts of how "The Inferior Defeats the Superior" are claimed to be unique to China, and to have [sic] developed by Chinese strategists over thousands of years. For this reason, PLA authors employ extensive examples from Chinese ancient military campaigns which they claim are the heart of Mao's military doctrines. Westerners are presumed to be ignorant of these Chinese "lessons learned" about Assassin's Mace employment concepts and the doctrines of "The Inferior Can Defeat the Superior."

Pillsbury further explains why the Chinese shroud assassin's mace programs in a veil of secrecy:... some of the doctrines are considered to be highly classified in China, especially as they are taught in classified courses in military operations in the senior PLA schools. Available open sources thus only hint at the full set of concepts of the Inferior Defeats the Superior. Nor do open sources necessarily provide a full set of Assassin's Mace Weapons, either. After all, the need to surprise and even paralyze the opponent is an explicit goal of both these weapons and this doctrine. It is hardly to be expected that they would be fully described for the opponent to read and study in advance.

Having gained awareness of one of China's assassin's mace concepts and how the Chinese leadership has intentionally shrouded it in secrecy, one can better understand that Chinese military developments, as seen by Western observers, may indeed only be what the Chinese want outside observers to see. The Chinese do not try to hide the fact that they have been downsizing the PLA's end strength. The most recent troop reductions brought the PLA down to 2.3 million personnel. That figure is almost identical to that of the U.S. Armed Forces. It is interesting to note that a country of over 1.3 billion people has the same number of soldiers as the United States with a population of only 300 million.

There are other sweeping changes occurring in China's military. The PLA, PLAN (navy) and PLAAF (air force) are undergoing a Chinese version of Goldwaters-Nicols in order to function more along the lines of U.S. joint operations. Additionally, the Chinese have coined a term: "informationalization" or what the United States calls "command, computers, control, communications, intelligence, reconnaissance and surveillance (C 4ISR)." The white paper stresses satellite and airborne sensors, unmanned aerial vehicles and information warfare. The Chinese have been funding these changes by increasing its military budget at a rate of 10 percent for the past 20 years. This year's defence budget's increase is 18 percent over last year's. There is more money for technology while there are fewer troops in the field.

THE ROLE OF CONFIDENTIALITY AND DECEPTION IN CHINESE MILITARY STRATEGY

The stress on seizing the initiative in conflicts and keeping the adversary off balance in Chinese military strategy gives rise to a strong emphasis on deception at the strategic, operational, and tactical levels. Chinese doctrinal materials define strategic deception as "[luring] the other side into developing misperceptions... and [establishing for oneself] a strategically advantageous position by producing various kinds of false phenomena in an organized and planned manner with the smallest cost in manpower and materials."

In addition to information operations and conventional camoufiage, concealment, and deception, the PLA draws from China's historical experience and the traditional roles that stratagem and deception have played in Chinese statecraft. Recent decades have witnessed within the PLA a resurgence of the study of classic Chinese military figures Sun-tzu, Sun Pin, Wu Ch'i, and Shang Yang and their writings, all of which contain precepts on the use of deception.

The Chinese Communist Party's heavy reliance on secrecy acts in tandem with military deception to limit transparency in national security decision-making, military capabilities, and strategic intentions. However, over-confidence may result from military leaders enamored with the uncertain benefits of stratagem and deception. In addition, the same skills commanders use against adversaries can be used to cover up or slow the transmission of bad news internal to the PLA system, a chronic problem in the PRC. Secrecy and deception may therefore be a double-edged sword, confusing China's leaders as much as China's adversaries.

Force transformation Goals and Trends

China's leaders have stated their intentions and allocated resources to pursue broad-based military transformation to enable joint operations that encompasses force-wide professionalization; improved training; more robust, realistic joint exercises; and accelerated acquisition of modern weapons. For the moment, China's military is focused on assuring the capability to prevent Taiwan independence and, if Beijing were to decide to adopt such an approach, to compel the island to negotiate a settlement on Beijing's terms. At the same time, China is laying the foundation for a force able to accomplish broader regional and global objectives.

The Intelligence Community estimates China will take until the end of this decade or later to produce a modern force capable of defeating a moderate-size adversary. In building such a capability, China's leaders stress asymmetric strategies to leverage China's advantages while exploiting the perceived vulnerabilities of potential opponents using so-called Assassin's Mace programs. The January 2007 ASAT test could be viewed in this context.

The PLA's ambition to conduct joint operations can be traced to lessons learned from U.S. and Coalition operations since the 1991 Persian Gulf War. Since 2004, the PLA has conducted a number of exercises designed to develop the PLA's joint operational concepts and demonstrate new capabilities, command automation systems, and weapons. The PLA hopes eventually to fuse service-level capabilities with an integrated network for command, control, communications, computers, intelligence, surveillance, and reconnaissance (C4ISR), a new command structure, and a joint logistics system. However, it continues to face deficiencies in inter-service cooperation and actual experience in joint operations.

As PLA modernization progresses, twin misperceptions could lead to miscalculation or crisis. First, other countries may underestimate the extent to which Chinese forces have improved. Second, China's leaders may overestimate the proficiency of their forces by assuming new systems are fully operational, adeptly operated, adequately maintained, and well integrated with existing or other new capabilities.

Rising Area Denial/Anti-Access Capabilities

In the near term, China is prioritizing measures to deter or counter third-party intervention in any future cross-Strait crises. China's approach to dealing with this challenge centres on what DoD's 2006 *Quadrennial Defense Review* report refers to as disruptive capabilities: forces and operational concepts aimed at preventing an adversary from deploying military forces to forward operating locations, and/or rapidly destabilizing critical military balances. In this context, the PLA appears engaged in a sustained effort to develop the capability to interdict, at long ranges, aircraft carrier and expeditionary strike groups that might deploy to the western Pacific. Increasingly, China's area denial/anti-access forces overlap, providing multiple layers of offensive systems, utilizing the sea, air, and space.

PLA planners have observed the primacy of precision strike in modern warfare and are investing in offensive and defensive elements of this emerging regime. China is pursuing improved ISR assets ranging from unmanned aerial vehicles, satellite constellations, and "informatized" special operations forces which could provide targeting data for long-range precision strikes when linked with robust communications. The PLA envisions precision strike capabilities sufficient to hold at risk western Pacific airbases, ports, surface combatants, land and space-based C4ISR, air defense systems, and command facilities.

To prevent deployment of naval forces into western Pacific waters, PLA planners are focused on targeting surface ships at long ranges. Analyses of current and projected force structure improvements suggest that in the near term, China is seeking the capacity to hold surface ships at risk through a layered defense that reaches out to the "second island chain" (i.e., the islands extending south and east from Japan, to and beyond Guam in the western Pacific Ocean). One area of apparent investment emphasis involves a combination of medium-range ballistic missiles, C4ISR for geo-location of targets, and onboard guidance systems for terminal homing to strike surface ships on the high seas or their onshore support infrastructure. This capability would have particular significance, owing to the preemptive and coercive options it would provide China in a regional crisis.

Chinese military analysts have also concluded that logistics and mobilization are potential vulnerabilities in modern warfare, given the heavy requirements for precisely coordinated transportation, communications, and logistics networks. To threaten in-theatre bases and logistics points, China could employ its theatre ballistic missiles, land-attack cruise missiles, special operations forces, and computer network attacks. Strike aircraft, enabled by aerial refueling, could engage distant targets using air-launched cruise missiles equipped with a variety of terminal-homing warheads.

Advanced mines, submarines, maritime strike aircraft, and modern surface combatants equipped with advanced ASCMs would provide a supporting layer of defense for its long-range anti-access systems.

Planned Capabilities

Nuclear Deterrence. China is qualitatively and quantitatively improving its legacy strategic forces. These presently consist of approximately 20 silo-based, liquid-fuelled CSS-4 ICBMs (which constitute its primary nuclear means of holding continental U.S. targets at risk), approximately 20 liquid-fuelled, limited range CSS-3 ICBMs, between 14-18 liquid-fuelled CSS-2 intermediate range ballistic missiles (IRBMs) and upwards of 50 CSS-5 road mobile, solid-fuelled medium range ballistic missiles (MRBMs) (for regional deterrence missions), and JL-1 SLBMs on the XIA-class SSBN.

By 2010, China's strategic nuclear forces will likely comprise a combination of enhanced CSS-4s; CSS-3s; CSS-5s; solid-fuelled, road-mobile DF-31s (which achieved initial threat availability in 2006, and will likely achieve operational status in the near future, if it has not already done so), and DF-31A

ICBMs ; and the JL-1 and JL-2 SLBMs. The addition of the DF-31 family of missiles and the JL-2 and JIN-class SSBNs will give China a more survivable and flexible nuclear force. New air- and ground-launched cruise missiles that could perform nuclear missions will similarly improve the survivability and flexibility of China's nuclear forces.

China's 2006 Defense White Paper states that: 1) the purpose China's nuclear force is to "deter other countries from using or threatening to use nuclear weapons against China;" 2) China "upholds the principles of counterattack in self-defense and limited development of nuclear weapons;" and, 3) China "has never entered into and will never enter into a nuclear arms race with any other country." The paper reiterated China's commitment to a declaratory policy of "no first use of nuclear weapons at any time and under any circumstances," and states China "unconditionally undertakes not to use or threaten to use nuclear weapons against non-nuclear-weapon states or nuclear weapon-free zones." Doctrinal materials suggest additional missions for China's nuclear forces include deterrence of conventional attacks against the Chinese mainland, reinforcing China's great power status, and increasing its freedom of action by limiting the extent to which others can coerce China. China's assertion of a nuclear "no first use" policy, therefore, is ambiguous. This ambiguity is compounded with the juxtaposition of the "no first use" declaration and the stated commitment to adhere to the principle of "counter attack in self defense."

Periodic military and civilian academic debates over the future of China's nuclear doctrine have questioned whether or not a "no first use" policy supports or detracts from China's deterrent, and whether or not "no first use" should remain in place. The Chinese government has provided public and private assurances that its "no first use" policy has not and will not change. Nevertheless, coupled with the debates themselves, the introduction of more capable and survivable nuclear systems in greater numbers suggest Beijing may be exploring the implications of China's evolving force structure, and the new options that force structure may provide.

Space and Counterspace. China's space activities and capabilities, including anti-satellite programs, have significant implications for anti-access/area denial in Taiwan Strait contingencies and beyond. China further views the development of space and counter-space capabilities as bolstering national prestige and, like nuclear weapons, demonstrating the attributes of a world power.

China has accorded space a high priority for investment. Premier Wen Jiabao, marking the 50th anniversary of China's aerospace industry in October 2006, stated that "China's aerospace industry is standing at a new starting point and facing a new situation and tasks." It is now necessary, he said, "to implement the principle of independent innovations, leaps in key areas... carry out major state science and technology special projects in manned space flights and a lunar probe, and achieve new breakthroughs in research and development [of] aerospace equipment and... space technology."

Reconnaissance. China is deploying advanced imagery, reconnaissance, and Earth resource systems with military applications. Examples include the CBERS-1 and -2 satellites and the Huanjing disaster/environmental monitoring satellite constellation. China is planning eleven satellites in the Huanjing program capable of visible, infrared, multi-spectral, and synthetic aperture radar imaging. In the next decade, Beijing most likely will field radar, ocean surveillance, and high-resolution photoreconnaissance satellites. In the interim, China probably will rely on commercial satellite imagery (e.g., SPOT, LANDSAT, RADARSAT, and Ikonos) to supplement existing coverage.

Navigation and Timing. China has launched four BeiDou satellites with an accuracy of 20 meters over China and surrounding areas. China also uses GPS and GLONASS navigation satellite systems, and has invested in the EU's Galileo navigation system.

Manned Program. In October 2005, China completed its second manned space mission and Chinese astronauts conducted their first experiments in space. Press reports indicate China will perform its first space walk in 2007-2008, and rendezvous and docking in 2009-2012. China's goal is to have a manned space station by 2020.

Communications. China uses foreign providers, like INTELSAT and INMARSAT, for communications, but is expanding indigenous capabilities in this area. China may be developing a system of data relay satellites to support global coverage, and has reportedly acquired mobile data reception equipment that could support more rapid data transmission to deployed military forces and units.

Small Satellites. Since 2000, China has launched a number of small satellites, including an oceanographic research, imagery, and environmental research satellites. China has also established dedicated small satellite design and production facilities. China is developing microsatellites – weighing less than 100 kilograms – for remote sensing, and networks of imagery and radar satellites. These developments could allow for a rapid reconstitution or expansion of China's satellite force in the event of any disruption in coverage.

Anti-Satellite (ASAT) Weapons. In January 2007, China successfully tested a direct-ascent ASAT missile against a Chinese weather satellite, demonstrating its ability to attack satellites operating in low-Earth orbit. The direct ascent ASAT system is one component of a multi-dimensional program to generate the capability to deny others access to outer space.

In a PLA National Defense University book, Joint Space War Campaigns (2005), author Colonel Yuan Zelu writes: *[The] goal of a space shock and awe strike is [to] deter the enemy, not to provoke the enemy into combat. For this reason, the objectives selected for strike must be few and precise...[for example] on important information sources, command and control centres, communications hubs, and other objectives. This will shake the structure of the opponent's operational system of organization and will create huge psychological impact on the opponent's policymakers.*

China's nuclear arsenal has long provided Beijing with an inherent ASAT capability. However, in recent years Beijing has pursued a robust, multidimensional counterspace program. UHF-band satellite communications jammers acquired from Ukraine in the late 1990s and probable indigenous systems give China today the capacity to jam common satellite communications bands and GPS receivers.

In addition to the direct ascent ASAT program demonstrated in January 2007, China is also developing other technologies and concepts for kinetic (hit-to-kill) weapons and directed-energy (e.g., lasers and radio frequency) weapons for ASAT missions. Citing the requirements of its manned and lunar space programs, China is improving its ability to track and identify satellites – a prerequisite for effective, precise physical attacks.

Information Warfare. There has been much writing on information warfare among China's military thinkers, who indicate a strong conceptual understanding of its methods and uses.

For example, a November 2006 *Liberation Army Daily* commentator argued: *[The] mechanism to get the upper hand of the enemy in a war under conditions of informatization finds prominent expression in whether or not we are capable of using various means to obtain information and of ensuring the effective circulation of information; whether or not we are capable of making full use of the permeability, sharable property, and connection of information to realize the organic merging of materials, energy, and information to form a combined fighting strength; [and,] whether or not we are capable of applying effective means to weaken the enemy side's information superiority and lower the operational efficiency of enemy information equipment.*

The PLA is investing in electronic countermeasures, defences against electronic attack (e.g., electronic and infrared decoys, angle reflectors, and false target generators), and computer network operations (CNO). China's CNO concepts include computer network attack, computer network defense, and computer network exploitation. The PLA sees CNO as critical to achieving "electromagnetic dominance" early in a conflict. Although there is no evidence of a formal Chinese CNO doctrine, PLA theorists have coined the term "Integrated Network Electronic Warfare" to prescribe the use of electronic warfare, CNO, and kinetic strikes to disrupt battlefield network information systems.

The PLA has established information warfare units to develop viruses to attack enemy computer systems and networks, and tactics and measures to protect friendly computer systems and networks. In 2005, the PLA began to incorporate offensive CNO into its exercises, primarily in first strikes against enemy networks.

7

China's Strategic Forces Today

China is also developing a submarine-launched variant of the DF-31, called the JL-2. China has built at least two new ballistic missile submarines since 2007. The Office of Naval Intelligence believes China may build as many as five of the new submarines to replace China's lone Xia-class nuclear-powered ballistic missile submarine, which is not believed to be operational. Although the JL-2 may become operational as soon as 2010, China appears to have rather limited capabilities for communicating with submarines at sea and probably has not established operational practices for conducting deterrent patrols. The growth in China's ballistic missile arsenal is not confined to China's nuclear forces. China has also developed new conventionally armed solid-fuel short-range ballistic missiles, the DF-11 and DF-15, which it deploys in very large numbers near Taiwan. China has also deployed a conventional variant of the DF-21, the DF-21C, and is further developing a fourth modification to serve as an anti-ship ballistic missile. Finally, China has deployed a new land-attack cruise missile—the ground-launched DH-10—as part of a broad effort to acquire ground-, air-, and sea-launched cruise missiles.

This process of replacing liquid-fuelled ballistic missiles with solid-fuelled ballistic and cruise missiles underpins China's ongoing strategic modernization. Although many observers have linked the deployment of the DF-31 and DF-31A to recent U.S.

missile defence deployments, it is important to keep in mind that these programs date to the mid-1980s and were supposed to have been completed many years ago.

China is not developing new warheads for its new ballistic missiles. The warheads for the new nuclear delivery systems—the DF-31, DF-31A and JL-2—were tested during the 1990s, before China signed the CTBT in August 1996. Since that time, China has observed a moratorium on nuclear tests. Without resuming yield testing, China would have significant difficulty in designing and certifying a new design, such as those incorporating insensitive high explosives. China does appear to have a significant stockpile stewardship program that may make use of hydro-dynamic experiments at the Lop Nor Test Site.

China may also have a small stockpile of gravity bombs for delivery by aircraft, but no aircraft appear to have the primary mission of nuclear warhead delivery, and nuclear warheads do not appear to be deployed at Chinese airbases. Before permanently moving its nuclear testing underground in the 1980s, China tested numerous nuclear weapons by dropping them from aircraft; however, Chinese officials have stated that the purpose of "airdrop" tests was to reduce test debris that would assist foreign intelligence agencies in analysing the test results.

China probably does not deploy tactical nuclear weapons, although it has the capability to do so and successfully tested an enhanced radiation weapon or "neutron bomb" in 1988. If China's modernization seems unusual, perhaps it is because China is only now completing the deployment capabilities that other countries have possessed for decades.

This is not to suggest that missile defence and other aspects of U.S. strategic modernization have no effect on Chinese decisions. China has developed and flight-tested a sophisticated suite of penetration aids for the DF-21 and DF-31 family of ballistic missiles. Some Chinese specialists have argued that China may increase the number of nuclear warheads capable of reaching the United States, rather than simply replacing the

DF-4 and DF-5 on a one-to-one basis. It remains to be seen whether China will increase its number of nuclear warheads as much as current U.S. intelligence community predictions, which anticipate very large increases in Chinese nuclear forces to respond to U.S. missile defence efforts. In 2001, the U.S. intelligence community asserted that the number of Chinese warheads capable of reaching the United States could grow to 75–100 by 2015. In 2006, the National Air and Space Intelligence Centre warned that the number of Chinese nuclear warheads that could reach the United States "could expand to well over 100 in the next 15 years."

Although such increases are within China's economic and industrial capabilities, especially if China were to deploy as many as five new ballistic missile submarines, it is also possible that China's modernization will occur within the general parameters of its overall force posture, characterized by keeping warheads in storage and a restrictive nuclear no-first-use declaratory policy.

China's nuclear arsenal also stands out from the other nuclear powers not merely due to its small size, but also because China keeps its nuclear forces off alert and under the strictures of a no-first use pledge.

By all indications, Chinese nuclear warheads are not normally mated to their missiles. Robert Walpole, then national intelligence officer for strategic and nuclear programs at the CIA, stated in 1998 that "China keeps its missiles unfueled and without warheads mated." The warheads are stored at nearby, but separate, bases. Press reports of Chinese mobile ballistic missile exercises published by the state-run Xinhua News Agency indicate that nuclear warheads would be mated in the field to mobile ballistic missiles before launch, similar to the procedure used by Soviet Mobile Technical Rocket Bases (PRTB, in Russian) stationed in East Germany and elsewhere during the Cold War.

Anecdotal evidence from public descriptions of Chinese exercises and doctrinal materials suggest that Chinese forces expend considerable effort training to conduct retaliatory missions in the harsh environment after a nuclear strike. One Chinese textbook that is used to train cadres is forthright about the difficulty of maintaining a survivable retaliatory capability under a no-first-use doctrine. "According to our principle of no first-use of nuclear weapons," the text *Zhanyi Xue* (Operational Studies) warns future commanders, "the nuclear retaliation campaign of the Second Artillery will be conducted under the circumstances when [the] enemy has launched a nuclear attack on us. ... The personnel, position equipment, weapons equipment, command telecommunication system and the roads and bridges in the battlefield will be seriously hurt and damaged."

Whether Chinese leaders will change these features of their nuclear posture is difficult to predict. Western analysts have long predicted, for example, that China would eventually move away from a no-first-use posture—yet China's political leaders continue to appear committed to the policy. In part, the judgment that China would dump no-first-use has been based on voluminous criticisms of no-first-use in Chinese military writings. The considerable ink spilled in Chinese military publications complaining about "no-first-use" is probably the best evidence that the policy remains in place. Dissatisfaction among some Second Artillery commanders with no-first-use might also explain the growing deployments of conventionally armed ballistic missiles, which are presumably subject to less doctrinal interference from senior leaders and Chinese nuclear weapons scientists.

Fundamental changes are more likely to result from ongoing changes in China's domestic politics, rather than as a mechanistic response to changes in U.S. strategic capabilities such as missile defence or conventional strike. China's small cadre of scientists and engineers continue to play a significant role in matters relating to nuclear policy—but today, unlike in Nie's era, they are no longer the only voices on nuclear policy. As part of an effort to ensure that military priorities are better reflected in defence science and technology investment, the General Armaments Department replaced the Commission on Science and Technology for National Defence, which was run by Nie's son-in-law as late as the mid-1990s. Although the GAD itself may be a distinct interest group, relative to the Second Artillery or the Navy, it is presumably much less independent than in Nie's day.

Moreover, the Second Artillery and the Navy are vastly more professional today than even ten years ago. In the past it would have been difficult to imagine the parochial service interests overriding a desire for central control over China's nuclear forces—as embodied in aphorisms such as "the party must control the gun, the gun must never control the party." But today China is very different: the PLA is far more professional than ever before, and China's leaders were children when the United States subjected China to nuclear threats.

DEVELOPMENT OF CHINA'S ARMED FORCES

China's armed forces are composed of the People's Liberation Army (PLA), the People's Armed Police Force (PAPF) and the militia. They play a significant role in China's overall strategies of security and development, and shoulder the glorious mission and sacred duty of safeguarding national sovereignty, security and development interests.

Over the years, the PLA has been proactively and steadily pushing forward its reforms in line with the requirements of performing its missions and tasks, and building an informationized military. The PLA has intensified the strategic administration of the Central Military Commission (CMC). It established the PLA Department of Strategic Planning, reorganized the GSH (Headquarters of the General Staff) Communications Department as the GSH Informationization Department, and the GSH Training and Arms Department as the GSH Training Department. The PLA is engaged in the building of new types of combat forces. It optimizes the size and structure of the various services and arms, reforms the organization of the troops so as to make operational forces lean, joint, multi-functional and efficient. The PLA works to improve the training mechanism for military personnel of a new type, adjust policies and rules regarding military human resources and logistics, and strengthen the development of new- and high-technology weaponry and equipment to build a modern military force structure with Chinese characteristics.

The PLA Army (PLAA) is composed of mobile operational units, border and coastal defence units, guard and garrison units, and is primarily responsible for military operations on land. In line with the strategic requirements of mobile operations and multi-dimensional offense and defence, the PLAA has been reoriented from theater defence to trans-theater mobility. It is accelerating the development of army aviation troops, light mechanized units and special operations forces, and enhancing building of digitalized units, gradually making its units small, modular and multi-functional in organization so as to enhance their capabilities for air-ground integrated operations, long-distance maneuvers, rapid assaults and special operations. The PLAA mobile operational units include 18 combined corps, plus additional independent combined operational divisions (brigades), and have a total strength of 850,000. The combined corps, composed of divisions and brigades, are respectively under the seven military area commands (MACs): Shenyang (16th, 39th and 40th Combined Corps), Beijing (27th, 38th and 65th Combined Corps), Lanzhou (21st and 47th Combined Corps), Jinan (20th, 26th and 54th Combined Corps), Nanjing (1st, 12th and 31st Combined Corps), Guangzhou (41st and 42nd Combined Corps) and Chengdu (13th and 14th Combined Corps).

The PLA Navy (PLAN) is China's mainstay for operations at sea, and is responsible for safeguarding its maritime security and maintaining its sovereignty over its territorial seas along with its maritime rights and interests. The PLAN is composed of the submarine, surface vessel, naval aviation, marine corps and coastal defence arms. In line with the requirements of its offshore defence strategy, the PLAN endeavours to accelerate the modernization of its forces for comprehensive offshore operations, develop advanced submarines, destroyers and frigates, and improve integrated electronic and information systems. Furthermore, it develops blue-water capabilities of conducting mobile operations, carrying out international cooperation, and countering non-traditional security threats, and enhances its capabilities of strategic deterrence and counterattack. Currently, the PLAN has a total strength of 235,000 officers and men, and commands three fleets, namely, the Beihai Fleet, the Donghai Fleet and the Nanhai Fleet. Each fleet has fleet aviation headquarters, support bases, flotillas and maritime garrison commands, as well as aviation divisions and marine brigades. In September 2012, China's first aircraft carrier Liaoning was commissioned into the PLAN. China's development of an aircraft carrier has a profound impact on building a strong PLAN and safeguarding maritime security.

The PLA Air Force (PLAAF) is China's mainstay for air operations, responsible for its territorial air security and maintaining a stable air defence posture nationwide. It is primarily composed of aviation, ground air defence, radar, airborne and electronic countermeasures (ECM) arms. In line with the strategic requirements of conducting both offensive and defensive operations, the PLAAF is strengthening the development of a combat force structure that focuses on reconnaissance and early warning, air strike, air and missile defence, and strategic projection. It is developing such advanced weaponry and equipment as new-generation fighters and new-type ground-to-air missiles and radar systems, improving its early warning, command and communications networks, and raising its strategic early warning, strategic deterrence and long-distance air strike capabilities. The PLAAF now has a total strength of 398,000 officers and men, and an air command in each of the seven Military Area Commands (MACs) of Shenyang, Beijing, Lanzhou, Jinan, Nanjing, Guangzhou and Chengdu. In addition, it commands one airborne corps. Under each air command are bases, aviation divisions (brigades), ground-to-air missile divisions (brigades), radar brigades and other units.

The PLA Second Artillery Force (PLASAF) is a core force for China's strategic deterrence. It is mainly composed of nuclear and conventional missile forces and operational support units, primarily responsible for deterring other countries from using nuclear weapons against China, and carrying out nuclear counterattacks and precision strikes with conventional missiles. Following the principle of building a lean and effective force, the PLASAF is striving to push forward its informationization transform, relying on scientific and technological progress to boost independent innovations in weaponry and equipment, modernizing current equipment selectively by applying mature technology, enhancing the safety, reliability and effectiveness of its missiles, improving its force structure of having both nuclear and conventional missiles, strengthening its rapid reaction, effective penetration, precision strike, damage infliction, protection and survivability capabilities. The PLASAF capabilities of strategic deterrence, nuclear counterattack and conventional precision strike are being steadily elevated. The PLASAF has under its command missile bases, training bases, specialized support units, academies and research institutions. It has a series of "Dong Feng" ballistic missiles and "Chang Jian" cruise missiles.

In peacetime, the PAPF's main tasks include performing guard duties, dealing with emergencies, combating terrorism and participating in and supporting national economic development. In wartime, it is tasked with assisting the PLA in defensive operations. Based on the national information infrastructure, the PAPF has built a three-level comprehensive information network from PAPF general headquarters down to squadrons. It develops task-oriented weaponry and equipment and conducts scenario-based training so as to improve its guard-duty, emergency-response and counter-terrorism capabilities. The PAPF is composed of the internal security force and other specialized forces. The internal security force is composed of contingents at the level of province (autonomous region or municipality directly under the central government) and mobile divisions. Specialized PAPF forces include those guarding gold mines, forests, hydroelectric projects and transportation facilities. The border public security, firefighting and security guard forces are also components of the PAPF.

The militia is an armed organization composed of the people not released from their regular work. As an assistant and backup force of the PLA, the militia is tasked with participating in the socialist modernization drive, performing combat readiness support and defensive operations, helping maintain social order and participating in emergency rescue and disaster relief operations.

The militia focuses on optimizing its size and structure, improving its weaponry and equipment, and pushing forward reforms in training so as to enhance its capabilities of supporting diversified military operations, of which the core is to win local wars in informationized conditions. The militia falls into two categories: primary and general. The primary militia has emergency response detachments; supporting detachments such as joint air defence, intelligence, reconnaissance, communications support, engineering rush-repair, transportation and equipment repair; and reserve units for combat, logistics and equipment support.

MILITARY STRATEGY AND DEVELOPMENT OF CHINESE ARMED FORCES

Paper outlines the military strategy of active defence to guard against and resist aggression, contain separatist forces, safeguard border, coastal and territorial air security, and protect national maritime rights and interests and national security interests in outer space and cyber space. It reiterates PLA's doctrine of 'local wars under the conditions of informationization, intensify integration and joint employment of different services and arms, and enhance war fighting capabilities based on information systems.

Reading in between the lines it appears that there is an attempt to strengthen the role of Chinese Central Military Commission in shaping the politico – military discourse. Creation of the Department of Strategic Planning is significant, implying harmonizing political and military objectives in shaping national security objectives. Chinese White Papers routinely highlight cliché's related to strategies and tactics of people's war, advance integrated civilian-military development, and enhance the quality of national defence mobilization and reserve force building', this practice continues.

The doctrine of winning local wars under informationised conditions was mentioned in detail in its 2004 White Paper and subsequent papers wherein considerable details had been given as to how PLA intends to proceed with the process of military modernisation. It appears that a local war under informationised conditions has been adopted as central doctrine by the Chinese armed forces together with the concept of 'active defence'. It needs to be noted that while China purports active defence as a "defensive military strategy", it is in effect pro active in nature. Essentially implying China can initiate hostilities on mere perception of the intent of the adversary which Chinese leadership may perceives as detrimental to its interests.

For the first time the PLA has provided an outline structure of its armed forces. It is a different matter that much of it was already available in the open domain, however, what has been revealed by the PLA varies only in a limited sense from the estimates made by analysts and researchers. Structurally PLAA (PLA(Army) is aiming to create small, modular and multi functional organizations with conceptual shift from "Theatre Defence" to "Trans Theatre Mobility". Implying thereby on growing focus on rapid mobilization, rapid deployment and quick launch in what in Indian parlance can be referred to as 'cold start' doctrinal thinking. Infrastructural development, enhanced C4ISR and space based systems are seen to enhance these capabilities.

The paper states that the PLAA mobile operational units include 18 combined corps, plus additional independent combined operational divisions (brigades), often referred to as rapid reaction forces or task oriented 'battle groups'. Combined strength of PLAA has been placed as 850,000. The combined corps, composed of divisions and brigades, are respectively under the seven military area commands (MACs): Shenyang (16th, 39th and 40th Combined Corps), Beijing (27th, 38th and 65th Combined Corps), Lanzhou (21st and 47th Combined Corps), Jinan (20th, 26th and 54th Combined Corps), Nanjing (1st, 12th and 31st Combined Corps), Guangzhou (41st and 42nd Combined Corps) and Chengdu (13th and 14th Combined Corps). Creation of four "strategic zones" (northern, eastern, western and southern), supplanted upon seven MAC, as part of overall rationalization of armed forces (as some reports in Chinese media suggested) however does not find mention? Notably of the 18 combined corps only four are deployed in MAC's opposite India; Chengdu and Lanzhou. Thus for any India specific contingencies China will be forced to undertake large scale trans-theatre force mobilization together with build up of logistic capabilities. Such moves will no doubt leave large footprints making enhanced ISR capability by India a strategic necessity.

The modernization and growing role of PLAN is of particular interest. Paper highlights the efforts being made to develop naval capabilities. It mentions PLAN training for as combined task forces composed of new types of destroyers, frigates, ocean-going replenishment ships and shipborne helicopters" in what it terms as complex battlefield environments. Paper also highlights training for "remote early warning (space based systems), comprehensive control, open sea interception, long-range raid, anti-submarine warfare and vessel protection at distant sea". It is obvious that PLAN is preparing itself for what it calls "Distant Sea Operations", highlighting that since 2007, the PLAN has conducted training in the distant sea waters of the Western Pacific involving over 90 ships.

Given the above focus China could be expected to be more assertive in safeguarding its perceived maritime interests and incrementally enhance its influence in the Indian Ocean with growing focus on security of sea lines of communication, and force projection. This by implication means China will seek and develop Rand R facilities which could overtime be upgraded into bases in the IOR littoral. India cannot remain impervious to these developments and would need to take steps to keep Chinese activities under surveillance and continually weigh its own strategic options.

The paper alluding to tensions in South China Sea highlights organization of coastal forces to carry out live force-on-force training for air defence, anti-submarine, anti-mine, anti-terrorism, anti-piracy, coastal defence, and island and reef sabotage raids, etc. The Chinese propensities at escalating tensions were at full display in March 2013. In a commentary noted China specialist Andrew Erickson highlighted "four foreign policy fumbles" in Mar 2013 that led to escalation of tensions in South China Sea, these include, two incidents of firing by Chinese Marine Surveillance vessels on Vietnamese fishing vessels, maneuvers by four vessel, PLAN flotilla, near Parcels at a place called "James Shoal", 80 Km from Malaysia. Fourth pertained to loading up crude from China in violation of current embargoes on Iran.

So far as PLA Air Force (PLAAF) is concerned the paper mentions that the PLAAF now has a total strength of 398,000 officers and men, and an air command in each of the seven Military Area Commands (MACs). The focus of PLAAF modernization is on developing and improving early warning command and communication networks, to raise strategic early warning, and for deterrence and long distance strike capabilities. It is also developing range of new generation fighters, ground to air missiles and radar systems. For strategic intervention role it poses a one airborne corps with adequate strategic lift capability. PLAAF appears to be developing strong operational capabilities underscored by upgradation of air defence networks, developing number of airfields in Tibet and adjoining Lanzhou and Chengdu MAC, and strengthening its air defence cover. It is obvious that based on its capability development programme PLAAF could in the next couple of years develop credible interventionist capabilities, with formation like the 15 Airborne Corps providing the desired strategic airlift capabilities.

White Paper bills "PLA's Second Artillery Force (PLASAF) as the core force for China's strategic deterrence". It comprises both nuclear and conventional missile forces and operational support units, primarily responsible for ensuring functional efficacy of Chinese strategic deterrence and preventing coercion. According to the paper Second Artillery Force (SAF) is striving' at 'enhancing the safety, reliability and effectiveness of its missiles, improving its force structure of both nuclear and conventional missiles, strengthening its rapid reaction, effective penetration, precision strike, damage infliction, protection and survivability capabilities'. The Second Artillery is responsible for war planning and training based on the assumption that China will absorb first nuclear strikes and use its nuclear forces only to retaliate. Its strategic forces are complimented by large conventional missile force capable of precision attacks based on well developed space based ISR systems which further enhance the credibility of its no-first-use pledge. Science of Second artillery Campaign explicitly highlights the interface between nuclear and conventional missile forces by underscoring "during future joint combat operations Second Artillery will not merely act as the main force in providing nuclear deterrence and nuclear counter-strike power, but will also act as the backbone force in conventional firepower assaults".

The current political leadership has been paying particular attention to SAF. After having taken over as Chairman of the Central Military Commission in November 2012, Xi Jinping visited Second Artillery Force and observed that "the artillery force is the core strength of China's strategic deterrence, the strategic support for the country's status as a major power, and an important cornerstone safeguarding national security". Many advanced versions of ballistic and cruise missiles are being fielded with appropriate integration with C4ISR assets which are both ground and space based. PLA carried out second anti-ballistic missile test in January this year indicating that it is moving towards acquiring a ballistic missile defence capability. Although this is primarily aimed at degrading the American strategic capabilities it would no doubt also impact the value and worth of India's nuclear deterrent.

The paper also gives insights into China's nuclear posture though to a limited degree. It states "If China comes under a nuclear threat, the nuclear missile force will act upon the orders of the CMC, go into a higher level of readiness, and get ready for a nuclear counterattack to deter the enemy from using nuclear weapons against China. If China comes under a nuclear attack, the nuclear missile force of the PLASAF will use nuclear missiles to launch a resolute counterattack either independently or together with the nuclear forces of other services. The Chinese government insists that modernization of its nuclear forces is only to maintain a reliable second-strike retaliatory capability. The focus therefore is to ensure that the "nuclear deterrent" is "safe, reliable, and credible" under "any" circumstance and China is capable of effective counter attack in self defence, an interesting perspective however is debate on the nature of response – proportional or massive.

The conventional missile force is able to shift instantly from peacetime to wartime readiness, and conduct conventional medium- and long-range precision strikes". By inference it means that China will employ precision nuclear strikes as part of its conventional war fighting doctrine and is unlikely to resort to first use of nuclear weapons. If we were to take the NFU declaratory doctrine of China at face value as also that of India's this would essentially mean nuclear weapons as tools of deterrence are outside the equation of any conventional conflict scenario. Given the growing state of conventional asymmetry, Chinese with their superior conventional and missile force will always be at an advantage and force decisions on their terms in a limited conflict scenario, putting India at a disadvantage. Following from above the manner in which Indian strategic deterrence in the scenario of growing conventional asymmetry would play require deeper analysis in India.

The paper also describes the role of People's Armed Police Force (PAPF) which is a Para military force meant for internal security duties and to assist the PLA in war time. Some of its main tasks include performing guard duties, dealing with emergencies, combating terrorism and participating in and supporting national economic development. It is also employed for national development tasks and is composed of some special forces assigned for various miscellaneous civil and military tasks. Possibly, the Chinese troops which have been sent to POK for so called development activities are from PAPF.

An aspect that has been emphasised in 2013 Paper is PLA's role in aid of the people and national development so that PLA can be truly seen as peoples' army. Since 2004 this role of PLA is being stressed upon more and more. The paper says that "The Constitution and relevant laws entrust China's armed forces with the important tasks of safeguarding the peaceful labour of the Chinese people, taking part in national development and serving the people wholeheartedly". During the CPC's 18th Congress conclave in November, 2012 the party leadership had emphasised that "We must unwaveringly adhere to the principle of the Party's absolute leadership over the armed forces and continue to educate them in the system of theories of socialism with Chinese characteristics". The paper goes to considerable length in portraying PLA as peoples and not the Party's army.

Defence Expenditure

Notably the most important thing missing in the paper is any mention of the defence expenditure which has been invariably mentioned in all the white papers issued so far. China's defence expenditure according to its 2006 paper was US dollars 36 billion; this year the budget according to figures released in 12th National People's Conference in early March was estimated to be between US dollars 115 to 117 billion, more than three times the size of 2006 figures. Last year the defence budget was around 107 billion dollars. However, according to a US Defence Intelligence Agency Report of 17 April 2013 China spent as much as 215 billion dollars on military related services and goods in contrast to the last year's official budget of 107 billion dollars. One of the major factors contributing to rise in the defence expenditure in Asia-Pacific is the double digit growth in PRC's defence budget from 1990 to 2013 as China's neighbours remain wary of its growing military might and enlargement of its 'core interests'.

Major conclusion that emerges is China is embarked on building all round comprehensive military capabilities to emerge as the dominant military power in Asia with ability to challenge even the US in its core areas of interest. The manner of its engagement in international peace keeping and anti piracy operations highlights its global ambitions as a responsible stake holder.

So far as India is concerned it is quite evident that military asymmetry with China will increase and if not addressed would become unbridgeable. India has to accelerate its military modernization which has been stymied due to politico-bureaucratic inertia, inadequate and outdated system and processes. India's long term integrated perspective plans for its armed forces remain an amalgamation of individual respective perspective plans since there is no shared vision among the services in the absence of coherent national security policy and military strategy. Though inadequacies and gaps military capabilities are well known yet sufficient effort has not been put in filling the voids and gaps in military capabilities. India needs to improve its ground holding capabilities, C4ISR capabilities, accretion of space assets, missile warfare capabilities, long range precision capabilities besides infrastructure development in border regions. Further, China through its various manoeuvres has been aspiring to dominate Indian Ocean region which is critical to Indian security; this challenge needs to be met both through diplomacy and modernisation of our maritime capabilities.

CHINESE ARMY MODERNIZATION

The Chinese People's Liberation Army (PLA) is in the third decade of a comprehensive program of modernization and transformation that began in 1979 after the PLA's last major campaign against a foreign enemy, its "self-defensive counterattack" against Vietnam. The program continues with renewed vigore into the new century.

Chinese military modernization encompasses all four services with priority of effort directed toward the PLA Navy (PLAN), the PLA Air Force (PLAAF), and the strategic missile force (known as the Second Artillery). The ground army, which previously had been the centre of gravity of the Chinese Armed Forces, remains the largest service and still provides the bulk of senior leadership for the military, but it has felt the brunt of force reductions as the PLA's mission emphasis has shifted. U.S. Army personnel who served in the post-Vietnam and post-Gulf War military should be able to appreciate the scope of what the Chinese are attempting and understand the time period required to achieve their goals. The strategic underpinning for a long-term military modernization process was set in 1985 when China's supreme military command, the Central Military Commission (CMC), headed by paramount leader Deng Xiaoping, declared the most likely military contingency China faced to be "local, limited war" (replacing the threat of the "early, major, and nuclear war" foreseen by Mao Tse-tung).

Because the threat of major war was deemed low, senior Chinese leaders made the critical strategic decision to subordinate military modernization to other aspects of national economic development, such as agriculture, industry, and science and technology. Thus, in the 1980s and early 1990s, the Chinese Government did not spend vast sums of money and national resources to rapidly modernize the PLA. The "bloated" PLA could take its time to reform, focusing first on downsizing its 4-million-plus force.

For the first 10 years of modernization, China perceived its major potential foe to be the Soviet Union. Using force to reunify Taiwan with the mainland was low on the list of China's military priorities. By the mid-1990s, the situation between the mainland and Taiwan had changed considerably. A multiparty democratic form of government was taking hold on the island, and voices for independence had risen. After the 1995-1996 crisis in the Taiwan Strait, China's leaders decided they needed to develop military capabilities more rapidly to prevent what Beijing perceived as further steps toward Taiwanese independence.

Although Chinese leaders preferred peaceful reunification of the island with the mainland, they knew Taiwan and its supporters in the United States had to see China's military power as credible. As a result, after 1999 the intensity of the PLA's modernization process increased, focusing principally on the goal of deterring Taiwan's independence and, if necessary, on imposing the will of Chinese leaders by force. Although the Taiwanese scenario became the top planning priority, training for a variety of military missions continued throughout the country and in all PLA units.

The acceleration of PLA modernization after 1999 became possible to a large extent because of the confluence of a more specifically defined mission, the availability of increased resources, a smaller force, and 20 years of previous effort that had laid the groundwork for what was to follow.

In particular, many advances in the PLA since 1999 have taken advantage of the Nation's impressive economic growth during the 1990s, especially developments in the Chinese electronics industry. The end of the Soviet threat, along with the availability of advanced military weapons from a cash-strapped Russian Government, also contributed to changes in China's strategic posture in the late 1990s. Still, despite some marked improvements in China's military capabilities, the effectiveness of PLA modernization has yet to be proven in battle against a hostile force.

Elements of Modernization

By the turn of the 21st century, several distinct but interrelated elements have been seen in the PLA's modernization program. The following components of modernization were directly linked to developments of the previous two decades and enhanced by increased resources available since 1995:

* Reduction in force size.
* Changes in force structure.
* Reform of the structure and missions of the reserves and militia.
* Changes in the personnel system.
* An influx of new equipment.
* Doctrinal revision to prepare the PLA to fight and win Local Wars Under Modern High-Technology Conditions or Local Wars Under Informationalization Conditions.
* Improvements in the frequency, content, and methods of military training, with emphasis on joint operations.
* Transformation of the PLA logistics system.
* Enhancement of all soldiers' standard of living, pay, and lifestyle.

* Modification of the professional military education system.

Members of the U.S. Army will appreciate the complexity of the PLA's transformation, its long-term nature, and the difficulty of the tasks Chinese military leaders face. The PLA is also pursuing modernization with a much smaller resource and combat experience base than did the U.S. Army in the 1970s and 1990s. On the positive side, the PLA's modernization goals are more manageable because, unlike the U.S. Army, the PLA does not seek to project force across oceans, and it limits its scope of operations to what it considers protection of Chinese sovereignty (which, by definition, includes Taiwan and much of the South China Sea). The PLA does not have to man foreign bases and respond to a web of defence commitments throughout the world. Moreover, unlike the U.S. Army, the PLA remains a party-army bonded by loyalty to the Chinese Communist Party.

Security apparatus. The PLA is one of three elements of the Chinese Armed Forces, each of which is a separate, distinct organization, although all are closely related. According to China's National Defence Law of March 1997, Chinese Armed Forces are composed of the—

* PLA, both active and reserve units.
* People's Armed Police (PAP) Force.
* People's militia (ordinary and primary units).

The PLA is primarily responsible for defending China from external threats, with the secondary mission of domestic security in accordance with the law; that is, when requested by local authorities and approved by the central leadership. The ultimate command authority for the PLA is the CMC, with command running through four general headquarters departments in Beijing to the forces deployed in seven military regions throughout the country. The PLA, PAP, and militia wear similar but distinct uniforms, have similar organizational and rank structures, and undergo similar basic training, but they have separate systems for command and control, funding, promotion, education, and training. All three support national economic development with labour and service projects and can be mobilized to provide rescue and relief support in the event of floods, earthquakes, and other natural disasters. The PAP and militia are paramilitary organizations. By law and in practice, the PAP is not part of the PLA, although it is sometimes mistakenly called military police by Chinese and foreign sources alike. The PAP's primary mission, worked in conjunction with the Ministry of Public Security police force, is internal security. The PAP has a dual command structure that includes the CMC and the State Council through the Ministry of Public Security. Its secondary mission is to help the PLA in local defence against external enemies.

The militia supports the PLA in time of war and also helps maintain public order when necessary. The PLA chain of command and local civilian governments are in the militia's command structure. They cooperate through established joint civilian-military organizational mechanisms. The 1.7-million-person civilian Ministry of Public Security police force is primarily responsible for law enforcement and domestic security. It and the Ministry of State Security, with the missions of counterespionage and domestic and foreign intelligence, respond to the State Council and are not part of the Chinese Armed Forces. However, in its annual human fights reports, the U.S. Department of State (DOS) includes the Ministry of Public Safety with the PLA, the PAP, the Ministry of State Security, and "the state judicial, procuratorial, and penal systems" as part of the Chinese Government's security apparatus.

According to a recent DOS report, "[c]ivilian authorities generally maintained effective control of the security forces." What kind of control they exercised is not altogether clear because "[s]ecurity policy and personnel were responsible for numerous human rights abuses.... At times, police used excessive force against demonstrators." There is no recent confirmed evidence of the PLA being used routinely to control domestic demonstrations or dots, although that could change if the civilian police force and PAP fail in their missions.

The PLA is also distinct from the civilian-run (but mostly government-owned) defence industrial sector composed of some

2 million workers and thousands of enterprises that produce and sell military equipment and civilian goods and services.

Reductions in force. The PLA has undergone two large reductions in force in the past decade, starting with about 3 million people in 1995 and losing 500,000 people from 1997 to 2000 and another 200,000 from 2003 to 2005. By the end of 2005 the PLA have about 2.3 million people on its active duty roster.

As the largest component of the PLA with the lowest priority in modernization, army ground forces suffered the largest proportion of cuts. Current estimates put the number at 1.6 million—town about 500,000 from 1995. Reserve personnel, most of whom are in reserve army units, number about 800,000. The PAP might have up to 1.5 million in its ranks. The primary militia, according to a 2004 defence white paper, has 10 million members, but the number of ordinary militia, presumably a larger force, was not announced.

While PLA active duty forces have been cut by approximately 23 percent over the past 10 years, the officially announced defence budget has nearly quadrupled from about 64 billion yuan in 1995 to 248 billion yuan in 2005.

Yet these figures do not account for the total funds available to the PLA from extra-budgetary sources, such as support from local governments and special budgets for the purchase of foreign weapons.

The PLA-watching community has debated exactly what should be included in estimates of actual Chinese defence expenditures and what factor should be applied to announced budget numbers to arrive at true defence spending.

Estimates range from about 1.5 to 3 times (or greater) the announced figure. Whatever the true amount of funds available, such a large force is still relatively resource-constrained; thus, PLA leaders constantly look for ways to save money as new equipment enters the force and training opportunities increase.

Future personnel reductions with increased defence budgets would not be surprising.

PROJECTING POWER

China's rulers have adopted what is known as the "two-island chain" strategy of extending control over large areas of the Pacific, covering inner and outer chains of islands stretching from Japan to Indonesia. "Clearly, they are still influenced by this first and second island chain," the intelligence official said. The official said China's buildup goes beyond what would be needed to fight a war against Taiwan. The conclusion of this official is that China wants a "blue-water" navy capable of projecting power far beyond the two island chains. "If you look at the technical capabilities of the weapons platforms that they're fielding, the sea-keeping capabilities, the size, sensors and weapons fit, this capability transcends the baseline that is required to deal with a Taiwan situation militarily," the intelligence official said. "So they are positioned then, if [Taiwan is] resolved one way or the other, to really become a regional military power as well."

The dispatch of a Han-class submarine to waters near Guam, Taiwan and Japan was an indication of the Chinese military's drive to expand its oceangoing capabilities, the officials said. The submarine surfaced in Japanese waters, triggering an emergency deployment of Japan's naval forces. Beijing later issued an apology for the incursion, but the political damage was done. Within months, Japan began adopting a tougher political posture toward China in its defence policies and public statements. A recent Japanese government defence report called China a strategic national security concern. It was the first time China was named specifically in a Japanese defence report.

Energy Supply a Factor

For China, Taiwan is not the only issue behind the buildup of military forces. Beijing also is facing a major energy shortage that, according to one Pentagon study, could lead it to use military force to seize territory with oil and gas resources. The report produced for the Office of Net Assessment, which conducts assessments of future threats, was made public in January and warned that China's need for oil, gas and other energy resources is driving the country toward becoming an expansionist power. China "is looking not only to build a blue-water navy to control the sea lanes [from the Middle East], but also to develop undersea mines and missile capabilities to deter the potential disruption of its energy supplies from potential threats, especially in the case of a conflict with Taiwan," the report said. The report said China believes the United States of America already controls the sea routes from the oil-rich Persian Gulf through the Malacca Strait. Chinese President Hu Jintao has called this strategic vulnerability to disrupted energy supplies Beijing's "Malacca Dilemma."

To prevent any disruption, China has adopted a "string of pearls" strategy that calls for both offensive and defensive measures stretching along the oil-shipment sea lanes from China's coast to the Middle East. The "pearls" include the Chinese-financed seaport being built at Gwadar, on the coast of western Pakistan, and commercial and military efforts to establish bases or diplomatic ties in Bangladesh, Burma, Cambodia, Thailand and disputed islands in the South China Sea. The report stated that China's ability to use these pearls for a "credible" military action is not certain.

The rapid Chinese naval buildup includes the capability to project power to these sea lanes in the future. "They are not doing a lot of surface patrols or any other kind of security evolutions that far afield," the intelligence official said. "There's no evidence of [Chinese military basing there] yet, but we do need to keep an eye toward that expansion." The report also highlighted the vulnerability of China's oil and gas infrastructure to a crippling U.S. attack.

"The U.S. military could severely cripple Chinese resistance [during a conflict over Taiwan] by blocking its energy supply, whereas the [People's Liberation Army navy] poses little threat to United States' energy security," it said. China views the United States as "a potential threat because of its military superiority, its willingness to disrupt China's energy imports, its perceived encirclement of China and its disposition toward manipulating international politics," the report said.

'Mercantilist Measures'

The report stated that China will resort "to extreme, offensive and mercantilist measures when other strategies fail, to mitigate its vulnerabilities, such as seizing control of energy resources in neighbouring states." U.S. officials have said two likely targets for China are the Russian Far East, which has vast oil and gas deposits, and Southeast Asia, which also has oil and gas resources.

Michael Pillsbury, a former Pentagon official and specialist on China's military, said the internal U.S. government debate on the issue and excessive Chinese secrecy about its military buildup "has cost us 10 years to figure out what to do" "Everybody is starting to acknowledge the hard facts," Mr. Pillsbury said. "The China military buildup has been accelerating since 1999. As the buildup has gotten worse, China is trying hard to mask it."

Richard Fisher, vice president of the International Assessment and Strategy Centre, said that in 10 years, the Chinese army has shifted from a defensive force to an advanced military soon capable of operations ranging from space warfare to global non-nuclear cruise-missile strikes. "Let's all wake up. The post-Cold War peace is over," Mr. Fisher said. "We are now in an arms race with a new superpower whose goal is to contain and overtake the United States."

CHANGE IN FORCE STRUCTURE

To accommodate the loss of over 500,000 troops and to prepare for new missions, the PLA ground force has changed its structure greatly since the mid-1990s, when the main combat force was organized into 24 group armies (corps equivalent), approximately 90 maneuver (infantry and tank) divisions, about 15 brigades (mostly tank), plus scores of artillery, antiaircraft artillery (AAA), combat support, and local/border defence units.

Soviet unit structure provided the organizational pattern for many PLA units. Currently the PLA ground force is organized into 18 group armies, along with a number of independent units that do not belong to any group army. Maneuver forces consist of approximately 40 divisions and about 43 separate brigades, supported by roughly 42 artillery, AAA, and air defence divisions and brigades, and various Special Operations Forces (SOF), reconnaissance, helicopter, engineer, communications, chemical defence, electronic warfare (EW'), and high-technology units.

While the two most powerful group armies retain their maneuver division structure, most group armies now have combinations of infantry and armor divisions and brigades, while four have an all-brigade structure. With the Soviet model no longer the pattern for the future force, many units are still undergoing experimentation. PLA divisions are considerably smaller than U.S. equivalents and have less firepower.

A number of new mechanized divisions and brigades have been formed since the late 1990s, including a light mechanized infantry division and two amphibious mechanized infantry divisions. Heavy armoured and mechanized infantry divisions and brigades comprise over 40 percent of ground force maneuver units, doubling the percentage of a decade ago. The army now has more amphibious forces than the PLAN, which has two marine brigades. At the same time, in the Nanjing Military Region a traditional army artillery brigade was transformed into a conventionally armed short-range ballistic missile brigade (with 12 to 16 launchers).

New air-defence brigades were also created by adding tactical surface-to-air missiles (SAMs) to AAA gun formations. (A number of AAA units without SAMs remain.) The number of helicopters of all types in the army has increased from about 135 in the mid-1990s to approximately 400 today. This still-small number is organized into units of about 25 to 30 aircraft, with the units spread throughout the country.

In the 1990s, each military region formed an SOF unit of roughly 1,000 persons. These units can be delivered by parachute, helicopter, or sea. They principally conduct raids and long-range reconnaissance. (The bulk of the Chinese airborne force is in the PLAAF, which has an airborne army comprised of three divisions and a SOF unit.) Also, over the past decade a few psychological warfare units and high-technology communications, intelligence, and EW units have been created. In addition to targeting enemy communications and computer systems, high-technology units aim to interfere with or jam the guidance systems of enemy precision-guided munitions. Logistics support units have not been forgotten; the PLA understands its new equipment increases fuel, ammunition, and technical support requirements.

The PLA has adopted the term "revolution in military affairs (RMA) with Chinese characteristics" to describe primarily how it will build a smaller, more technologically advanced force through "mechanization and informationalization." Mechanization is the foundation for informationalization, which focuses on applying information technologies to procedures and equipment to enhance capabilities. The PLA acknowledges that its concept of RMA with Chinese characteristics is considerably different from more advanced militaries' visions of RMA.

Reserves and militia. The active duty PLA has undergone major change, and the reserve force has undertaken similarly radical reforms in structure and mission since 1998. Army reserve units are estimated to include about 42 infantry, artillery, and AAA divisions; 16 infantry, artillery, and logistics support brigades; and 7 chemical defence, engineer, and communications regiments. Reserve infantry divisions are found in nearly every province and autonomous region, often with additional artillery and AAA reserve units. Since 1999, each military region has established a reserve logistics support brigade to sustain reserve and active duty operations. While many soldiers in the PLA reserve have served in active units, many reserve units recruit specialized civilians without prior service to fill specific technical needs. In time of war, reserve units can augment active forces or operate independently as local defence forces. Over the past decade, militia forces have undergone major reorganization and reorientation, focusing mainly on the primary militia (ages 18 to 28) and less on the ordinary militia (ages 18 to 35), which is reportedly being reduced in size. Militia units are found in villages and cities and in factories and commercial enterprises, including some foreign-owned companies. Many militia members have no active-duty service and receive only a few weeks of training per year. Militia units still perform the traditional roles of light infantry (especially in rear area support operations), air defence, and logistics support (particularly transportation and maintenance). In recent years, the role of urban militia has been highlighted, emphasizing air defence and repair of infrastructure damaged by long-range enemy attack. A variety of high-technology militia units have been formed to provide communications support and repair, as well as to conduct information operations.

In times of emergency, such as external defence, domestic unrest, or natural disaster, PLA reserves and militia elements are mobilized to support the active force. Manpower mobilization is one of the major responsibilities of the system of National Defence Mobilization Committees, which extends from national to county level and integrates military, government, and Communist Party leaders at all echelons. These committees are involved in all aspects of civilian mobilization (equipment, materiel, communications, transportation, air defence, national defence education, and so on), and many are prepared to set up military-civilian command posts in time of crisis.

Personnel system. The PLA is a conscript force led by a contingent of volunteer noncommissioned officers (NCOs) and officers. In 1999 the conscription period was reduced to 2 years for all PLA conscripts. The government brought in new soldiers from the countryside and cities in proportion to the population breakdown (70 percent rural/30 percent urban). Some conscripts were posted near their homes, although many serve in units assigned to other parts of the country. Near the end of their service period, some tactically proficient and politically reliable conscripts can volunteer to become NCOs and serve up to 30 years.

Also in 1999, the PLA implemented a new NCO system, NCO duties expanded, and the number of NCOs increased as the numbers of officers and conscripts were reduced. In recent years the PLA began enlisting limited numbers of civilians with special skills to become NCOs (enlistees undergoing only short, introductory training), but most NCOs come up from the ranks. In 2003, the CMC instituted a two-decade program to improve the quality of officers and NCOs through education and training. This program was influenced, in part, by the study of foreign military systems, especially the role of the NCO, and recognizes that professional NCOs and officers cannot be created overnight.

Most NCOs receive training at NCO schools or at some officer academies. They are divided into six grades, each with a specified term of service that is extended on promotion. As their numbers increase, NCOs are assigned new leadership and technical jobs. For example, NCOs are gradually replacing company mess officers (whose duties are similar to U.S. company supply sergeants).New PLA officers come from four sources: graduates from civilian universities who elect to join after graduation; "national defence students" from civilian colleges who attend on scholarships and are committed to serve in repayment for their scholarships; cadets from PLA military universities and academies; and soldiers selected from the enlisted ranks.

Officers are assigned duties in five categories: military (or operational), political, logistics, armaments, and specialist-technical. Their rank structure is similar to the U.S. Army's (second lieutenant through colonel), but the PLA adds a senior colonel rank (division commander) and does not have brigadier generals. Instead, its major generals wear one star, lieutenant generals two, and full generals three. In addition to military ranks, officers are assigned duty position grades, or posts, which extend from platoon leader through each level of command to CMC vice chairman. Duty position grade takes precedence over military rank. In the PLA, unit commanders serve side by side with political officers who, as a rule, hold the same duty position grade and have the same military rank (although occasionally one officer might outrank the other). The commander and political officer are jointly responsible for the performance of their unit.

Weapons and equipment. Since 1999, PLA ground forces have received a variety of new Chinese-made weapons and equipment, including main battle tanks, amphibious tanks, armoured personnel carriers, self-propelled artillery, tactical SAM and AAA systems, and small arms.

A number of new support vehicles and items have also been deployed (forklifts, maintenance vans, fuel tankers, field kitchens, and ambulances). Of significance is that Chinese electronics and aviation industries have provided computers, satellite and microwave communications, optical fiber links, night-vision goggles, frequency-hopping radios, battlefield surveillance equipment, and unmanned aerial vehicles. Imports from Russia are limited mostly to Mi-17-series helicopters and precision-guided munitions and technology. Many of the above items were displayed at a large military parade in Beijing on 1 October 1999. A good source for photographs and technical descriptions of PLA equipment is the Chinese Defence Today website.

Not all units can be reequipped at the same time. Most still have a mix of high-, medium-, and low-technology equipment. Initially, the Army assigned new equipment to divisions, but by 2002 a few newly formed brigades received new equipment. The PLA recognizes that it takes time to achieve combat readiness after units receive new weapons; it has therefore set the general goal of achieving combat readiness with new equipment to within a year of its arrival at a unit. The PLA also accepts that it remains technologically less advanced than many other militaries. As a result, leaders often challenge soldiers to find new ways to use existing equipment to defeat a high-technology enemy. In 1999, the CMC replaced 1980s regulations with new doctrine outlining how the PLA will make "preparations for military struggle" and conduct future military operations. Based in large part on careful examination of foreign military campaigns of the 1990s, updated doctrine emphasizes joint operations and incorporates lessons learned about the effectiveness of modern technology while still emphasizing the importance of man and the support of the Chinese population.

The PLA also retains other traditional concepts, such as speed, surprise, deception, stratagem, and the decisive role of the offense. The conduct of joint operations is an important element of all levels of professional education, and the PLA has published many books and articles to explain it.

Training. The Military Training and Evaluation Program (MTEP), which sets standards for training and evaluation of all types of units and headquarters elements, guides PLA training for both active and reserve units. The MTEP is modified according to new requirements and the acquisition of new capabilities. The General Staff Department formulates annual training tasks, which vary according to military region and service. Units often receive specific topics for experimentation in order to develop and refine tactical procedures such as night, high-altitude, or logistics operations. Units study successful lessons learned, and if they are applicable to other units, they are disseminated throughout the force. Many experiments are discarded.

Chinese ground forces are involved in a range of training activities throughout the country. Units prepare for missions appropriate to local situations (coastal, interior, desert, mountain, and so on) and train to defend against external threats, to foil terrorists, and to conduct disaster-relief operations. Many tasks are highlighted during field deployments, but nearly every major exercise includes rapid mobilization and deployment from garrison and defence from long-range air or missile attack. Units might be in the field for several months while undergoing progressive training from small-unit to group-army exercises.

Since 1996, the PLA's main training focus seems to be on amphibious operations. Four major amphibious training bases have been designated along the coast, and many units have built smaller amphibious training areas locally. Over the past 5 years approximately one-quarter or more of all army maneuver divisions and brigades have trained to some extent for amphibious operations. The Nanjing and Guangzhou military regions opposite Taiwan are the sites of most amphibious training, but some units from the Jinan, Shenyang, and Beijing military regions also participate. In contrast to 10 years earlier, units have crossed military region boundaries during a few exercises.

Live-fire and force-on-force confrontation exercises are integral elements of the training cycle, which culminates in annual evaluations. In garrison, unit training halls are equipped with computers and weapons simulators to prepare for all aspects of field training. Computer wargames, often played from multiple locations, are becoming common.

Logistics. Functions considered logistics in the U.S. Army are managed by two PLA systems, one headed by the General Logistics Department, the other by the General Armaments Department.

The PLA is developing joint logistics structures centred in the military regions to support forces of all services. Logistics units provide general-purpose supplies (food, water, uniforms, transportation, medical support, and so on) while armaments units provide specialized supplies (such as ammunition) and services (maintenance and repair support). A major component of reform is outsourcing, or contracting, with civilian enterprises for goods and services such as dining facilities management, grain storage, fuel and some spare parts provision, and some maintenance. Also, in the event of war, the PLA will mobilize and integrate civilian personnel and materiel into the force at least in the war zone and possibly throughout the Nation to support any campaign lasting more than a few days. Such mass mobilization is another of the traditional People's War concepts that have survived into the 21st century.

Soldiers' standard of living. The Chinese Government states that a large part of official defence budget increases in recent years has gone to improving the standard of living for all PLA personnel. This statement is true. Improving living standards is especially important in maintaining troop morale as most of the rest of the country gets richer and fatter. Accordingly, soldiers have been issued new uniforms, including Kevlar-type helmets, and berets, and units have developed colorful identification patches to be worn on uniform sleeves. Pay and benefits have increased substantially, albeit from a low base. Ration allowances have been consistently increased to provide a greater variety of food and beverages in garrison and in the field. Barracks throughout China have been rebuilt and refurbished and conveniences such as washers, dryers, and air conditioners added. Modern communications, entertainment equipment, and computers are available to troops in numbers unimagined a decade before.

Education. To keep up with the changes in force structure and doctrinal developments, the PLA has also reformed its system of schools and academies. Like the rest of the force, the system has decreased in size. Many institutions have been consolidated with others, reassigned to local governments, or closed down altogether. Courses of study have been modified to reflect new joint doctrine and new missions such as disaster relief and peacekeeping operations. New schools for NCOs have been established and long-distance learning encouraged using the Internet. Officers now can pursue advanced degrees in over 50 PLA institutions and in civilian schools in China and abroad. As its equipment becomes more advanced and its doctrine more complex, the PLA understands the need for highly educated, technically proficient personnel. Chinese leaders also accept that achieving their goals will take years, perhaps decades, to accomplish.

More Changes Ahead

Despite the slow, long-term nature of PLA modernization, Chinese military officers will obey their civilian leaders' orders and execute assigned missions to the best of their ability. The longer they have to modernize and prepare for those missions, the greater their chance of success.

Beijing's own estimate of another 10 to 20 years for the modernization program to reach advanced standards is realistic. In the meantime, ground forces will focus on building SOF, long-range missile, helicopter, and high-technology units to be used in the early stages of a campaign to support the missile, air, and naval forces that most likely will engage the enemy. Large-scale amphibious operations will probably not come early in future campaigns, but nevertheless, the PLA continues to prepare for that contingency, just as it prepares to repel threats along its land borders.

By monitoring Chinese media, observers can follow to some extent the type, size, and content of some PLA training; however, accurately judging the quality of training or proficiency of units is problematic. While the PLA has certainly improved its capabilities over the past decade, much of its training still appears to be relatively rudimentary. For example, despite the emphasis on joint operations, no PLA officer has actually planned for or commanded under combat conditions the type of operations the new doctrine envisions. Tellingly, in the past 2 years the PLA has created the term integrated joint operations to remind commanders that they must include all elements of combat power in exercise scenarios and training. Furthermore, the PLA does not train for or even have the doctrine to execute what the U.S. military considers close air support, and the number of helicopters in the force is so small as to severely limit the size and frequency of airmobile training. The PLAAF's large-transport fleet is also extremely small, which significantly affects force projection. Nonetheless, PLA leaders understand its capabilities and shortfalls—better than most outside analysts do. The U.S. military's experiences in modernizing and transforming should provide us some appreciation for the difficulty the PLA faces in executing a modernization program composed of so many parts. But the Chinese are patient and resolute. With the country continuing to apply more money to the process, the PLA's progress deserves close study and objective analysis.

EVALUATING CHINA'S MILITARY STRENGTH

The Department of Defence recently released its long-overdue annual report on China's military power. The document tells us much about how the Democratic Congress and the Obama administration would like to approach relations with China, and not nearly enough about China's military modernization. It suggests we have a Congress that does not take the China challenge seriously and a White House that is uncertain how to tackle it.

The problems started with the 2010 National Defence Authorization Act (NDAA), which revised the 2000 NDAA—the law that requires an annual DOD report to Congress on China's military power—in a number of ways. Most noticeably, the 2010 NDAA changed the report's title from "Military Power of the People's Republic of China" to "Military and Security Developments Involving the People's Republic of China," which obscures the report's purpose by framing China as a passive actor. China's development of an anti-satellite (ASAT) capability, for example, is not a military development involving China; it is a decision by China to enhance its military power.

Also, before the 2010 NDAA, the report's scope included "the tenets and probable development of Chinese grand strategy"; now, Congress has stripped away every mention of "grand strategy." DOD had in the past been instructed to provide analysis of "trends in Chinese strategy that would be designed to establish [China] as the leading political power in the Asia-Pacific region and as a political and military presence in other regions of the world." Now, DOD must report on "trends in Chinese security and military behavior that would be designed to achieve, or that are inconsistent with," "the goals... shaping Chinese security strategy and military strategy."

Further, since its inception, the report's purpose has been to inform the Senate and House about Chinese military power so that Congress can adequately fund U.S. defence needs; this is why the law requires that the report be submitted by March 1 of each year, long before the NDAA debates take place. But this year, not wanting to anger the Chinese—who have complained about the report year after year—the White House delayed its release, presumably excising declassified information that it deemed too provocative. (The Chinese complained anyway.) By the time the administration released the report to the public, Congress was in recess and the rest of Washington on vacation. Published too late to have the impact that it should on the congressional debate over the 2011 NDAA, and at a time when few members of Congress are likely to comment, the report has failed in its purpose: to inform Congress as it prepares the coming year's defence-spending bill.

It seems that the White House wishes to avoid an open, honest, and public debate about China's military modernization and intentions in Asia. Such a debate might make it more difficult for the administration to pursue a cooperative approach to relations with Beijing. While the recent decisions to wade into the South China Sea territorial disputes and to send the USS George Washington to exercise in the Yellow Sea—both of which elicited strident Chinese objections—suggest that the White House might be abandoning that approach, the report's handling should make outside observers think twice. At best, it suggests a confused China policy; at worst, that the president prefers "business as usual"—or rather, business as in 2009. This president seems most comfortable when he is extending an open hand; he is unlikely to quickly set aside the "strategic reassurance" policy articulated last year. If that means manipulating the public's perceptions of a rising China, then so be it.

The irony of this state of affairs, unfortunately, seems to be lost on this administration. It is Beijing—not any report produced by the Defence Department—that is primarily responsible for how China is perceived. As the new report notes, "the limited transparency in China's military and security affairs enhances uncertainty and increases the potential for misunderstanding and miscalculation." Beijing fails to satisfactorily explain the reasoning behind its aggressive military modernization, thus generating concern and suspicion amongst its neighbors and in the United States.

Unfortunately, the DOD report also fails to adequately explain Chinese military modernization. A close reading reveals that the modernization is robust, and is occurring across all of the service branches. But the report (like its predecessors) does not explain how these developments are related to each other or to Beijing's strategic goals. What role will they play in China's security strategy? In China's military strategy?

For example, this year's report, like last year's, notes that China is developing an aircraft carrier and that its navy has already started training pilots for carrier-borne aviation. But it does not explain that aircraft carriers are the quintessential instrument of military power projection. A nation does not build them if it does not see a need to project air power to distant shores. With Chinese carriers patrolling the seas, Guam, Australia, all of Southeast Asia, and the entirety of India will for the first time be in range of People's Liberation Army tactical aircraft.

The 2010 report similarly lacks analysis of the developments in China's missile force. While it mentions the 2nd Artillery Corps's development of an anti-ship ballistic missile (ASBM), few details are provided, and no attempt is made to explain the impact it will have on the U.S. Navy's ability to operate in the Western Pacific.

The report is vague about the PLA's overall missile buildup as well. It notes that "China is fielding an array of conventionally armed ballistic missiles [and] ground-and air-launched land-attack cruise missiles... to hold targets at risk throughout the region." But again, there is no explanation of what this might mean for U.S. forces in the region. Can those missiles hit American bases and those of our allies? What kind of damage can they inflict?

Though you wouldn't know it from reading the report, China likely envisions using ASBMs, other ballistic and cruise missiles, future carriers, and other capabilities—including nuclear and quiet conventional attack submarines, cyber-and space-warfare assets, and an integrated air-defence system—in pursuit of its regional goals.

Those goals are, in short, to unify Taiwan with the mainland, to settle East and South China Sea disputes in China's favour, and, more broadly, to assert its primacy in the region.

In a Taiwan Strait crisis, for example, the PLA could use its missile force to strike American aircraft carriers in the Western Pacific, and airbases in Japan and potentially on Guam.

Strike-group ships that survived could be stalked by multiple, increasingly stealthy submarines. Meanwhile, the now-limited number of tactical aircraft that the U.S. could send to the fight would face a highly sophisticated air-defence system on the Chinese mainland, but only if they could bypass or punch through combat air patrols launched from Chinese carriers in the East China and Philippine Seas. Chinese cyber and space operations would further complicate American efforts to bring force to bear. This would leave China's air force, ground forces, and smaller surface warships to focus their efforts on Taiwan.

This is a relatively straightforward story, and one that the DOD reports have failed to tell over the years. China, thankfully, has a long way to go before it will be able to successfully pull off such an operation.

But American forces in Asia are vulnerable, and increasingly so as Chinese military modernization continues. The administration should provide the American people and the U.S. Congress with a full accounting of PLA modernization and Chinese strategic goals, and of how they are linked; armed with such an accounting, Congress would be in a position to fund the military America needs for the Asia-Pacific region.

Congress, of course, also has a responsibility to ensure that it is getting the information it requires. Last year's changes to the DOD China report were ill considered and should be revisited.

When it comes to China, this administration seems to be pulled in two directions. It spent much of 2009 trying to reassure China that the U.S. welcomes its rise; the White House's handling of the report was one effort in that broader campaign. At the same time, there has been the occasional glimpse of a more confrontational approach to Beijing: Secretary Clinton's Internet-freedom speech, arms sales to Taiwan, Secretary Gates's remarks at the International Institute for Strategic Studies' Asia Security Summit (also known as the Shangri-La Dialogue), and the recent diplomatic contretemps over the South China Sea.

Hopefully, the president is learning that these two approaches need not be mutually exclusive. With an honest recognition that the United States and China share some interests but not others, the president should, sooner or later, settle on the proper course: to cooperate with China on issues where goals intersect, and to vigorously defend those U.S.

interests that China threatens. If the two countries can find a way to cooperate on climate change or in international economic forums, they should do so. But Washington should be less concerned with "reassuring" Beijing and more concerned with deterring it from upsetting the American-led international order.

This requires both an unwavering commitment to the security of U.S. allies and partners in Asia—including Taiwan—and the maintenance of an American preponderance of military power in the region. The role of U.S. forces in the Asia-Pacific region should be, first and foremost, to deter Chinese aggression. Absent a robust, resilient force in the region, Beijing will be tempted to resort to force to achieve its goals. And absent an honest public debate in this country about China's rise—a debate the report fails to foster—that robust, resilient force may one day be a thing of the past.

ARMY OF THE FUTURE

In the past, some defence specialists insisted a Chinese attack on Taiwan would be a "million-man swim" across the Taiwan Strait because of the country's lack of troop-carrying ships. "We left the million-man swim behind in about 1998, 1999," the senior Pentagon official said.

"And in fact, what people are saying now, whether or not that was ever useful, is that it's a moot point, because in just amphibious lift alone, the Chinese are doubling or even quadrupling their capability on an annual basis." Asked about a possible Chinese attack on Taiwan, the official put it bluntly: "In a time frame, a capability was there that a year ago we would have said was very, very unlikely.

We now assess that as being very likely to be there." Air Force Gen. Paul V. Hester, head of the Pacific Air Forces, said the U.S. military has been watching China's military buildup but has found it difficult to penetrate Beijing's "veil" of secrecy over it. While military modernization itself is not a major worry, "what does provide you a pause for interest and concern is the amount of modernization, the kind of modernization and the size of the modernization," he said during a recent breakfast meeting with reporters. China is building capabilities such as aerial refueling and airborne warning and control aircraft that can be used for regional defence and long-range power projection, Gen. Hester said.

It also is developing a maneuverable re-entry vehicle, or MARV, for its nuclear warheads. The weapon is designed to counter U.S. strategic-missile defences, according to officials who spoke on the condition of anonymity. The warhead would be used on China's new DF-31 long-range missiles and its new submarine missile, the JL-2. Work being done on China's weapons and reconnaissance systems will give its military the capability to reach 1,000 miles into the sea, "which gives them the visibility on the movement of not only our airplanes in the air, but also our forces at sea," Gen. Hester said.

Beijing also has built a new tank for its large armed forces. It is known as the Type 99 and appears similar in design to Germany's Leopard 2 main battle tank. The tank is outfitted with new artillery, anti-aircraft and machine guns, advanced fire-control systems and improved engines. The country's air power is growing through the purchase of new fighters from Russia, such as Su-30 fighter-bombers, as well as the development of its own fighter jets, such as the J-10.

Gen. Hester compared Chinese warplanes with those of the former Soviet Union, which were less capable than their U.S. counterparts, but still very deadly. "They have great equipment. The fighters are very technologically advanced, and what we know about them gives us pause for concern against ours," he said. Missiles also are a worry.

"It is their surface-to-air missiles, their [advanced] SAMs and their surface-to-surface missiles, and the precision, more importantly, of those surface-to-surface missiles that provide, obviously, the ability to pinpoint targets that we might have out in the region, or our friends and allies might have," Gen. Hester said. The advances give the Chinese military "the ability... to reach out and touch parts of the United States — Guam, Hawaii and the mainland of the United States," he said.

To better deal with possible future conflicts in Asia, the Pentagon is modernizing U.S. military facilities on the Western Pacific island of Guam and planning to move more forces there. The Air Force will regularly rotate Air Expeditionary Force units to Guam and also will station the new long-range unmanned aerial vehicle known as Global Hawk on the island, he said.

It also has stationed B-2 stealth bombers on Guam temporarily and is expected to deploy B-1 bombers there, in addition to the B-52s now deployed there, Gen. Hester said.

8

Investment Strategy for Research and Technology Development in Army

CONCEPT FOR ARMY AFTER NEXT OPERATIONS

In the last decade, the Army's modernization efforts have focused on achieving "information dominance" of the battlefield by making full use of information technologies. The evolving "digitized" force, known as Army XXI, will be realized in 2010. Beyond Army 2010, TRADOC has been charged by the Chief of Staff to investigate revolutionary capabilities achievable for an AAN in the year 2025. The AAN will depend on accelerated changes, even revolutions, in mobility, lethality, survivability, and sustainability that will dramatically increase the Army's capabilities to achieve full-spectrum dominance of the battlefield. Requirements for the systems that will be added to Army XXI to make up the AAN have not yet been determined.

In fact, at the time of this study, the AAN concept is becoming a cyclical process involving war games, analyses, and evaluations by the Army. This process was described to the committee as a concept exploration to define characteristics of a future Army capable of deploying a highly lethal battle force anywhere in the world on short notice.

With technological superiority, the AAN battle force would collapse an opponent's center of gravity before opposing forces have had time to "set," that is, to "dig in" following an act of aggression. The self-sustained battle force would be capable of delivering a devastating surgical blow in 14 days or less. Then, depending on the mission, the battle force would be followed by Army XXI forces.

The AAN tactical concepts and technologies are still notional but are considered possible in the 2025 time frame. Army 2010 is a major milepost on the road to the AAN along with operational concepts promulgated by the Joint Chiefs of Staff in *Joint Vision 2010* (DoD, 1996).

To ensure its success, the AAN must project forces with superior tactical and operational mobility, highly lethal and survivable weapons, and systems that exhibit new standards of reliability and sustainability. Key ingredients will be superior intelligence capabilities (information dominance) and operational airlift capability to transport armaments, vehicles, and soldiers fully prepared to engage in immediate battle over long distances.

The AAN concept proposes an Army made up of the AAN battle force (up to 20 percent) and Army XXI forces (80 percent). The rapidly deployable battle force will respond to contingencies from the continental United States within 48 hours, and, if necessary, be followed by the heavier Army XXI forces. The battle force would consist of units of up to 8,000 soldiers equipped with highly sophisticated weapons and vehicles capable of engaging and defeating a heavily armored enemy force. Compared to conventional operations, which averaged 40 km/h in the Gulf War, the battle force would move from a staging area and engage the enemy at speeds averaging 200 km/h (Scales, 1997).

The battle force would normally be part of a joint (multiservice) or combined (multinational) combat operation and would be capable of operating in densely populated urban areas when necessary. Operational emphasis will be on the vertical dimension for the inherent advantages of owning the "high ground." The vertical battle space will enable other forces to focus essential capabilities in general support (GS) of the

AAN battle force, including ground and air platforms to deliver supporting fire, unmanned aerial vehicles (UAVs), and command, control, communications, and intelligence (C3I) for information dominance provided by low-, mid-, and high-orbit satellites.

This study focuses on logistics support requirements for systems used by the AAN battle force. These include highly mobile, lethal, and survivable combat vehicles and other weapons platforms.

The battle force will also have sophisticated communications capabilities that will enable soldiers to maintain full situational awareness (SA), including near real-time damage assessment. The battle force will usually be augmented by supporting firepower and transport provided by the Air Force and Navy. All vehicles and equipment will necessarily be designed to require minimal logistics support because battle force units will have to be self-sustaining (i.e., require no support from logistics organizations external to the battle force) for up to 14 days.

In establishing a baseline for applicable AAN technologies, the committee assumed that between now and 2025 Army doctrine and culture will evolve in parallel with technology and that the Army XXI forces will evolve from the fully-digitized units now being formed. The committee also assumed that planned improvements in logistics support capabilities would enable coherent logistics support of both the AAN battle force and the follow-on Army XXI forces.

SCIENCE AND TECHNOLOGY INITIATIVES TO REDUCE ENERGY-RELATED LOGISTICS BURDENS

Based on the preceding analyses of the logistics burdens associated with the fuel and energy demands of AAN operations and the technological opportunities for reducing these burdens, the committee concluded that the Army should pursue the following areas of scientific research and technology development. The order of the numbered items reflects a rough order of priority.

Increasing the Energy Supply

1. Systems Analysis of Alternative Fuel Supply Systems. An efficient and reliable fuel supply system is critical for a modern land combat force. An investigation of significant changes in the existing fuel supply system to enable AAN operations and to decrease logistics burdens should be based on a model of the entire fuel supply system, including a realistic simulation of all significant logistics burdens and their effects on the supply system and the war-fighting organization. AAN wargames have begun to incorporate realistic modeling of fuel supply logistics at the strategic, operational, and tactical levels. An immediate objective should be to couple a fuel supply model to the fuel demands of the AAN system being used in a wargame. System(s) to achieve this modeling capability could also be used for fuel system trade-off analyses, mission planning, and training exercises.
2. High-Density Hydrogen Storage. The Army should monitor the progress of research on high-density hydrogen storage. If new technologies can be scaled and have the potential for future applications, the Army should foster industry partnerships, a joint-service program, or another mechanism for investigating the implementation of this new technology. A reasonable next step would be applied research to determine the feasibility of using technology based on high-density hydrogen storage to make hydrogen a battlefield fuel competitive with diesel fuel.
3. Modular Nuclear Power. The Army should investigate the feasibility of scaling modular, transportable, field-rugged, "walk-away safe" nuclear power plants to sizes suitable for use at an AAN staging area. A key consideration is whether an energy density in the range of 0.4 kW/kg can be maintained for modules of practical size (10 to 100 MW) that meet other critical performance, safety, and reliability objectives.

4. Fuel Cell Technology. The Army should continue its support of research and applications development in fuel cell technology. If the investigations into the feasibility of fieldable nuclear power plants and high-density hydrogen storage *lead to favorable results,* the Army should expand its participation in and sponsorship of applied research and development for large fuel cells, perhaps through partnerships with the automotive industry. *Assuming that the prerequisite investigations into nuclear energy as a primary source and hydrogen as a storable battlefield fuel are successful,* the Army should investigate an electrochemical process for converting electrical energy to fuel energy in hydrogen (reverse of a hydrogen fuel cell).

Reducing Energy Demand

1. Information on Lightweight Substitute Materials. The Army should find ways, through the information and research and development networks in which it already participates, to promote and support the development of information resources that would help system designers acquire data on lightweight materials. Information resources could include industry-wide databases of materials properties and user-friendly tools, such as graphical interfaces, for selecting and comparing data on substitutes for conventional materials.
2. Lowering the Cost of Lightweight Materials. The ongoing development of low-cost synthesis and processing technologies to extract, refine, and process lightweight materials (e.g. magnesium) warrants the Army's close observation, involvement, and encouragement. Similarly, the Army should monitor commercial developments for lowering the cost of ceramics and organic composites. Work being undertaken with the encouragement of the auto industry should be monitored and supported, as appropriate. The Army can leverage resources by keeping abreast of progress by potential commercial users and

by promoting joint-service and DoD-wide participation with industrial and academic partners.

3. Vehicle System Weight as a Design Criterion for Trade-off Studies. In an ideal scenario, vehicle system weight could be reduced without sacrificing other performance objectives. However, it appears that the stringent requirements proposed for AAN combat vehicles will probably require some trade-offs between system weight and other desirablebut not mission criticalcapabilities. The use of armor to protect against advanced high-velocity projectiles probably will be one of these capabilities. The general requirement of protecting combat vehicles against projectiles can be addressed in many ways and to varying degrees. The integrated, hierarchical modeling environment will be essential for evaluating the many technology options for AAN vehicles and for making sound decisions on the optimum strategy for balancing vehicle weight against effective protection. The lower levels of this hierarchical modeling environment could also assist designers in evaluating candidate materials for armor building blocks and new armor architectures. Feeding these vehicle protection designs up to force-on-force simulations in the hierarchy would allow the testing of assumptions about the most effective combination of characteristics in AAN wargames.

Efficient Energy Management

1. Fuel Economy as a Functional Specification. Faced with expensive developmental trade-offs, contractors will not design fuel economy into Army combat vehicles unless the Army specifies clear and unequivocal limits for maximum fuel consumption and holds the contractors to those limits. All vehicle procurement contracts should specify readily measurable limits on vehicle fuel consumption.
2. System Analysis of Hybrid Vehicles. Whether an electric hybrid power plant improves the fuel economy of a

vehicle depends on the vehicle duty cycle. Based on the qualitative descriptions to the committee of how an AAN battle force would operate and a general automotive engineering rule of thumb on the kind of duty cycle in which a hybrid power plant improves overall fuel economy, it seems unlikely that a hybrid vehicle would reduce fuel consumption *in an AAN operation.* However, a quantitative analysis based on realistic modeling of representative duty cycles and the distribution of energy sinks would resolve this issue. Furthermore, other factors in system design might favor a hybrid vehicle. Once again, this decision calls for a vehicle system trade-off analysis that realistically represents the duty-cycle demands on the power plant, including nonrecoverable energy losses during prolonged, high-speed, off-road operation.

SCIENCE AND TECHNOLOGY INITIATIVES TO REDUCE MOBILITY LOGISTICS BURDENS

Based on the preceding analysis of the logistics burdens associated with mobility requirements for AAN-style operations and the technological opportunities for reducing these burdens, the committee concluded that the Army should pursue the following areas of research and technology development. The order of the numbered items under a heading reflects a rough order of priority.

Operational Mobility

Air Mobility Alternatives. The committee is not optimistic that the Army's current or planned aircraft programs will provide the operational mobility necessary for AAN missions. The R&D risks in this area are high, and the acquisition costs may be prohibitive. In addition, even if the R&D objectives are realized, the resulting aircraft will add significantly to overall logistics demand for the AAN battle force mission. Nonconventional, novel concepts for air mobility, however, might lead to a revolutionary breakthrough. The WIG concept is one example of an approach that seems to warrant a careful and open-minded evaluation. Although WIG technology has been demonstrated to some extent, both fundamental research on the aerodynamic principles and thorough feasibility studies would be essential before the Army could make a commitment to technology development. A similar combination of foundational research and exploratory testing for feasibility in military operations would apply to other novel air mobility concepts. The search for new approaches to air mobility should be a joint effort; at the same time, the Army must ensure that Army requirements are fully met in the process. (This initiative pertains to reducing logistics demand for the *operational mobility* requirements for the AAN battle force. Obviously, the battle force will also have a continuing need for a limited number of aircraft for combat and support missions the battle area.)

Tactical Ground Mobility

1. Mobility M&S Environment for System Design and Trade-off Analyses. Decisions regarding vehicles will be critical to determining AAN logistics needs. These decisions must be made from a total systems perspective. The choice of fuel, for example, cannot be made without considering the vehicle power plant. The choice of vehicle power plant cannot be made without careful consideration of the vehicle duty cycle. The choice of power plant may also determine the main gun; conversely, the choice of the main gun may influence the choice of power plant.

The development of a family of vehicles that weigh 15 tons or less is not only feasible but also desirable for meeting AAN operational goals. The technologies for an advanced wheeled vehicle can be developed in the near term because many of them have already been implemented and could be integrated into a total system with relative ease.

Unfortunately, the current vehicle mobility models (the NRMM) are inadequate to assess the performance and logistics benefits of active suspension and traction control, electric drive power trains, or other advanced subsystem technologies. These models cannot simulate cross-country speeds as high as 130 km/h, certainly not 200 km/h. They cannot be used to optimize route planning for both speed and fuel conservation. Therefore, the NRMM is only a starting point for the development of AAN mobility concepts.

Developments in M&S technology that would support off-road mobility analyses are listed below:

- traction models for high-speed vehicles on soft soils that can represent the effects of prior vehicle action on soil and the interaction of tires or tracks with the soil and can incorporate soil characteristics, terrain geometry, and cultural features
- enhanced NRMM with an updated VEHDYN simulation subsystem
- high-fidelity, real-time motion simulators for hardware-and-soldier-in-the-loop simulations that can be used as virtual proving grounds for advanced vehicle technologies and design concepts, as well as for modeling human-vehicle interactions and for driver training
- air mobility models, integrated with next-generation mobility analysis software, to analyze the in-theater mobility of an AAN battle force
- M&S capability for fuel consumption that accounts for energy dissipation at the tire or track interface with soil, for vehicle interaction with cultural terrain features, and for assessing candidate technologies and design concepts for AAN vehicles

2. Technology Development to Support a 15-Ton Wheeled Combat Vehicle. In contrast to the aircraft program, major improvements in ground vehicle mobility are possible and not excessively challenging. The committee considers a number of advanced technologies and design concepts to be well within the realm of near-term development. Use of these technologies would enable the expanded use of wheeled vehicles for AAN, achieve the principal AAN objectives, and enable meaningful logistics trade-offs during system design. The committee recommends that a research and development program be established to demonstrate these capabilities within a five-year period.

TARDEC and WES are currently doing some research in ground mobility; however, the Army has not placed a high priority on developing a wheeled vehicle, and the WES program has suffered from lack of financial support.

3. Look-Ahead Sensor Systems to Increase Vision-Controlled Speed. Sensors for cross-country mobility have enormous potential and little technical risk. A program in this area would require the resources and cooperation of WES, TARDEC, the Corps of Engineers Topographic Laboratory, and perhaps others.

4. Reducing Crew Size through the Evolution of Automated Systems Technologies. Fully autonomous ground vehicles will be important for performing specialized functions, but UGVs will not replace crewed vehicles and will not lessen the logistics burden. In the long term, as automated subsystems are incorporated into manned systems, UGVs may become a component of platoon-like fighting units, in which fewer vehicles will require human operators. The UGVTEE Demo III programs previously discussed appear to be worth pursuing for the specialized capabilities it could offer an AAN battle force, although logistics burdens may not be immediately reduced.

5. Mission Rehearsal Extensions to Mobility M&S Tools. Mission rehearsal mobility analyses will be essential for tactical planning and for determining logistics support requirements. A mission rehearsal capability based on mobility M&S tools can be helpful for designing supportable vehicles, forecasting fuel requirements for AAN operations, and minimizing mission logistics.

6. Driver Training Extensions to Mobility M&S Tools. The high-fidelity models and simulators required to train drivers without risk to them or their vehicles could be developed along with M&S simulators for mobility trade-off analyses. However, running training simulators in real time will require computational advancements.

ROLE OF DEFENSE RESEARCH AND DEVELOPMENT

The political and economic context of DoD's basic research has changed dramatically. Industrial competition has become global, and the commercial market has become much larger than the military market. These changes have had several implications for defense-related research and development. First, the commercial sector is driving many, if not most, of the near-term advances in components and systems. Second, DoD must incorporate commercial products into defense systems, adding ruggedness and military specialization as an overlay, rather than developing military-specific components. Third, international competition and the desire for near-term profits have reduced longer-term investments by industry in many areas of basic and applied research.

These changes have affected one specific area, semiconductor integrated circuits (IC), which are a critical aspect of the information dominance and near-perfect SA on which the AAN is predicated. Similar examples could be cited in other technology areas, such as wireless communications and turbine engines. In 1976, U.S. military purchases accounted for 17 percent of IC sales worldwide ($700 million out of total sales of $4.2 billion)a significant market share that gave DoD leverage in defining product specifications and directions. In the next 20 years, the U.S. military market increased only marginally, to $1.1 billion, while the commercial market exploded to $160 billion (ICEC, 1998). The military market now accounts for less than 1 percent of sales, and the commercial market has become the dominant force in setting IC product directions. Although lower prices have resulted, the DoD is now compelled to use commercial IC products and adapt them to meet military requirements, as necessary.

At the same time, competitive pressures have shortened industry's development horizons to one or two product cycles. As former director of defense research and engineering, Dr. Anita K. Jones, has observed, "... industry research and development horizons are increasingly near term." The horizon for the information technology industry sector, for example, is typically three years or less (Signal, 1997). In a cycle that begins with S&T (science and technology) and runs through development and production to life-cycle support, DoD has little to gain by adding a few additional dollars to industry's profit-driven, near-term development. Except for requirements that are truly unique to defense applications, DoD can exert much more influence by leveraging its dollars either at the front end in the enabling S&T phase or at the back end by adapting commercial technology to meet DoD needs.

Nevertheless, commercial industry remains dependent on the federal government for investments in long-term, higher risk S&T research. Historically, DoD has provided 15 to 20 percent of the total federal investment. In fiscal year 1997, expenditures by all of the services accounted for almost $8 billion in basic and applied research and advanced technology development (Touhy, 1998). This amount represents 40 percent of federal spending for basic research and includes more than 70 percent of all federal investment in microelectronics and electrical engineering (Signal, 1997).

U.S. industry has become increasingly dependent on the crucial leverage of government-funded research conducted at universities and in federal laboratories.

Although DoD's research investment has declined in constant dollars, the percentage of the DoD budget has remained stable since World War II because the relationship with industry has served the needs of the DoD, the research community, and the commercial sector. The imperatives of national defense have enabled DoD to invest directly in important new ideas with adequate resources to make a difference. Although this focused approach has not led to success in every project, it has led to enough successes to foster enormous progress in new technologies for both the military and commercial sectors. Early-stage development of new technologies is almost always applicable to both sectors. Therefore, by investing wisely, DoD can influence the directions of research and guarantee an adequate research base for technologies to meet its future needs. DoD can also leverage its investments by coordinating teams drawn from federal laboratories, industry, and universities for demonstration projects to develop new defense applications based as much as possible on commercially available components and software. The S&T advantage of U.S. forces will increasingly depend on adaptations of commercial products with a defense overlay, rather than on expensive military-specific designs.

INVESTMENTS TO REDUCE LOGISTICS SUPPORT REQUIREMENTS FOR AAN SYSTEMS

The preceding section described the research emphases of the Army's existing S&T program. This section describes areas of research and technology development that the committee recommends for investment because of their importance for reducing logistics support requirements for AAN systems.

Road Map Objectives

The committee derived road map objectives based on the burden reduction goals from the technology assessments. Whereas burden reduction goals are broad and can be pursued in various ways, the road map objectives require moving in the direction of reducing logistics demand. Through the technology assessments, the committee identified several areas of research or technology development as key enablers for achieving the road map objectives.

The burden reduction goals, the road map objectives for each goal, and the recommended areas for research and technology development. For many of the reduction goals, the committee identified several road map objectives. The areas of technology development and research with the most potential for meeting the road map objectives listed in the middle column.

The committee focused most of its efforts on ways to reduce the principal weight-and-volume logistics burdens of fuel and ammunition; however, it also considered maintenance, repair, and refitting (particularly reducing the personnel and infrastructure needed to provide support capabilities), and spare parts. The associated reduction goals for fuel are reduced fuel demand, improved system energy management, increased fuel energy density by weight, and reduced weight of lethal systems. The reduction goals for the ammunition burden are fewer rounds of ammunition per target and reduced ammunition weight. Improved reliability of systems was identified as the key goal for reducing maintenance and spare parts burdens.

Logistics support for individual soldiers is a critical burden for any army, past, present, or future. The significance of this burden cannot be measured in terms of total weight or transport volume. The committee identified two goals for reduction of soldier logistics: lightweight, compact systems for individual soldiers and increased soldier effectiveness.

The Army has begun a major effort to improve logistics delivery systems in response to *Joint Vision 2010*, and the Statement of Task for this study required that the committee focus on technologies that would reduce logistics support requirements of AAN combat systems. Because of this, the committee did not assess technological opportunities to improve the logistics supply and distribution process itself. Nevertheless, technologies to improve logistics operations are very important. The reduction goal of "just-right" logistics to underscore the importance of SA technologies to logistics operations, as well as to combat operations.

Finally, a major theme of this report is the importance of system analysis of the kind associated with systems engineering. System analysis should begin early in the design process and continue through the stages of prototyping, testing, engineering development, and manufacturing. This capability is critical for weighing all of the requirements for reducing logistics burdens against one another, as well as for weighing the larger goal of logistics burden reduction against other AAN performance goals and requirements. Specialized forms of system analysis are also necessary for achieving many of the other road map objectives.

For many important road map objectives, the key S&T needs identified by the committee are primarily technology developments or applied research for specific technology applications, rather than basic research. The committee identified a number of areas where basic research is essential to fill gaps in what is known (e.g., advances in hydrogen storage that might allow much higher energy per mass of storage system or innovative concepts for operational or tactical air mobility). However, some of these basic research areas are fairly narrow and limited (e.g., hydrogen storage). Others are better suited to strong Army participation in joint research (e.g., operational mobility) or to leveraging limited Army resources through partnering, rather than becoming a major focus of Army research.

Distributed M&S Technology

The committee found that distributed M&S technology, in various forms, can contribute to nearly all of the road. This finding was not a presumption when the study began; it emerged gradually, in one functional area after another, from the information gathered and assessed by committee members. Although calls for increasing support for M&S have become commonplace in studies for the Army and other defense agencies, *this report focuses on improving and extending existing M&S tools to provide a useful and reliable environment for making system trade-offs that incorporate burden reductions with the performance goals of other primary systems.*

Trade-off analyses must be done at several stages prior to making the decision to field a system, especially in the early stages of requirements definition and design, as well as in the prototyping and other phases of design implementation. The committee recognizes that not enough is known about logistics support requirements, which are characteristics of entire systems, to predict them accurately from basic design elements (i.e., from first principles). Nevertheless, experience has shown that when logistical considerations are not addressed until the engineering and manufacturing development phases, design alternatives that could have significantly reduced logistics while maintaining adequate levels of other essential characteristics have already been eliminated from consideration.

Given the time frame and resource constraints of fielding AAN systems, M&S appears to be the best way for the Army to perform the requisite systems analyses. However, *the tools must be adequate to the task.* Only a few of the existing tools can provide realistic, quantitative modeling of the logistics associated with the operating conditions being modeled for a system or subsystem. Unless M&S tools have the capability to relate logistics impacts to other performance characteristics, they will be unusable for most of the purposes advocated in this report. For this reason, the committee believes that developing *adequate* analysis tools is a matter of the highest urgency and priority for achieving AAN capability by 2025.

The committee does not advocate that the Army develop one large M&S system, or even a tightly integrated "system of systems." In any given area, M&S tools must be able to pass data back and forth, creating a "distributed M&S environment." In some instances, closer coupling of several models, using one simulation or modeling "run" on coupled models, may be advantageous or even essential. But for most M&S applications discussed in this report, tight integration of modeling tools is not necessary, or even desirable.

Furthermore, M&S environments (sets of M&S tools) will vary, depending on the application area in which logistics burdens must be analyzed to optimize burden reduction and other performance goals. For example, an environment in which energy supply and distribution logistics can be effectively simulated, along with details of the AAN operational concepts that determine the "when, where, and how much" of energy demands. Also calls for an energy system management approach, incorporating M&S, for assessing technology options for reducing vehicle fuel demand. These two applications for M&S probably constitute two different "distributed M&S environments," with some capability for exchanging results and assumptions. The environment for modeling vehicle fuel demand is, however, the same as the distributed environment for vehicle design.

Another application area in which one or more M&S environment will be needed is in the analysis of alternative lethal systems. The M&S tools in this area must not only give realistic results about the logistics burdens associated with various options, but must also correlate the energy demand for these options with the overall energy supply and distribution M&S environment. Assumptions and results from lethal systems M&S can then be translated into operation-wide energy demands, and vice versa. Despite the necessity for data to be moved back and forth, the two environments are distinct with respect to the kinds of tools they must have to resolve logistics trade-offs. Assumptions and results of the lethal systems M&S environment(s) and the vehicle system M&S environment must also be transferable because the lethal systems will ultimately be subsystems of a vehicular platform.

Technology Development Areas

The most important factor in reducing the demand for fuel on the battlefield is reducing the weight of battlefield vehicles. However, deciding how to reduce vehicle weight and still meet other performance requirements will require systems analysis using a distributed M&S environment for vehicle design.

Substituting lighter weight materials for more conventional materials should be one of the objectives of vehicle design, as should increased reliability, defined in terms of AAN battle force mission requirements. A frequent obstacle to the evaluation of lightweight substitute materials is the lack of information or the difficulty of accessing information about them. The Army should promote and support the development of information resources to help system designers obtain data on alternative materials.

The substitution of lightweight materials that also offer improved reliability or other performance advantages over more conventional choices is an area of broad applicability for reducing logistics burdens. Designing systems with lightweight, multifunctional materials and knowing how to manufacture them with high reliability and cost effectiveness are essential for developing combat systems with lower fuel burdens, as well as the other system performance characteristics required for AAN operations.

Research Areas

The committee selected two research areas related to substituting lightweight materials in vehicle systems. One is advanced armor and protection concepts; the other is the use of M&S tools to design microstructural versions of materials and the processing techniques to manufacture them efficiently.

The diversity of projectile threats and of possible combinations of technological approaches to protecting a ground or air vehicle will require designers of AAN vehicles to think in terms of a vehicle protection as a subsystem of the vehicle. For instance, the protection system of an AAN vehicle might combine components of stealth and active protection with a lighter weight reactive armor. The Army should explore options for an optimal protection subsystem considering the mission requirements of the vehicle and taking into account the full range of projectile threats. *The weight of the protection subsystem components and the implications for fuel demand must be design criteria.* New armor building blocks and new architectures for armor should be investigated in the context of this broad perspective.

Some elements of biomimetics are relevant to this broad perspective, but other approaches to materials research, such as the development of lightweight alloys and functional-gradient intermetallics, ceramics for both organic-matrix and metal-matrix composites, and microstructured ceramics, should also be included. In the future, materials for components and substructures should be chosen to meet the full complement of performance objectives, such as structural and low-observable values, reduction in fuel demand through lighter system weight, and greater mission reliability, as well as the more traditional projectile defeat (armor) values.

The Army is currently considering a new SRO focused on advanced armor and protection concepts that reduce or eliminate dependence on heavy materials and vehicle structures. The SRO should include *materials research to increase the overall mission reliability of AAN systems as well as reducing weight.* A substitute material that can reduce the weight of a vehicle system must also meet all of the performance requirements of the particular application and must add less mass to the total system than conventional options. If known materials lack one or more of the required characteristics, computational approaches and modeling tools can be used by materials scientists to study, and even design, new materials with microstructures that can be controlled during processing.

Electronic substrates, for example, depend on M&S tools for design and assessment of candidate microstructures and processing methods so that they can be efficiently produced in large quantities. The current SRO in biomimetics addresses some aspects of this research. It includes research, for example, in which a biologically formed microstructured material is the starting point for replicating or adapting structural patterns that have been selected through natural evolution to provide high values in certain functional properties. Often the structural patterns of these biological materials are the reason these functional characteristics can be achieved with much less weight than conventional industrial materials with the same characteristics.

In computational approaches to materials design and in M&S of innovatively structured materials, as well as in biomimetics, the Army should continue to stimulate research, continue to be involved in the information and application-development networks with academic and industrial partners, and look for opportunities to leverage its resources by actively participating in joint-service and other programs to increase the knowledge base in this field. One opportunity for leverage might be in the commercial development and use of microstructural models to design manufacturing processes.

Airframe and Engine Designs

The committee discussed the problem of providing an AAN battle force with the operational mobility required by the AAN concepts. There are no airborne (or off-the-ground) candidates for providing tactical mobility for an entire AAN battle force that can maneuver in three dimensions at five times the speed of current ground combat vehicles, and use less fuel. To meet these requirements, *the Army will have to find novel, nonconventional air mobility concepts.* Even a demonstrated technology like the WIG (wing-in-ground) aircraft will require a great deal of both basic and applied research. Therefore, the committee listed airframe and engine design.

Whether or not the Army finds promising novel options for operational and tactical air vehicles, reducing the fuel demand of air vehicles must be an objective. A distributed, hierarchical M&S environment can help in designing airframes and engines for increased fuel economy. The importance of this kind of M&S environment for ground vehicles, but an analogous argument can be made for air vehicle system design and logistics trade-off analyses. Foundations for some of the engineering-level components of this environment already existfor example, the IHPTET program for the commercial development of high-performance turbine engines and the airframe design environments used by the aviation industry.

The Army should ensure that it has access to tools that can simulate the logistical performance, as well as other performance characteristics, of its airborne systems. Like the M&S environment for ground mobility, the "air mobility M&S environment" must provide links from the engagement levels down to the subsystem and component levels of air vehicle design, with the capability of feeding design results from lower levels back up to the vehicle system and engagement levels. If a search for nonconventional air mobility does turn up promising candidates, the M&S environment will be essential for maturing the technology and fielding logistically competent systems by 2025.

Unmanned and Minimally Crewed Vehicles

Reducing crew size can reduce the fuel demand of battlefield vehicles primarily by decreasing the amount of vehicle structure (hence weight) required for substructures, such as the cockpit and the protection subsystem (armor). The potential for reducing the total system weight and the design trade-offs with other performance objectives will have to be analyzed and optimized using a distributed M&S environment.

Although UGVs are likely to have many uses in both AAN and Army XXI operations, subsystem automation appears to be a more reasonable, evolutionary approach to reducing the crew complement in general-purpose combat vehicles. If a combat unit of vehicles (a squad) is considered as a "fighting system," one or more of the vehicles could be an uncrewed subsystem controlled and supervised by a human unit commander in another vehicle. As Army and DARPA technology demonstrations of UGVs for specialized functions continue, the technology of subsystem automation can be converged with the technology of specialized uncrewed vehicles with a human controller/commander nearby.

For the sake of simplicity, the general field of research relevant to subsystem automation and autonomous mobility as "robotics." Relevant aspects of research include control theory and control system engineering, which are considered a part of the field of artificial intelligence.

Mobility Systems

Designing and fielding AAN combat vehicles that incorporate highly efficient energy management while meeting other performance requirements will require thorough evaluations of the vehicle as a system from the concept design forward. Although some technologies, such as hybrid drive vehicles, have been widely accepted in the Army community as increasing vehicle fuel economy, *the committee believes that total system evaluations shall be done in the context of AAN mission requirements and operational concepts.* Evaluations should not be focused on maximizing any one performance goal, even fuel economy. With new technologies in intelligent engines, energy storage and recovery, active suspension, and terrain SA, system energy demands can be managed more efficiently. The capability of dynamic management must be designed into the vehicle system.

For ground vehicles, the capabilities of the driver will be a significant factor. Driver training for AAN operations will have to include the management of energy demand in the context of the cross-country mobility goals for the AAN battle force.

The committee endorsed a recommendation that has been made in previous Army-sponsored studies but has not yet been implemented. This is probably the simplest way to ensure that evaluations of mobility systems take fuel demand seriously and that optimum energy management systems are incorporated into AAN vehicles. *All vehicle procurements should include a clear, unequivocal, and easily measurable limit on vehicle fuel consumption.*

Terrain Awareness

Terrain awareness, like SA generally, is very important to meeting performance goals other than in logistics supportability. For example, a high level of terrain awareness will be essential to tactical planning and high cross-country speeds. Terrain awareness to emphasize its importance for improving the energy management of ground vehicles. The key enabling technology areas for terrain awareness are look-ahead sensors and systems. Mobility models will also facilitate the design and assessment of terrain awareness technologies.

Look-ahead sensor systems will be one subsystem of the SA system for terrain awareness. Real-time data on current terrain conditions in the vicinity of the vehicle and the vehicle's projected course will be used to update the terrain database and SA sensor information stored in the vehicle. Technology for terrain awareness is being developed at TARDEC, WES, and the U.S. Army Corps of Engineers Topographic Laboratory.

Potentially relevant research on new sensing methods and processing methodologies for assessing soil conditions, penetrating foliage and ground cover, and evaluating other terrain factors is being conducted by academic-industrial networks, which are motivated primarily by potential commercial applications but which offer the Army an opportunity to leverage its resources.

The Army's SRO for intelligent systems is also a venue for tapping into broader research in sensing and imaging.

The mobility models will provide a virtual test bed for assessing the logistical consequences of specific aspects of terrain awareness coupled with maneuver doctrine and tactics to conserve fuel while meeting other performance goals.

The mobility models will have to incorporate the terrain conditions that are recognizable to the candidate terrain awareness system and realistically simulate the consequences of the vehicle's interaction with the terrain on performance (e.g., ground speed, maneuverability, and avoiding or traversing obstacles) and fuel consumption.

New Energy Delivery Systems

A reliable fuel supply system is critical for a modern land combat force. The Army's exploration of significant changes in the fuel supply system to facilitate AAN operations and decrease logistics burdens should be based on an adequate model of the entire fuel supply system. The model should include a realistic simulation of the significant logistics considerations and their impacts on the fuel supply system and the war-fighting organization. The AAN war-gaming process has recently begun to incorporate modeling of fuel-supply logistics at the strategic, operational, and tactical levels. *An immediate objective should be the realistic coupling of a fuel-supply model to the fuel demands of AAN system concepts being tested in a war-game.* The techniques and systems used to achieve this modeling capability could also be used for fuel-system trade-off analyses, mission planning, and training exercises.

The modeling of energy system capabilities and energy requirements, based on trade-off analyses, including quantified logistical savings, may lead to totally new energy delivery paradigms for the AAN battle force. As a radical alternative to the current delivery system, which is based on transporting a petroleum-based fuel (diesel) for use in internal combustion engines, the committee investigated using hydrogen as a battlefield fuel for combustion engines and fuel cells. A hydrogen production facility at the staging area could be powered by a compact nuclear reactor.

Technological developments to support this radical alternative include scaling up the existing technology for compact nuclear reactors and improving the energy output per unit mass of electrolysis units that produce hydrogen from water. Although these developments seem feasible in the AAN time frame, a more difficult obstacle will be the development of lightweight, compact storage facilities for the hydrogen fuel. Unless all of these issues can be resolved in favor of this radical alternative, the existing system will be difficult to beat, although it can be improved by careful system optimization.

Lethal Systems Performance and Reduced System Weight

The principal focus of reducing logistics demands for lethal systems is reducing the ammunition burden. However, large lethal systems have substantial weight and require energy (fuel) to move them strategically and operationally, as well as tactically (on the battlefield). Some of the proposed alternatives to conventional chemically propelled projectile systems, such as the EM and ETC concepts, in effect trade part of the ammunition burden for increases in fuel. Both of these concepts require that fuel energy be converted to electrical power to propel the projectile, which means more fuel is required to move the heavier system, which must include an energy conversion and management subsystem.

Depending on the details of the technology and its operational profile, trading ammunition weight for an increase in fuel weight may increase or decrease the total logistics burden. The committee found no evidence that these trade-offs are being considered systematically. In fact, the committee was unable to find data on the quantities of fuel and ammunition used in past military operations that would be adequate to study past burden trade-offs. The objective is intended to remind the Army that the logistics trade-off analyses for any system should include *all* logistical considerations. Comparisons of alternative systems with respect to logistics burdens and performance characteristics including logistics should address all of the relevant burdens.

Situational Awareness and Precision Guidance

AAN operational concepts, as reflected in terms such as "precision maneuver" and "precision fires," assume a *near perfect* level of SA. From a logistical standpoint, this essential SA is not a burden that can be measured in weight or volume. Rather, it is a critical necessity, a logistical choke-point; *any loss or degradation in the supply of SA information to AAN combat units can have cascading consequences, up to and including total defeat.* Although the committee was primarily concerned with logistics burdens reflected in weight and volume, this critical requirement for near-perfect SA was so ubiquitous across AAN technology applications that the committee felt compelled to note areas where AAN planners seem to be taking SA for granted.

In addition to the need for near-perfect SA in all aspects of AAN engagement concepts, SA technologies and their applications could significantly reduce the ammunition burden. With near-perfect SA, force dispositions and environmental conditions would be known precisely, which would improve the effectiveness of precision guided lethal systems and reduce the number of rounds required (and the number of rounds fired) per target. *SA and precision guidance have the most potential to reduce the ammunition logistics burden of all technology applications assessed by the committee.*

ARMY SCIENCE AND TECHNOLOGY PROGRAM

Army and DoD S&T programs include basic research (budget line item 6.1), which increases scientific understanding, applied research (budget line item 6.2), which identifies and exploits technology opportunities based on new knowledge and evaluates their technical feasibility to increase war-fighting capabilities, and advanced technology development (budget line item 6.3), which demonstrates applications to specific military systems, to speed the transition to maturity and insertion.

The Army share of DoD funding for research in all three categories. Like overall DoD investments, funding for research has remained a constant proportion of Army appropriations, although investment in constant real dollars has declined steadily since the end of the Cold War along with the rest of the defense budget.

The research and technology development needed for the AAN will require a cooperative effort. As the Army has fewer and fewer dollars to invest, it will become increasingly important for the Army to leverage the research activities of industry, government, and the other services. Army dollars should be invested principally in projects that will meet Army-specific requirements or that will be undertaken only if they are funded by the Army.

Strategic Research Objectives and S&T Objectives

The Army and DoD use the term "Strategic Research Objective" (SRO) to refer to an area of scientific research selected for emphasis because of its potential relevance to military operations, particularly for long-range, high payoff applications.

The relatively small number of Army (and DoD) SROs should not be confused with the roughly 200 Army Science and Technology Objectives (STOs). An STO states a specific, measurable technology advance funded by applied research or exploratory development dollars (budget line items 6.2 or 6.3) and is to be achieved by a specific fiscal year. By contrast, Army SROs focus and guide the S&T community on predominantly basic research (budget line item 6.1) that can be linked, although more tentatively than an STO, to Army requirements for technology development (DA, 1997c).

Strategic Research Objectives and AAN Situational Awareness

Based on the critical role of the technologies for enabling the near-perfect SA required to achieve "one-round, one-target" lethality for the AAN, as well as other operational efficiencies, including terrain awareness, operational energy management, and just-right logistics support, the committee believes that the current SROs in nanoscience, mobile wireless communications, intelligent systems, and compact power have the potential to support logistics burden reduction. The research areas that should be given the most emphasis are discussed below.

Nanoscience

The historical trend of increasing computational power at decreasing cost (according to Moore's Law) has been based entirely on the integration of increasingly large numbers of metal-oxide-on-silicon semiconductor devices on a given area of silicon substrate. For this trend to continue beyond the presently perceived physical limits on decreasing the size of silicon-based transistors (e.g., approximately 50-nm gate widths for CMOS [complementary-metal oxide on silicon] devices), new device concepts and computing architectures will have to be invented. Decreasing the size of transistor devices below these physical limits is likely to involve quantum devices with scales on the order of electronic wave functions (1 to 10 nm) or devices based on Coulomb blockade effects.

Army Strategic Research Objectives

Biomimetics. novel synthetic materials, processes, and sensors through advanced understanding and exploitation of the design principles found in nature

Nanoscience. innovative enhancements in the properties and performance of structures, materials, and devices that have controllable features on the nanoscale (tens of angstroms)

Smart Structures. advanced capabilities in modeling, predicting, controlling, and optimizing the dynamic responses of complex, multi-element, deformable struc-tures used in vehicles and systems

Mobile Wireless Communications. rapid, secure transmissions of large quantities of multimedia communications

Intelligent Systems. systems that can sense, analyze, learn, adapt, and function in changing hostile environments

Compact Power Sources. improved batteries and fuel cells, as well as the identi-fication of new concepts relating to energy density, operating characteristics, reliability, and safety of portable power (DA, 1997c)

So far, no device has emerged as a clear competitor to conventional silicon technology, although alternatives do exist (e.g., gallium-nitride for wide-bandgap semiconductor applications). Also, decreasing the size of interconnections between the devices, referred to as packaging, will become as significant a challenge to engineers as decreasing the size of the individual devices.

Even if nanoscience does not lead the way to new paradigms for the fundamental elements of computing circuitry, it will have an impact on a wide range of sensor technologies. Especially important areas for research include (1) detectors for chemical and biological agents and (2) materials for focal plane arrays to detect and image electromagnetic radiation, particularly in the infrared region.

Mobile Wireless Communications

AAN SA will rely heavily on communications, and the Army urgently needs a total systems simulation of these communications needs, along the lines of a distributed M&S environment that can realistically simulate functionality under combat conditions. The engagement and system level simulations need to be linked to the protocols for available and projected hardware and software subsystems, so that modeling results can flow up and down the structural hierarchy. These simulations should be updated as experience is gained from Army XXI and as planning for the AAN continues.

An important SA issue that the Army must address for both Army XXI and the AAN is the communications burden of new sensor systems. Proliferation of sensor systems with high data-link requirements on platforms, such as UAVs or UGVs, located remotely from the point where the sensor information is used, will compete for available communications bandwidth with other essential communication functions, such as command and control. Sensor fusion and advanced signal processing on the remote platform will add complexity and cost to the individual sensor applications but may be essential for capacity and robustness of the overall C4ISR system.

Intelligent Systems and Compact Power

The intelligent systems SRO is directly applicable to autonomous vehicles as AAN sensor platforms and to automated subsystems to reduce AAN crew size and manage energy demands. AAN soldiers can be expected to play critical roles as sources, processors, and recipients of sensor data under battlefield conditions even more fluid than those anticipated for Army XXI. Compact power sources could reduce the logistics burden for the AAN battle force and increase the effectiveness of soldier systems. Combined with energy-efficient technologies in future soldier systems, research under the compact power SRO should lead to the development of compact power technologies that would simplify soldier-level logistics requirements (NRC, 1997a).

Strategic Research Objectives and Lightweight Materials

Two of the SROs, biomimetics and smart structures, could lead to the development of new and novel lightweight materials, but the time frame for incorporating the resulting innovations into fielded systems extends beyond the rapidly approaching date required for initial operational capability of AAN systems.

If research is directed toward reducing weight and increasing reliability, the results could significantly reduce overall logistics burden. Some of the applicable materials research will be undertaken by the civilian sector in pursuit of commercial aims, but the impetus and direction for the development of military materials, especially new armor building blocks and architectures for incorporation into protective systems, must come from the Army, perhaps with joint-service participation.

Strategic Research Objectives for Logistics

The Army sponsor of this study asked the committee to identify candidate research topics for a new SRO that would focus on reducing logistics demand for the AAN. Representatives of the Army logistics community further suggested to the committee that an SRO dedicated to logistics technologies and incorporating research into areas such as "ultrareliable" systems, prognostics, or fuel efficiency might be an appropriate focus for basic research. However, the committee was asked to address technologies to reduce the logistics demands of AAN systems, not technologies to improve logistics operations.

Fuel economy and system reliability are important objectives for reducing logistics burdens, but the committee's analysis shows that they should be considered broad performance objectives of an entire system, and should be designed into AAN systems at every level of subsystem and component analysis, rather than as guides for research or S&T development.

Prognostics could improve system maintainability, but the committee considers prognostics to be one of several components of the broader area of materials research and structural design that could improve the maintainability and reliability of AAN systems.

During the course of the study, the Army proposed establishing a new SRO focused on designing new armor materials. The committee believes that advanced materials with lightweight, protective, high-performance characteristics will have to be available well before 2025 to be incorporated into AAN systems. Successful candidates *within that time frame* are, therefore, more likely to result from applied research and advanced development of known technologies, rather than from basic research. Whether or not the Army proceeds with an SRO in this area, which would be valuable in the long term, the Army should focus on applied research and technology development that facilitates the integration of new materials into future system designs because of the importance of reducing weight to logistics savings.

TECHNOLOGY DEVELOPMENT AREAS

There is considerable overlap in the technology development and research areas that would contribute to meeting the road map objectives of SA and precision guidance. Many of the basic electronic, electro-optical, and data processing technologies necessary for SA technology applications (communications and sensor systems, decision support aids, data integration and filtering) are also applicable to the affordable, small, integrated guidance systems required for precision guided missiles and munitions.

In the AAN time frame, UAVs and UGVs will be important sensor platforms for a wide range of C4ISR applications, ranging from intelligence preparation of the battle space and real-time communications at all levels of command, to tactical scouting and targeting for individual fighting units. The many active development programs for UAV and UGV sensor platforms throughout DoD and other government agencies, such as the NRO and NIMA, as well as the Army, should be reviewed periodically to determine whether they are collectively addressing AAN requirements. If necessary, the Army should identify and set priorities to redirect these programs.

Research Areas

All of the research areas on basic and applied knowledge relevant to the SA technology applications will contribute to the near-perfect SA for AAN missions. The committee chose to highlight research on C4ISR supportability and robustness because of the significant unresolved issues in these areas. Four current Army SROs (in nanoscience, smart structures, mobile wireless communications, and intelligent systems) support some (but not all) aspects of SA technology. Also, the intelligent systems SRO should enable the Army to focus on Army-specific basic research to support UGV technology. This research will continue to draw on advances first tested and used in UAVs or undersea vehicles (assuming that support continues for defense-relevant research in robotics, control theory, and engineering for unmanned vehicles and the C4ISR enabling technologies that apply to UGVs and UAVs). Other research areas to support advances in precision guidance, include the fusion of on-board sensors, reliable, inexpensive compact packaging, and sensor-actuator integration and control.

Reducing the Ammunition Burden through Lethal Systems Performance

Besides SA and precision guidance, other performance characteristics of weapon systems (e.g., range and reproducibility of propelling force) also contribute to reducing the number of rounds required per target. Significant trade-offs (with respect to reducing the weight of a round) among alternative designs for a given concept or competing concepts might be possible. Reductions in ammunition burden must be considered along with the fuel requirement for moving or energizing alternative weapon systems. Another logistics-related consideration is the size of the crew required for the weapon system, compared to alternative systems with similar functionality. The factors related to reducing logistics burdens should be assessed along with lethality performance characteristics in the context of clearly identified AAN lethality requirements.

The committee found no obvious winners among the potential alternatives for major weapon-systems, such as the main armament of AAN "front line" combat vehicles or the fire support systems that might be integral elements of a battle force. *This absence of clear winners reflects the lack of relevant data rather than equal potential performance of the enabling technologies or system concepts.* Even at the level of broad technology options, such as liquid propellants versus modular solid propellants, the available information on AAN requirements and logistics-relevant performance of the competing technologies is insufficient for the Army to make an informed choice.

The projectile weapon-system concepts and enabling technologies reviewed by the committee have already been in development for more than the time remaining until system choices must be made for the first generation of AAN platforms. So the lack of relevant data (even of estimates or reasonable guesses) cannot be explained by the novelty of the technologies or basic system concepts. The ongoing development programs have simply not provided the base of data for making systems-level comparisons and trade-off decisions that take logistics burdens into account. *To remedy this situation, the Army should leverage the existing R&D programs in projectile weapons and supporting technologies to provide data for modeling system alternatives and making rational trade-offs.*

Data on logistics support requirements should be compiled for each enabling technology or system concept. By assessing these disparate programs and development efforts from the standpoint of their contributions to a hierarchical simulation of system options and informed design trade-offs, the Army will be able to determine where modifications or additions should be made to the S&T base.

Energetics and Warhead Materials

Improving the performance of the energetics (propellants and explosives) in a missile or projectile round can reduce the mass and volume per round without compromising lethality or can reduce the number of rounds required to achieve the desired effect. Improving uniformity of burn, for example, can improve precision thereby reducing the average number of rounds required to hit a target. Energetics with higher energy density may enable the delivery system to be lighter and smaller. Less obvious, but equally important in terms of burden reduction for a given technology investment, are the indirect effects of less sensitive munitions. The best chances for burden reduction are from technological advances that would improve the performance of an energetic as a propellant or explosive while decreasing its sensitivity to heat or shock.

The Army should continue (or increase) its participation in the IHPRPT program while focusing on meeting the needs for AAN systems, including missile systems that can be launched from small vehicles, reach high velocity quickly (Mach 6 and greater), produce minimal smoke, and are insensitive to thermal and shock threats. These systems must also be throttleable and adaptable to various missions. Solid-fuel ramjets are an option to explore for high-speed, relatively low-cost missiles for AAN operations.

The development of energetics that are insensitive to shock and thermal threats must be based on a basic understanding of the mechanisms of insensitivity. This understanding can be achieved through studies in quantum chemistry, chemical and thermal decomposition, and improved computer modeling of shock and thermal events. The Army should keep abreast of ongoing research at the national laboratories on new, high-energy energetic materials (such as metastable interstitial composites) that may offer tailorable output and improve energy-density over current energetic fills.

The Army should develop insensitive, high-energy warhead fills and novel mitigation-barrier materials to eliminate fratricide. The Army should also support the development of reactive, three-dimensional detonation physics hydrocodes for warhead design and target interactions.

Systems Design for Reliability

The reliability requirements for AAN systems should be defined first at the functional level of meeting mission requirements. The war-fighters and technologists engaged in the AAN process should work together to define objective, quantifiable, accountable terms for mission reliability, beginning at the highest levels of engagement analysis and proceeding down to reliability requirements for individual systems (platforms or vehicles). The S&T community should ensure that the lower levels of system analysis include reliability-related performance metrics during design and system trade-off studies. The committee identified two technology development areas as critical for designing systems for reliability. First, the distributed M&S environments used to support system design and logistics trade-off analysis should be extended to provide the following five elements, which are not included in current M&S tools used by the Army:

- models that represent the system properties and environmental conditions that affect AAN mission reliability requirements
- measurable reliability-related requirements for models at every level in the M&S hierarchy
- iterative simulations up and down the hierarchy of models in the design and engineering process
- provisions for obtaining valid data on lesser-known design options that could contribute to meeting combinations of AAN performance goals (including mission reliability)
- maintenance of mission reliability, defined by assessable reliability requirements, as a performance objective for design and engineering development

As the committee noted in the discussion of the road map objective of lightweight materials for air and ground vehicles, necessary improvements in information resources for materials selection at the component level of the hierarchy include improved data and representations for assessing the reliability-related features of materials.

The discussion of lightweight materials also covered a research area that is important for the long-term innovation of materials that are more reliable for specific applications, as well as lighter in weight and able to meet other performance requirements.

If reliability requirements are conveyed down the structural hierarchy from the systems level to the level of requirements for materials for components and structures, materials research could contribute decisions about a range of candidates already available to designers.

The areas of materials research relevant to improving reliability are (1) the mechanisms of failure and the incorporation of this knowledge into M&S tools, (2) the selection or design of materials that can meet AAN requirements, including reliability requirements, that familiar materials cannot meet, and (3) embedded prognostic sensing technology in designing structures and components. The Army should continue to leverage its resources in these areas of research through networking with industry and academic partners and through active participation in joint-services programs.

Compact Power

Personal power sources for the dismounted soldier is a major logistics concern, not because of the tonnage involved but because the effectiveness of individual soldiers is a combat necessity. For meeting this objective, the committee supports the recommendations on research areas and relevant technologies of an in-depth NRC study of energy-efficient technologies for the dismounted soldier (NRC, 1997a). Long-term research to increase dramatically the amount of energy stored per unit weight carried by soldiers will require a different approach than traditional electrochemical batteries. The compact power SRO has focused research on fuel cells and on microturbines, a high-risk, high-payoff alternative to batteries.

Prototypes of rechargeable fuel cell systems with high potential for soldier application have already been demonstrated. A fundamental departure from electrochemical batteries would be nuclear batteries providing for direct conversion of low-level nuclear energy to electrical power, which may be feasible with icosahedral borides or another semiconductor with photovoltaic properties.

Lightweight Protection Systems for Individual Soldiers

The ideal protective garment for the soldier of the future will have to be multifunctional.

In addition to preventing or minimizing injury from small-caliber rounds and shrapnel, it should also protect the wearer from biological and chemical threats and from residual radiation following a nuclear blast.

Protection from the NBC (nuclear, biological, and chemical) threats requires a barrier to air exchange with the external environment, which implies that thermal management and purification of respirable air will also be necessary. At the same time, this garment or protective system must not impede the soldier's ability to see and hear or to move and react quickly to the physical demands of a combat environment. Indeed, the advantages of personal sensor systems and exoskeleton arrays is to enhance the perceptions and physical strength of soldiers.

For each of these functional requirements in isolation, there are technologies that at least offer promise, if not near-term practical implementation.

From the perspective of decreasing logistics demand, the more difficult challenge is to meet all of the functional requirements and objectives in one set of protective gear. A suitable level of functionality in each area must be integrated into an optimally performing, highly reliable, protective and supportive system of combat gear. Since weight is a primary consideration for soldier logistics, the system may have to be modular so different combinations of functionality could be supplied and distributed for use on the AAN battlefield.

The Army has been successful in meeting Army XXI soldier requirements by approaching the "soldier as a system." Technology development programs to address these needs, including programs in chemical and biological defense and the Twenty-First Century Land Warrior Program, are developing technologies that can be inserted into functional open-system architectures. A similar strategy that incorporates AAN logistics trade-off analyses is recommended to minimize logistics support requirements for AAN soldier systems.

Advances in Combat Medicine, Nutrition, and Soldier Fitness

The logistics of sustaining an individual soldier *physiologically* for the duration of an AAN combat pulse or mission are more complicated than identifying technological possibilities for meeting one or another requirement or advancing toward one or another desirable capability. The human soldier is the Army's most complicated system. Attempts to alter radically the proven methods of sustaining soldiers under combat conditions will require a careful assessment of the effects on overall performance. The consequences may be indirect, delayed, or cumulative and may have little or no immediate or easily observable effects.

The Army is pursuing many avenues in this area; most of those briefed to committee members should be ready for extensive testing well before the AAN time frame. The area clearly has high potential for increasing the combat effectiveness of AAN soldiers. However, the committee did not have the expertise to make an in-depth assessment of technological opportunities in this area.

AAN Logistics Trade-off Analyses across Burden Reduction Goals

This report has repeatedly emphasized that burden reduction goals should not be pursued in isolation from other performance objectives, and vice versa. It is equally true that any burden reduction goal cannot be pursued in isolation from other logistics burdens that affect the performance profile of a system.

The small unit and force-on-force engagement levels of the distributed M&S environment can be particularly valuable for the design analyses for assessing consequences in terms of logistics burdens (as well as other performance objectives) and for making necessary trade-offs. However, the results will only be as realistic and dependable as the relationships built into each level of the M&S hierarchy.

9

Indian Army Vision 2020

ROLE OF THE INDIAN ARMY

Armies are maintained by countries in order to safeguard their core values and national interests from external aggression and internal subversion. The Primary and Secondary roles of our Army are as under :-

- Primary Role. Deter external aggression and, if deterrence fails, defeat it by force.
- Secondary Role. Assist the Government in overcoming internal threats, foreign sponsored or indigenous, and aid the civil authority when requisitioned for the purpose.

Capabilities Entailed by the Role

The capabilities that the Army must posses to fulfil its role must be identified in accordance with our 'Vision' for the Army. The capabilities, thus identified are as under :-

- Deterrent Capability. The Army should be so strong in both conventional and nuclear weapons, that potential aggressors are deterred.
- War Fighting Capability. If deterrence fails, the Army should be able to fight a successful war against the enemy, over any terrain, and in conventional as well as NBC warfare situations.
- Internal Security Management Capability. The Army should be able to deal with and manage internal security

situations of various types like insurgency, grave law and order situations; and also render aid to civil power, when requisitioned under various situations including disasters, both natural and man-made.

- Force Projection Capability. The Army should be capable of operating 'out-of-area' as part of an integrated task force, when ordered by the Government.
- Peace Keeping Operations Capability. The Army should be able to undertake UN Peace Keeping Missions in any part of the world and inter-operate with Army components of other countries in such operations.

Though we presently posses all these capabilities in some measure, the desired level is yet to be realised in many areas. Resource inadequacy, lack of clear policy directions from the Government, frequent 're-thinks' on the part of the Army, failure of timely supplies of material and shoddy quality of what has been supplied, are some of the reasons attributable to the Army's inability to achieve and retain the desired level of capability at all times. Perhaps, even more important reason, is the knowledge driven Revolution in Military Affairs (RMA), which accelerates the process of obsolescence of equipment, doctrines and tactics. It is in this critical area of RMA that a lot of work needs to be done so that we can have adequate levels of the desired capabilities, at all times. Let us now examine whether the present structure of the Army needs to be altered to enable the Army to fulfil its assigned role better.

ARMY'S CAPABILITY ACCRETION

The challenges that the army is expected to face in the next decade are not likely to be any less formidable. An appraisal of the emerging threats in fact indicates an increasing complexity of the missions that the army may be expected to execute.

The basic character of the Army's responsibilities is unlikely to witness significant changes. Till the boundary disputes with China and Pakistan remain unresolved, Army's most important role of ensuring the nation's territorial integrity will retain primacy. Concurrently, as in the past, the Army will continue to remain embroiled in combating militancy, insurgency and terrorism. With the prevailing instability in the immediate and near neighbourhood, and the growing regional and global role of our country, the Army must also be prepared to undertake missions beyond our borders. It may be added that however much the Army may want to resist, it will continue to be drawn to tackle internal law and order situations and national manmade or natural calamities.

How has the Army fared in the last two decades in the discharge of its responsibilities? At considerable cost to itself it has barely managed to keep the lid on. Given the serious shortage of junior officers, and the indifferent and insufficient weaponry at its disposal, the Army it can be contended, has done exceedingly well. Regrettably the problems of the Army, and the stresses it is subjected to, are understood only by those who are in it. The MOD and the political leadership, or for that matter also the strategic community have a vague awareness, nowhere close to the ground realities. This explains the decades of inertia.

Exploiting the progressive decline of our conventional military capability all through the decade of the eighties, Pakistan launched a well orchestrated offensive through irregulars in Kashmir from about the beginning of 1990. When the momentum of this offensive seemed to be petering out Pakistan did not hesitate to gamble for higher stakes by resorting to Kargil. The Kargil fiasco and the growing domestic instability, however, did not dampen Pakistan's appetite for fomenting trouble for us. The terror attack on our Parliament in 2001 and 26 Nov. 2008-Mumbai is still fresh in our memory.

Over the last few years China too has begun to demonstrate bellicosity, tinged with arrogance, against us. Border intrusions with the purpose of intimidation coupled with force accretions in Tibet and along the LAC, portend problems for us. Its aggressive posturing on other fronts compounds the basket of our concerns.

Viewed from the national security perspective it emerges that our concept of military deterrence has failed or is failing.

Clearly then, the Army's conventional war fighting capabilities must be brought to levels that promise if not absolute, sufficient deterrence.

So how do we go about building a credible dissuasive conventional military deterrence? For the past two to three decades the three services have been unsuccessfully trying to drive the process. It would be mindless to persist with the same approach. The responsibility must shift to the PM and his Cabinet Committee on Security. This is not going to happen without some precipitate action. How this is to be brought about is a matter that the services must address?

The Army could do with a totally fresh appraisal to cover its overall strength, its structure and equipment profile, the quality of its man power, its leadership and its training. Such a review could perhaps be relevant and necessary for the Navy and the Air Force as well.

Technological advancements are taking place rapidly. Correspondingly the rate of obsolescence is also increasing. It is therefore imperative that we manage change with much greater sophistication so as to ensure available funds are utilized optimally. It follows that individuals charged with formulating qualitative requirements, induction plans and evaluation of systems must be competent and have the requisite grooming and experience. Even though this issue has been debated before no concrete remedial steps have yet been taken.

DRDO AND FORCE MODERNIZATION

Since the 1970s the Defence and Research Development Organization (DRDO) championed the cause of 'Made in India' philosophy and assured the Armed Forces that by the turn of the century Indian Armed Forces would be 60 per cent self sufficient for its hardware needs. It reinvented the wheel in large projects to the determent of the army. This was the story of socialism and non-alignment, and the greatest sufferer was the Indian Army. The main battle tank Arjun failed to appear despite 15 years in the making, the T-72 tank could not get night fighting capability, the basic rifle for the soldier remained the 7.62 mm and in EW and in night vision devices and weapon locating radars (the Cymbiline was attempted for upgrade), the army found itself deficient and with unprotected vehicles. Russia bailed India out, by supply of essential hardware, and the Bofors 155 mm Howitzer saved the day in the 1999 Kargil war.

The Indian Army leadership has only now understood that it needs to plug the chinks in its own armour both for fighting terrorism and to have an upper hand in war, as analysts claim India has only a slight edge over Pakistan in conventional capability. It has therefore, imported T-90s tanks (with poor night fighting capabilities) and a host of other equipment and gone to the private sector for vehicles and other programmes. The DRDO is now collaborating with NPO Mach of Russia to jointly build the Brahmos missile. The DRDO has expertise and facilities, hence opportunities now exist to collaborate with Western defence companies for most unfinished projects. Herein lies opportunity for the army's modernization.

The IMF-led economic liberalization of India began in 1991 when its reserves fell to $1 billion. It resulted in neglect of the modernization needs of the Indian Army. Gen. V.P. Malik, who was the Army Chief during the 1999 Kargil War, stated, "The army's modernization Programmes are in a state of terminal illness. Our conventional combat edge over Pakistan has been eroding with every passing year. Unless additional funds are earmarked, future planning is not possible and the erosion in combat edge will soon become uncorrectable." In hindsight it is apparent that when the Indian Armed Forces were mobilized on 18 December 2001 in operation Parakram (Valour), the army was the first to realize how woefully short it was of spares, night vision equipment and lethal punch.

However, as strategic thought and long-sighted planning in India has been lacking, it has now come to light that the army never received any verbal or written directives on the aims of this massive mobilization, which lasted till 16 October 2002. Most training and peace-time activities suffered. The Government cloaked Op Parakarm as coercive diplomacy, but it tired the Army which lost 728 lives, some 130 first in laying over 1 million mines and then in clearing them.

Malik's successor Gen. S. Padmanabhan had this to say on 9 November 2002. "Whenever there is a situation calling for (the) army's help, the latter's role should be clearly defined to avoid confusion", hinting the army was not clear why it was mobilized. It is providential that India did not go to war. India's political leadership was jolted out of its slumber in the stand off with Pakistan, which threatened to use nuclear weapons if its territorial integrity was transgressed. India realized that it had to honestly reexamine its nuclear weapon credibility.

The Nuclear and Air Defence Challenges

In May 1998, the strident BJP government took courage and exploded five nuclear devices including three fusion devices heralding India into the thermo nuclear club. India and Pakistan have been *de facto* accepted as nuclear powers. The scientists of BARC (Bhabha Atomic Research Centre) and DRDO rode piggy-back on the Army Engineer regiments deployed at the test site Pokhran, to ensure that their experiments were a success, but the 'top brass' of the army were never brought into the loop to devise India's nuclear strategy or their deployment.

This led to a woolly approach to chart India's plans for its nuclear deployment and a draft 'No First Use' policy was espoused for the first five years, which no one in uniform ever questioned. It will be the Armed Forces that would be hurt by a first strike and yet they were tasked to deploy the second strike, in a flawed theory. Only early this year an Air Marshal was appointed as the C in C Strategic Forces and a Nuclear Command Structure for decision-making announced. The first Nuclear Op Management course for mid level officers was conducted in November 2003.

The premise of command and control of nuclear assets remains diffused, as the army believes in the principles of Artillery where Command means training, positioning and readiness of the gunnery forces, and control means 'control of fire'. Attempting to clarify SFC's position, the Chairman of the Chiefs of Staff Committee, Admiral Madhvendra Singh articulated three points and confirmed what this chapter is conveying. First, the training in nuclear weapons and servicing of delivery systems would be the responsibility of the individual services.

Second, the utilization and use of nuclear weapons would be the prerogative of the newly formed SFC. And third, while the 'control' of ballistic missiles will be transferred to the SFC initially, the Indian Air Force would soon decide on the transfer of its nuclear capable fighters to the SFC. So far this has not happened but the army missile forces have just been nominated for raising.

Raising Of Missile Forces

The Cabinet Committee on Security (CCS) that stands in for the National Security Council has cleared the raising of India's ballistic missile force. The Pakistan-specific 700 to 800 km range Agni-I and 2,000 km plus Agni-II manufactured by DRDO and Bharat Dynamics are designated as 334 and 335 Missile groups and based at Secundrabad where they are manufactured.

The scientists would help the army in the deployment. Two new Prithvi (150-250km) units for the army, which would be named 444 and 555 missiles groups will also be raised to augment the two Prithvi missile groups—the 222 and the 333, deployed in Central India, where the Command shelter for the top leadership is planned.

The new missile groups would be operational by the beginning of 2005. This decision offers the army its first opportunity to clarify the command and control structure by a revisit on all inter-services issues. The IAF-ARMY battle for nuclear assets and air defence has been simmering for long. India has received the first shipment of Green Pine AD radar and the plans for long range AD missiles including the Arrow and the Patriot and the Russian SU 300 series are in the melting pot. Aerostats are also due to be positioned soon by the IAF's Western Command.

India, USA and International Cooperation

A defence review was attempted to take a holistic view of India's military threats and security challenges in 1998 by the

National Security Advisory Board but the events of 9/11 and USA's lifting of sanctions and overtures has made the study redundant.

A new review is being attempted to look at the International World Order and how India can find a dominant position and voice its concerns. The Indian Army has close Infantry links with the British Army. An Indian Army Liaison Officer is stationed in HQ Infantry at Warminster in UK. More recently, USA is seeking cooperation and overseeing these interactions is the Defence Policy Group co-chaired by India's Defence secretary and the US Under Secretary of Defence for Policy. Under this is the Joint Technical Group between the two defence research establishments, the Military Cooperation Group between the US Joint Staff and the Indian Chief of Integrated Defence Staff, and the Executive Steering Groups of the Indian Army, Air Force and Navy, which interact with their counterparts.

The US Pacific Command is responsible for the region, which includes India. There is also a Joint Working Group on peacekeeping, a Security Cooperation Group formed after the 9/11 events to discuss counter-terrorism-related issues, and a regular exchange between the defence research and analysis communities in both countries. The Army is now exercising with US and other forces but it needs to take greater part in the international arena and opportunities now exist, with France too. Russian links are already strong. This will enable it to change its old mindset, and India can be a training hub to counter terrorism, as it already has facilities for training UN Peace Keepers.

ARMING THE INDIAN DEFENCE FORCES

It needs to be understood that defence modernization must imperatively respond to prevailing challenges and needs of our country. The technology environment is changing and unless the development cycle of new equipment is shortened, the Armed Forces will continue to remain in an operationally disadvantageous situation.

In the present strategic scenario, the sources of assured military supplies have dwindled. At the same time, the availability of a variety of new and alternate equipment has added to the complexities of procurement. Added to this is the fact that the environment has become conflict prone and uncertain, with the result that the forces have to be prepared to meet contingencies over a wide spectrum of conflict and a large physical area of operation.

Therefore, in addition to the security challenges from external threats, we need to be prepared to combat internal challenges and tackle cross-border terrorism. We have to develop a national strategy and an integrated response to effectively deal with threats to our national security. This calls for an integrated politico-military strategy for projecting our national power and building capabilities, both economic and military.

Building Military Capability

The strength, type and structure of the armed forces have to take into account the security environment facing the nation, both conventional as well as nuclear. Indian Armed Forces have to be organised to fight on two fronts, as our unresolved border with China in the north and northeast continues to pose a threat despite an improvement in relations.

The long drawn 'Proxy War' in J&K and our strained relations with Pakistan are serious challenges facing the nation. India has also to plan for dealing with threats to its sea coast and island territories. The size and shape of the defence forces has to take into account the threat to the sea-lanes and its trade routes. The non-state actors and terrorist groups are another factor to be considered.

There is, therefore, a compelling need for India to undertake military modernization, especially when we compare the rapid investment in military hardware and infrastructure by China. This is more noticeable in the infrastructure in our border region, in the air and maritime capabilities. Over 96 per cent of China's nuclear arsenal has relevance only for its neighbours. China has been aggressively expanding its missile defence and aerospace power.

Pakistan on the other hand is adding to its military power by diverting US aid meant for fighting the Taliban on the Pak-Afghan border. Post 9/11 Pakistan received 11 billion $ aid from the USA and 85 per cent of this has been spent on defence. Pakistan has been made a non-NATO ally and recipient of huge funds for counter-terrorism as part of Af-Pak strategy. It has also been transferred radars, Attack-helicopters, Harpoon missiles and F-16 aircraft, and has developed its nuclear capabilities significantly. Terrorism in Kashmir and elsewhere in India is supported by Pakistan. We must, therefore, have the capabilities to deter and defeat the external threats from our neighbours, as the war fighting potential of China and Pakistan has increased tremendously. The other factors that determine military capability are the state of indigenous defence industry and the induction of new technology.

Military capability takes time to be created and cannot be achieved in a hurry in times of war. Financial angle is another important consideration. Affordability and budgetary allocation in view of high costs of military equipment and manpower requirement have to be taken into account. The quality and speed of defence modernization is influenced to a large extent by political, economic, technological and strategic factors.

The Indian approach to defence modernization is, therefore shaped by geo-political and geo-strategic environment; economic interests; technology constraints and imperatives; and social and cultural factors. The security challenge facing India is diverse, complex and constantly evolving. Instability in our immediate and extended neighbourhood heightens the threat to our security. Indian strategic thinking is influenced by what happens in the Indian Ocean, West Asia, Central Asia and South-East Asia.

Prime Minister Manmohan Singh during his address to Combined Commanders' Conference in October 2005 had observed thus:

> " To meet national security challenge, our strategy has to be based on three broad pillars. First, is to strengthen ourselves economically and technologically; second to

acquire adequate defence capability to counter and rebut threats to our security, and the third to seek partnerships both on the strategic front and on the economic and technological front to widen our policy and developmental options."

Thus introduction of cutting-edge technologies, both in the field of defence and civil, becomes equally important. Even though preference to economic over military development is normally given, it is possible to proceed simultaneously in both the areas once a certain level in economic development and capabilities has been reached. Defence modernization is therefore, a necessity for the armed forces. However, priorities at the national level vary because of competing needs of other important social sectors that need funds for development. It is not the intention here to review the entire range of military modernization that needs to be undertaken but to highlight a few of the important aspects which illustrate the existing status of modernization.

This is being done in the succeeding paragraphs. Similarly a national strategy to fight tribal insurgencies, religious fundamentalism and Maoist activities needs to be formulated with a suitable mechanism for centralised control and synergy.

Joint Doctrine

n the forces and other
ɔnduct war and conflicts
ıot only gives a common
itative guidance for the
ogies which may be of
ıt has been termed a
ılated and released by
ɔectives, it is neither

ıber of task-oriented
rsary's territory from
:asks quickly within
sure can be brought
ines both emphasize

on the strategic reach of their respective services and the need to operate in joint service environment in order to achieve synergies of defence-effort. The Indian Navy was first off the block in achieving high speed connectivity between shore establishment ships, other naval platforms and even logistics installations. The army has also made strides in net-centric warfare and few of the formations have already been exercised. However, we have to factor the Chinese Ballistic Missile and anti-Satellite capabilities. Chinese counter-space capabilities are a threat to India's limited but valuable intelligence, surveillance, reconnaissance, and communication satellites.

While China continues to improve its space assets, it indirectly also makes Pakistan a proxy space power because of the close cooperation between the two. India is still miles away from validating a Ballistic Missile Defence System. We urgently need to create an organization for overseeing the entire gamut of militarization of space with a national perspective and integrate the Doctrines of the three Services under the long awaited Chief of Defence Staff. Such a step would assist in setting out critical national priorities in the acquisition of military-hardware and ensure best utilization of funds. This would also act as the nodal-point for providing single-point military advice, as also sorting out inter-service differences and fixing responsibility.

Streamlining Defence Procurements

The defence reforms were carried out in 2001 to evolve integrated and joint structures for higher defence organization in order to face the emerging threats and consequently achieve the desired levels of modernization. These reforms have achieved some degree of maturity and have been periodically updated. Formation of HQ Integrated Defence Staff has been instrumental for a joint approach towards building military capability.

Streamlining defence procurement procedures, involving private sector in defence-production, spurring research and development, taking long term perspective in defence planning and budgeting, upgradation of quality of personnel in the armed forces and rationalization of manpower were among many of the key reforms recommended by the Group of Ministers Report of 2001. However, these need to be implemented fully, as lack of a central policy planning staff and absence of Chief of Defence Staff greatly inhibit integrated effort in defence modernization. A few instances of malpractices in defence purchases should not derail the entire procurement programme; instead the guilty should be given suitable punishment and the planned inductions continued. Today the entire decision making apparatus appears paralysed once a scandal in the defence purchase is reported and the Capital budget for procurements remains unspent, adversely affecting the defence capability.

Technology Induction

At the present juncture, our armed forces are in transition from industrial age forces to knowledge age forces with a portion being equipped with the state-of-the-art weapons. While the Army is more manpower intensive, the Navy and the Air Force are more technology intensive forces and are much better on the equipment profile. Availability of state-of-the-art technology is dependent on international relations and strategic partnerships between us and the major militaries. A collaborative approach between the users, DRDO, the industry and foreign vendors is the only way ahead.

We must transform our buyer-seller relationship to joint-ventures. Transfer of technology being undertaken at the HAL aircraft manufacturing factory and some of the other joint ventures with countries like Israel, Russia and France for various weapon systems is the right step from the earlier days of licensed production system. Defence Public Sector Units and DRDO must adopt time bound processes and adopt bold management practices and scrap the process if it does not conform to a reasonable time-frame, rather than seeking frequent time extension, as shelf-life of equipment is becoming shorter by the day due to obsolescence.

Precision Guided Munitions (PGMs)

Precision engagement is considered one of the most

important aspects of the ongoing modernisation. And this is one of the niche capabilities which are being strengthened in our armed forces. The benefits of PGMs are well known. Precision weapons are a far more efficient substitute for heavy mass retaliation. They enable concentration of effects from geographically widely dispersed forces, contribute to reduced logistics tail, and help in reducing collateral damage. Therefore, increasing the accuracy and range of our missiles, and acquiring and developing a family of PGMs should receive greater attention in our armed forces.

However, long ranges of weapon platforms are of no use unless they are complemented by matching surveillance, target acquisition, battle damage assessment and weapon guidance capabilities. Therefore, besides ground based and air borne early warning systems, space based assets assume importance for imparting force-multiplication effects to air and surface forces.

In addition, space is another area which is being used basically for communications and navigations and we are in the process of increasing our capabilities in this area too. Aerospace capabilities have a long gestation period. It is necessary to carry out cost-effective replacements and selective upgradation of existing systems. All platforms including transport support aircraft and helicopters with residual life must be upgraded, along with the weapon systems.

Surveillance and Night Vision Devices

With the change of battlefield scenario, Indian Army is now equipping itself with latest state of the art technology and looking for night vision equipment between 3,000-5,000 metres range. This would give a tactical advantage for our forces which would enhance their night fighting skills and improve surveillance and reconnaissance capabilities greatly, but the numbers are large and would take time for induction.

Army feels that the night vision equipment will enhance combat potential to facilitate operations over 24 hours cycle. As a part of its modernization and upgrading weaponry, Indian Army has planned to equip all its battalions with night vision equipments but the progress is painfully slow. We need to push these on fast-track procurement procedure by intervention at the highest level.

'MBT- Arjun' Tank Production

The inordinate delay in the production of the ARJUN Tank and its design faults is a major cause of worry. Indian Defence Minister has admitted that frequent design modification and assembling format have also caused additional delay in its induction.

His assurance that necessary steps have been taken to ensure the timely availability of all critical aggregates, is still far from the reality. The Ministry of Defence in regular intervals comes out with promising statements only to justify the public-sector defence undertakings and to secure uninterrupted financial grants. Meanwhile, we continue to import the Russian T-90 and T-72 tanks, which are far superior but involve huge expenditure on imports from foreign sources.

Modernization of Field Artillery (155 mm guns)

As part of the field artillery modernization programme, army is looking to purchase artillery guns since mid-80s as well as increase domestic manufacture of field guns. Artillery modernization programme has been held hostage to various scandals and pressures and the army is even considering buying older models of 130 mm guns as a desperate measure. Despite the army repeatedly requesting for induction of 155 mm guns, due to irregularities in the procurement process and the unscrupulous role of middlemen and agents, this has not seen the light of day.

It needs to be realised that even after giving the go-ahead, it takes at least five years for the equipment to reach the Army units since these products are not available off-the-shelf and the numbers to be inducted are large. This is a matter of serious concern and the operational readiness of the army is jeopardized by continued inaction of the Government.

Building Maritime Capability

India's peninsular configuration invests her with an opportunity to project maritime power in the Indian Ocean.

This enables her to protect its sea-lanes as also to interdict hostile shipping, which traverse through the Indian Ocean. The rationale for an extensive PLA Navy build-up, development of Gwadar port in Pakistan, surveillance outposts on Myanmar islands, and beefing of ports in Sri Lanka and Bangladesh by the Chinese, suggest an intention to use these during forays of the PLA Navy into the Indian Ocean.

India, therefore, needs to enhance its naval build-up and expedite induction of the planned aircraft-carrier, the Scorpene submarines and the Maritime surveillance aircraft. Whereas, India can meet some of the challenges independently, others require rallying together Indian Ocean region Navies.

Air power

Air assets are best applied centrally and can be switched to other sectors speedily. The areas where IAF needs capability enhancement is its strike-forces, its space–assets, AWACS, airlift aircraft, air-rescue and air defence.

This would imply creating a composite capability to be able to strike strategic targets and sustain a rapid–reaction force in the Indian Ocean region. It would also necessitate expansion of air-ports and harbour infrastructure. It is well known that our defence budget allocation and our procurement policies have not been adequate to support our defence potential.

Budgetary Support

The future direction and pace of modernization would largely be dictated by budgetary constraints. Presently, the budget is at modest level of 2.3 per cent of the GDP. Even in current five years defence plan (2007–2012), the defence budget is expected to be around 2.5 per cent of the GDP.

If there is a sustained growth of eight per cent and above in the economy then additional budget for the defence must be allotted. This is especially important in view of the rapid modernization and increased defence budgets of our adversaries. Pakistan military budget is at 3.5 per cent and China has 4.5 per cent of the GDP and both countries hide actual expenditures, such as pensions and new procurements under different heads.

Additionally, PGMs, induction of force-multipliers, cyber security and achieving synergies in the field of information technology should continue to be the focus of our modernization programme.

However, a long-term perspective, accountability in decision making, a firm financial commitment and fast–track procurements procedure will have to be adopted to actually achieve our planned defence capabilities, otherwise the funds will remain unspent, eroding our combatedge adversely.

Fighting Internal Challenges

Challenges to internal security have been discussed at various forums and a national counterterrorism centre and a national investigative agency have been established. These are commendable steps which need to be effectively implemented. However, what ultimately matters is the political will to act and good governance.

An effective legal frame-work and modernization of Police Force along with fair and equitable economic development of all sections of Indian society, is equally necessary. The policy of appeasement needs to be replaced by a pro-active and positive response, to emerging situations. The intelligence agencies will have to be made more accountable and the State response more professional for timely intervention. National response cannot be the sole responsibility of the Security Forces and the government. Each and every citisen and civil society as a whole, including its commercial and business institutions would need to be involved in strengthening our nation's security.

Restoring Combat Edge

We are yet to buy a single artillery gun in 23 years. We have an aging naval fleet and dwindling numbers of advance jet fighters. Therefore, there is a compelling need to give a greater impetus to procurement of critical equipment. India also has a bitter experience of foreign vendors not fulfilling their contractual commitments once full payments are made. They fail to provide accepted after-sale support, arbitrarily increase cost of spares, and decline to honour transfer of technology commitments.

India's failure to negotiate foolproof contracts has allowed Russia to increase the cost of aircraft-carrier 'Gorshkov' manifold. Similar contractual flaws have resulted in delays in the deliveries of 'Hawk Trainers', T-90 tank kits, and 'Scorpene' submarines. It is essential that we develop critical technologies ourselves or enter joint-ventures with strategic partners. We also need to have professional teams to negotiate defence contracts. This would need the establishment of a dedicated procurement agency staffed by professionals, who are experts and are accountable to the Defence Minister. It is evident that the state of our defence modernization is unsatisfactory and there is urgent need for full implementation of the required institutional restructuring.

ARMY AVIATION IN INDIA

The Army Aviation Corps as we see it today was formally established on November 1, 1986. The proposal indicating a requirement for an integral army aviation was mooted by Gen. J.N. Chaudhry in February 1963 when the J.R.D. Tata Committee deliberated on the expansion and rationalisation of the air arm of India.

The case was submitted to the government in April 1968, with the underlying concept of induction of helicopters, including attack helicopters, with large scale mechanization, combining various arms, including armour, mechanized infantry, self-propelled artillery, all requiring integrated command for meshing elements into a cohesive fighting force. A memorandum of July 16, 1986, directed that the 31 Air OP Flights be transferred to the army by October 31, 1986, though the attack, medium and heavy lift helicopters were to remain assets of the air force, along with certain instructions not being elaborated here. The dedicated attack helicopter purports to counter the armour imbalance and, therefore, India's compulsion is not similar to that of Pakistan when we view the qualitative and quantitative aspects.

An Army Aviation Cell was created at Army Headquarters under Brig. (later Major General) Atma Singh who later became the first Additional Director General of Army Aviation. This nucleus was initially placed under the Director General Mechanized Forces. The air force continued providing logistic and maintenance support till October 31, 1989, for the 45 Chetak and 95 Cheetah helicopters. Regular expansion had been undertaken since the 1971 Indo-Pak conflict; even with the imposition of financial constraints and aviation development propositions by the government, 23 flights and 11 Squadron Headquarters have been established post 1971. In the meantime, the Indian Army became committed in Operation Meghdoot in the highest battlefield in the world, the Siachen Glacier.

The requirement of man and machine to operate in the rarified temperatures is phenomenal and this has been a continuous effort on the part of army aviation since April 1984. No other helicopter, till the date of induction and some several years after, except the Cheetah, has been able to make a landing at the highest of helipads at altitudes in the range of 24,000 feet. The air at Siachen's altitude is half as dense as at sea level, which means helicopters are able to lift only a quarter of their load or even less. A helicopter can carry only one soldier or a few boxes of ammunition or supply, and more so if it has to land. The Indian Peace Keeping Force (IPKF) had been inducted into Sri Lanka at the request of the Sri Lankan government in terms of the Agreement of July 29, 1987. By this time, the first All Arms Course, comprising officers of the armoured corps, infantry and mechanised infantry who joined the artillery officers to be trained at Air Force Academy at Dundigal in June 1987, had earned their wings in November 1988.

Select officers, after having qualified in the mandatory tests, would be trained by the air force, including the conversion to the rotary wing, and the final leg in gunnery and other tasks related with flying would be completed at Nasik Road under the squadron located there. The Combat Army Aviation Training School became operational at Nasik Road in September 2003.

Aviation support during Operation Pawan was invaluable. Helicopters were christened 'Ranjit' after being fitted with two medium machine guns fitted on either side. Directing artillery fire, evacuation of casualties, battle reconnaissance and surveillance were routine.

The army aviation units in support of the IPKF were as under:

- HQ 664 Air OP Sqn—Trincomalee.
- 10 Air OP Flt—54 Infantry Division, Jaffna Peninsula
- 26 Air OP Flt—36 Infantry and 57 Mountain Divisions Trincomalee.
- 31 Air OP Flt—4 Infantry Division, Vavunia.

The last elements of army aviation returned to India in March 1990 by which time, trouble was brewing in Jammu and Kashmir. The nomenclature air observation post (AOP) was changed to reconnaissance and observation (R&O) with the formation of this separate corps. Notable contributions have since been made by the army aviators since May 1990 (Operation Rakshak) in insurgency ridden Jammu and Kashmir, in reconnaissance, casualty evacuation and air observation shoots. Operation Vijay involved tremendous helicopter effort to provide support in terms of ammunition supply and casualty evacuation. Two Vir Chakras, one Yudh Seva Medal and seven Sena Medals were awarded to this corps to commend their contribution in the three-month conflict with Pakistan. Not only has the battlefield seen active participation and contribution of this corps but active involvement in United Nation missions and natural disaster management as well as in aid to the civil authorities.

Notable among these are the rescue of civilians on a Manasarovar trek at Malpa village (in Uttarakhand) when tragedy struck in August 1998, by way of a landslide, the Orissa cyclone in October 1999 and the Gujarat earthquake in January 2001. The acquisition programme for helicopters for army aviation is now a matter of much debate and choice. India emerges as a needbased country and, therefore, needs a balance in managing inter-relations, with not only neighbouring countries, but also its own standing as a military-politico-economic force to be reckoned with.

India had announced a preferred purchase of 197 helicopters at an approximate cost of US $550 million dollars, to replace the Cheetah and Chetak fleet of the 1970s vintage.

Unfortunately, the arrangements with Eurocopter of France could not see the light of day on account of procedural requirement shortcomings, and the end was sounded on December 6, 2007. The indigenous helicopter programme of developing the advanced light helicopters (ALH) named Dhruv (Pole Star) had met with considerable success with a demand for 120 helicopters.

The Combat Army Aviators Training School has been functioning in Nasik Road since September 1, 2003, to train army aviators.

As a paradigm shift to the training module, *ab-inito* training of aviators and instructors commenced at No. 664 Aviation Squadron (reconnaissance and observation) as rechristened, and the Rotary Wing Association at Bangalore, which was later discontinued.

THE FLIGHT AHEAD

The time had already come a decade ago when the ageing fleet of Cheetah and Chetak helicopters of nearly 40 years needed to be retired; however, a worthy heir to the Cheetah helicopter is still in waiting. The detailed process, commencing with paper evaluation and followed by winter and summer trials at present, has spread over a two-year period.

Keeping in mind the time lost and urgency required in view of delivery schedules, with inherent delay factors, it is certainly time to step up efforts, since all the aircraft are not be procured in 'flyaway' condition, and a significant number is expected to be built indigenously under a transfer of technology agreement at HAL. Significantly, a requirement of 115 helicopters by the air force to the 197 aircrafts that the army requires, pushes the value of the deal to $ one billion and the number of aircraft to 312.

It is interesting to note that there will be an addition of two squadrons of attack gunships and six heavy-lift helicopters to complement the expansion and modernization efforts, thereby, nudging the combined worth to $ 1.4 billion. Army aviation in India has been emblematic of significant contributions in terms of professional achievements and this would support a justification to sustain a capability-based organization rather than an equipment and inventory-based structure, implying commensurate induction of man, machine and infrastructure requirement, though not mentioned here in order of priority.

Optimum asset utilization and air space governance will require significant application and forethought. Application of aviation resources to disaster management has attained significance in the context of the requirement for growing economic and support stability operations and this would certainly require a doctrinal overview for optimum resource utilization as compared to insulated application for combat scenarios only. While the impressive modernization and replacement programme arouses enthusiasm, a more than soft look may be required at the indigenous development efforts. It has been remarked that the performance of the advanced light helicopter (*Dhruv*) has been satisfactory and a concerted effort has been made to improve the serviceability state. Certainly, early in the stage of a successful launch, its high terrain capability was questioned by Chile, and it also got into troubled waters regarding its maritime role due to 'payload and endurance limitations'.

The question is not in the efforts and credibility but the time penalty in terms of immediate upgrades at the doorstep of induction. We also see completion of the design for the light combat helicopter (LCH) and it will be ready for the first test flight by the end of the year, which translates into another prototype in the inventory. The questions hover around the requirement for it, inventory control becoming varied over a period of time, and a scheduled successful induction programme at the desired scale.

Intake and retention of army aviators has been a potential subject for animated debate. The average period of employment of an artillery officer on aviation duties was six years in the formative years, which has since increased to approximately eleven years for those in the support cadre. While in the permanent cadre, with induction, retention and recall rate of the support cadre caters to the minimum sustainable requirements of the aircrew, the manning level in the flight is still a matter of constant concern on account of an even-paced flying and administrative commitment on the part of those who constitute this corps.

This may certainly require a policy analysis, considering that the equipment strength and base is increasing with the announcement of the induction of the light utility tactical battle support helicopters (TBSH), armed and attack helicopters (AH) in a phased manner during the 11th Plan period and extending up to 12th and 13th Plans. Along with the induction of equipment, a recount of the infrastructural facility, existing and proposed, to obviate adhoc storage arrangements, will certainly need advance thinking in terms of planning, capital outlay and timebound completion. In the process of transition, what lies ahead is employability, not only in the battlefront but a milieu of multifarious tasking in all domains for potential realization and tangible unrestricted contribution so that the power and capability within is gainfully exploited.

THE FUTURE OF ARMY AVIATION

The entire Army Aviation (AA) in India is being modernized, in order to achieve a set of planned capabilities. These relate to directions given by military leaders based on the threat perception of India. Whilst numbers may not seem to be relevant on first thought, they have to be in consonance with the desired set of capabilities that the Indian armed forces seek to achieve. The numbers would preferably conform to a requirement that fulfils the total helicopter force that would be required by the armed forces, keeping in mind, of course, that some specialized type of aircraft may be required.

Our national policy does not support aggression in any form and, currently, we do not envisage deployments as expeditionary forces in any country. Whilst we do have missions under the auspices of the United Nations that are deployed and maintained by us, full scale support of foreign land forces in an out-of-area contingency is not currently envisaged in our plans. The role and employment of the rotary-wing aircraft has also undergone certain changes. Technology has contributed immensely both to, and as, a force multiplier. The helicopter forces of the Indian armed forces should, hence, be augmented and modernized.

Classic set-piece wars between states seem to have become a thing of the past, and over the years, have been influenced by many forms of warfare. These developments give us reason to rethink all our theories of not only of war and peace but also of the role and employment of the different corps and branches of the armed forces. What has been realised is that a comprehensive build-up of capability of the integral aviation arm of the land forces can eventually cater for all possible contingencies. Reminiscing on the ways to confront a changing world, Gen Dwight David Eisenhower had said that one cannot face the future simply by walking backwards, into the past. Since Army Aviation requires being at the forefront in the development of new methods for defeating adversaries of the future, incorporating lessons learned, adjusting force structure, evolving procedures and continued absorption of technologies will become ever so essential to enable Army Aviation to meet the current and future demands.

Issues that will have focus and a major share of attention in this writing, as a prelude to the current expansion phase of Army Aviation are:

- The nature of developments having a bearing on current trends in Army Aviation with respect to operational and technological advances.
- The requirements for adaptation.

NATURE OF DEVELOPMENTS AND TRENDS

Operational Trends

Army helicopters were sent to Vietnam to increase mobility and improvement in the concept of holding static defensive positions. Developments in guided missiles led to the combat role of the army from the air, including the facet of air-to-air combat. This was concurrent with providing infantry a platform to operate from the third dimension. The essence in application of force during the 1980s in Afghanistan was heavy reliance on aerial warfare, airborne troops and extensive use of armed helicopters. However, night and adverse weather operations were almost never attempted, even when air support was badly needed by troops in difficulty. They were also used in conjunction with conventional weaponry consisting of tanks (T-72) and artillery guns (152 mm self-propelled howitzers). The experience in Chechnya was somewhat different from the erstwhile concept.

Helicopters were now increasingly being utilised mainly for noncombat missions and approximately 90 per cent of the wounded were evacuated by helicopters. This gave enough evidence of the inherent potential to execute combat support operations, including medical evacuation duties, and combat search and rescue. Operationalization of the rotary-wing aircraft brings in the advantage of close contact operations in confined spaces and aerial observation. However, mere target acquisition by air observation posts lost relevance soon after World War I. Artillery ranges increased and it is evident that observation even now, with optical aids, is not meeting expectations.

So it was with the pace of operations where, first, the bulk of artillery pieces could not match the run of formations even during World War II, and where it has now matched the pace, with technology and ingenuity, the observation capability to enable direction of artillery is evidently becoming secondary and almost irrelevant except perhaps in the mountains where suitably placing observation posts is still an arduous task to achieve during operations. This is so because of the extraordinary ranges at which artillery can strike with accuracy without the intervention of the human eye. There are enduring images of the Korean War when helicopters evacuated the wounded and landed at the Mobile Army Surgical Hospitals (MASH)).

In sharp contrast, the Chinese and North Korean medical evacuation systems nearly collapsed by early 1951 because they relied on road and rail which was delay-prone and immensely time intensive. Today, an enormous amount of air effort is dedicated by the Indian Army Aviation in evacuating wounded soldiers in the Siachen, in Jammu and Kashmir (J&K), and the insurgency-prone northeastern states. The concept of air mobility has, ever since, remained attractive to armies the world over. The concept of tactical mobility is a cardinal feature of any military doctrine. It calls for extensive use of helicopters to transport both airborne and infantry units, together with supporting equipment, either across or along the edges of the battlefield. Armies all over the world have directed substantial efforts in improving their rotary-wing inventory and resources towards this end. The US apparently regards the chief function of the medium-lift helicopter as being carriage of equipment and weapons, Germany looks at troop lift operations of one battalion per corps in one operation. Attack helicopters have been designed keeping anti-tank roles as the foremost ones so that they may counteract any overwhelming numerical superiority of armour on the battlefield.

The strategy to counter armour is not always with attack helicopters, in particular where a favourable combat ratio exists. They are also to perform the infantry support role. However, in mountainous terrain, the entry, route and exit of such aircraft can be predicted with a fair degree of accuracy because when valleys are followed, the dangers increase, as also in any attempt to be close to the mountains for camouflage. Future battles can see unison of irregulars with conventional forces. Therefore, low and slow flying operations over hostile terrain against an adversary, whether in urban or mountainous terrain, will have to be weighed adequately against the vulnerabilities in such employment.

Technological Advances

The use of actual aircraft has become constrained by battlefield safety concerns. This becomes more evident with rapid urbanization and, thus, in the context of, and direct relation with, the conditions under which future warfare is going to surface and be contested. While survivability will be a requirement for any moment, a high level of attrition may seem a reality.

During Operation Iraqi Freedom 2003, over Karbala, 32 AH-64D Longbows were attacked in a classic ambush, by the Iraqi Medina armoured division. The outcome was significant when nearly all the aircraft were hit by ground fire.

The United States (US) Army has also lost more than 120 helicopters in the 'war on terror', about 25 per cent of them due to enemy engagements, resulting in 172 deaths, or about 5.5 per cent of total American deaths since the conflict began in March 2003. With technological advances, it is becoming exceedingly practical to utilise aircraft simulators to train certain critical skills before launching man and machine in actual operations. Rapid development in sensor and information technology is transforming Intelligence, Surveillance and Reconnaissance (ISR) capabilities, leading to greater effect-based operations. Reduced pilot workload, increased lift, better protection and enhanced survivability figure prominently in the cue to technological trends. The upgrades look into features of wire flight controls, full authority digital engine controllers, enhanced cockpit displays, while adding more horsepower, and allowing additional lift during external lift (sling load) operations. Flying under the cover of darkness is the preferred mode of operation. Therefore, there has been a pressing need for increased and more effective means of battlefield target acquisition by night and all-weather conditions.

As a result, night vision systems, both Night Vision Goggles (NVG) and Forward Looking Infrared (FLIR) systems, have become commonplace requirements. These devices offer the ability to 'see' down to levels of illumination two orders of magnitude below the capability of the human eye and, thus, have a considerable potential to contribute towards target acquisition by night. The high cost of purchase, and the operative and maintenance costs favour the utility of fixed-wing aircraft and had increased the attractiveness of its usage in Army Aviation.

Communication, troop carrying and photography missions are routine application for such fixed-wing assets. This led to the development of tilt rotors that aimed at harnessing the advantages of both fixed and rotary-wing aircraft. The reviews of tilt rotor V-22 Osprey aircraft were encouraging till weighed against their slow descent, limited protection, manoeuvrability and a bill of $100 million per unit. This does not favour investment in such assets by a country like India, at least till the middle of this century.

Neutralization of approximately 2,400 bombs and capture of some 141 planters without a single casualty on friendly forces in Afghanistan and Iraq, have substantiated the focus on the decentralised option towards the result oriented response of the *manned-unmanned* team. This has gained prominence after the success of Task Force ODIN (Observe, Detect, Identify and Neutralize). However, in the field of target acquisition from the air, there would at times appear little, if any, prospect of advances in technology providing means for penetrating the denser forms of natural cover except possibly in rather special cases where the target itself emits some helpful form of radiation. Urban terrain which is likely to be the arena for the battles of the 21 century, offers great opportunity for such cover and defence.

REQUIREMENTS AND ADAPTATION

Army Aviation is working on several material changes to its current and future aviation platforms. By far, the focus has been on acquiring platforms to replace the aging fleet. These costly acquisitions are expected to perform for a minimum two to three decades with suitable upgradation. Upgrades and key modifications that will need attention include the requirement to incorporate army digital network-centric connectivity. Without this, AA will become a standalone force incapable of fully integrating into the joint battlefield environment. Optical recognition and non line-of-sight communications are key areas which will determine the way AA is able to deliver in the future.

A self-protection suite, observation and targeting systems to include high definition imaging turrets, enhanced day and night capable helmet mounted displays, and night vision goggles are inevitable requirements. Management of dense air space will remain a complex challenge. The dense air defence over the battlefield environment necessitates tactical data links over voice control. Ground-based air defence batteries and aircraft should now be able to exchange digital information sufficiently and rapidly to fight the air-land battle.

The multitude and capability of air defence systems to detect and down low flying aircraft has achieved phenomenal magnitude. Also, large scale deployment of anti-aircraft weapons by both field units and fixed installations by own troops and adversary will lead to a highly intensive and 'saturated' air space where the Identification, Friend or Foe (IFF) system and coordination of air movements will increase exponentially. This will necessarily have a direct bearing on the aspects of survivability, target acquisition and engagement of hostile elements for neutralization. The command and control structure of Army Aviation should be able to furnish the prerequisites of participation in rapid response and small unit operations. The tendency to adapt present structures in the conventional mode to evolving challenges tends to provide only linear improvements to an organization. Countering terrorism and managing internal security has become a reality for the armed forces. "Every combat arms unit should have a limited, yet focussed capability to meet such challenges", as was expressed by Gen. Deepak Kapoor, Chief of the Army Staff. The country will continue to rely on the Special Forces (SF) of the three Services to tackle the threat from terrorists. Army Aviation has the potential to enhance the capability of SF and develop interoperability with the other Services, and National Security Guards where required.

The Indian Army modernization and expansion plan had envisaged a dedicated aviation wing for the SF way back in 2001. An internal exercise to examine various proposals from different agencies to get the maximum advantage seemed to have been truncated and shelved. Low cost and low maintenance fixed-wing aircraft operating with ground troops have their advantages. However, operations from the field imply having to be concerned with tactical dispersion, camouflage, enemy situation, assembly area security, ground- to-ground as well as ground-to-air communication issues, and maintaining aircraft in a field environment.

Factors that contribute to the operational attractiveness of these aircraft are associated with air base infrastructure and potential threats near forward and remote aircraft landing grounds. Whilst there are several existing ones, many will need activation and some additional ones will have to be created. Modernization and technology will catapult the demand for additional expertise.

Multi-track training programmes may require to be formulated where within each individual aircraft qualification course, there is a hierarchy of required skills, levels of simulation and individual training aids. As advanced electronics and systems packages get incorporated, the workload on the aircrew increases in terms of acquiring qualification and maintaining currency in the advanced expertise. So, either a new discipline of aircrew needs consideration or the present methods of specialized training need to be reworked to achieve the desired level of proficiency. This will have to be balanced with the state of availability of aircrew in units, their operational familiarization/utilization and, rest and relief.

Armoured carriers with Nuclear, Biological and Chemical (NBC) protection have been evaluated as useful but the ability to transport both troops and weapons in a nuclear battlefield with fair speed and be able to concentrate from dispersed landings is also a feature to be acknowledged while considering tactical mobility in affected areas. Troop movement and application in a nuclear battlefield has been thought through the years to be better executable with helicopters than any other mode when time is at a premium. There will be a requirement to focus on this aspect given the fact that India has two neighbouring countries which are nuclear powers.

The aviation logistics system has fielded the level of automation that is allowing commanders to see the logistics demands, movement and set conditions for success. To achieve the next step to 24x7 operational capability of a combat arm, the flexibility to plug into, and unplug from, a dedicated logistics network will be required. This may become more sustainable with the introduction of a modular maintenance package as it eliminates the ills of centralised and multiple level structures but retains the ability to meet the pace of modern warfare.

In summary, Army Aviation in India is undergoing one of the most significant initiatives in its history. It is an extremely crucial and exciting time as it tackles numerous challenges in its modernization and transformation. Its capability to restructure, leverage technological improvements in current and future systems will allow the army to respond better in a more effective and sustainable manner. Areas of special focus and structures have certainly been given due thought and action initiated in a highly professional manner but the workable recommendations have to be deliberated upon more deeply to complete the ambit of true and real integral aviation support to the Army.

DEFENCE FORCES OF INDIA

Let us briefly recapitulate the current defence forces fielded by India. The strength of the defence forces of India on the active list is approximately 1.3 million, with the Army dominating with nearly 1.1 million personnel. The Air Force has a strength of 140,000 and the Navy fields approximately 55,000 personnel. There is a Territorial Army component of approximately 40,000. The field force of the army comprises thirteen corps, three armoured divisions, four Reorganized Army Plains Infantry Divisions (RAPID), eighteen infantry divisions and ten mountain divisions, a number of independent brigades, and requisite combat support and service support formations and units.

The main combat and combat support units are sixty-two armoured regiments and there are over three hundred and fifty infantry battalions and three hundred artillery regiments (including two Surface to Surface Missile (SSM) units). Amongst major armaments and equipment, there are nearly 4,000 main battle tanks, 2,000 armoured personnel carriers, 4,300 artillery pieces and 200 light helicopters.

Unlike most modern armies, the Indian Army fields only reconnaissance helicopters in its aviation corps, with the air force still clinging to attack and medium lift helicopters, which should have been transferred to the army a long time back. The organizational structure of the army is generally on traditional lines, heavily influenced as it has been by the erstwhile colonial

British military. The Indian Army is competent in conducting both conventional as well as low intensity conflict (LIC) operations. The navy has 26 principal surface combatants, including one aircraft carrier; 49 patrol and coastal combatants and 16 submarines. The naval aviation has 35 combat aircraft and 97 helicopters. There is also a coast guard with 52 patrol craft of various types. The air force fields approximately 680 combat aircraft, grouped in 32 fighter ground attack and six fighter squadrons; 40 armed helicopters grouped in three squadrons; 12 transport squadrons; 19 helicopter squadrons and miscellaneous squadrons covering tanker, maritime attack, electronic counter-measures, survey, VIP movement, training and so on.

The growth of the defence forces of India in the past has usually been as a reaction to contemporary crises. Resultantly, the defence forces have generally remained unchanged, both structurally and in doctrinal terms, except for incremental changes to meet challenges as they arose. In recent years, however, there is a discernable doctrinal shift from attrition to manoeuvre warfare. Since the late 1980s, availability of funds has been a major constraint, with allocations for defence being less than 2.5 per cent of the GDP.

The three services are organised for conducting largely conventional operations, although a very large component of the army is heavily involved in Low Intensity Conflict operations. In all the three services, there has been some infusion of state-of-the-art equipment and armament, but much less than what is needed. India is a responsible nuclear weapon state, with an unblemished record of non-proliferation, which cannot be easily matched by even nuclear weapon states of long standing.

Our nuclear policy has two main components—minimum deterrence and no first use. Our higher defence structure is perhaps the weakest part of the defence forces of India. The defence forces are not part of the government of India, but are an attached 'office'. The implications of this formulation are obvious and need not be amplified, except to highlight that this arrangement effectively keeps them outside the policy formulation loop. No doubt, the service headquarters are consulted on security issues, but that is no substitute for being part of formulating policy. The highest policy formulation body in the country is the Cabinet Committee on Security (CCS). It gets its inputs from a variety of sources, viz., the National Security Council (NSC), the Cabinet Secretariat, different ministries, intelligence agencies and so on. The inputs from the services are channelled through the ministry of defence; neither the service chiefs nor the Chairman Chief's of Staff Committee are members of the CCS, although service chiefs may be called for consultations, like many others.

A National Security Council (NSC) was created in 1999. A National Security Advisor (NSA) was also appointed. We have had three incumbents so far for this appointment—two were retired diplomats and the third is a retired intelligence specialist. The NSA has a secretariat, which is headed by a Deputy NSA. This appointment too has been held by retired diplomats so far. As far as the secretariat is concerned, officers of various ranks hold senior, middle level and junior staff appointments, but the military is represented only by a handful of junior officers.

An ironical state of affairs, indeed! Within the Ministry of Defence, there is neither integration, nor any methodology for analyzing issues jointly. The Ministry of Defence asks service headquarters individually or jointly to submit their views on issues, whether they are on operational, intelligence or administrative matters or relating to personnel, and thereafter the Ministry deliberates on them, despite having little or no competence to analyze such military matters.

A similar situation prevails within service headquarters, wherein the stance of a particular service on an issue is first finalized in-house, including by obtaining inputs from their respective commands. Thereafter, it is forwarded to the Chief of Staff Committee for consideration. The Committee comprises the three service chiefs, with the seniormost being the Chairman. Such a structure and such formulations cannot hope to deliberate on issues objectively, as service biases are foremost in each member's mind. Since last year, the service headquarters have started calling themselves as Integrated Headquarters. It is a meaningless exercise in semantics, as there is hardly any integration of the three services, let alone with the ministry of defence. Even the establishment of the post of Chief of Defence Staff (CDS) continues to remain unimplemented.

VISION 2020

Modernising for an Era of Strategic Uncertainty

In the prevailing era of strategic uncertainty, while terrorism is gradually becoming the primary threat, the external and internal threats and challenges faced by India are such that a large army is still required to be maintained. Also, a high degree of preparation and operational readiness are still necessary as conventional war, though improbable, cannot be categorically ruled out due to unresolved territorial and boundary disputes with China and Pakistan.

At the same time, heavy capital investments in modern defence equipment are undoubtedly a drain on a developing economy that is ill equipped to handle the burgeoning defence expenditure. Several eminent analysts have recommended that qualitative upgradation should be accompanied by quantitative downsizing of personnel strength of the army to generate funds for modernisation. However, given its responsibilities for border management and the manpower-intensive sub-conventional operations that the army is involved in—this is easier said than done.

Future conventional conflict on the Indian sub-continent will in all probability result from the ongoing low-intensity limited war on the Line of Control (LoC) with Pakistan or the unresolved territorial and boundary dispute with China and will be predominantly a land conflict. The Indian Army lacks a potent firepower punch, especially in the mountain sector. Precision-guided munitions (PGMs) have still to enter service in numbers large enough to make a real difference.

The reconnaissance, surveillance and target acquisition (RSTA) assets necessary for the optimum exploitation of even the existing firepower assets are grossly inadequate. Automated command and control and decision support systems have been on the drawing boards for several decades but are yet to mature. According to former Vice Chief of Army Staff Lieutenant General (Retd.) Noble Thamburaj, the modernization focus of the 11th Defence Plan is on "precision fire power, air defence, aviation, Future Infantry Soldier as a System, infrastructure development, network centricity and achieving battlefield transparency through improved surveillance, night vision and target acquisition.... Considering the receding span of technological cycle, (the) right balance has to be maintained between state-of-art, current and obsolescent technologies."

Main Battle Tanks: T-90S replaces Arjun

On Army Day 2010, Chief of the Army Staff General Deepak Kapoor admitted that a large number of India's battle tanks are 'night blind'. The indigenously designed Arjun main battle tank (MBT) has been in the pipeline for over two decades. Though the tank has many good features, it has consistently failed to meet the army's General Staff Qualitative Requirements for an MBT and orders have been placed for only 124 tanks to be manufactured.

The Defence Research and Development Organization (DRDO) had been repeatedly pressing for comparative trials of the Arjun with the T-72M1 and the T-90S. Success in these trials has led to orders being placed for another 124 Arjun MBTs. Since the lack of progress on the Arjun MBT had significantly slowed down the pace of armour modernization, in 2000, India signed a deal with Russia to acquire 310 T-90S tanks and assemble 1,000 in India.

In 2008, the Ministry of Defence (MoD) decided to acquire another 347 T-90S tanks. The first India assembled T-90S (Bhishma) rolled off the production line on January 8, 2004. Ultimately, "The army's future armour profile could comprise approximately 1,700 T-90S, 1,800 upgraded T-72M1 and 250 to 500 Arjuns." Almost 1,800 T-72M1 (Ajeya) tanks are still awaiting modernisation. The lack of a suitable fire control system and night fighting capability are major handicaps. The upgradation of 500 to 600 of these has now commenced "at the rate of 200 tanks per year". The upgrade package includes a new fire control system comprising a TISAS (thermal imaging stand alone systems) night sight and TIFCS (tank integrated fire control system), new TADIRAN radios, a gyro-based navigation system and a Laser warning system. The ability to fire on the move is being improved with a better stabilization system. An add-on ERA (explosive reactive armour) package will enhance protection against APFSDS and HEAT rounds. Eventually, the T-90S 1,000 hp power pack, de-rated to 850 hp, will be retro-fitted.

The problem of defective indigenous ammunition is still to be resolved. The DRDO has commenced conceptual stage development of Future Main battle Tank and Future Infantry Combat vehicle for the 2020-25 time-frame. T-90S Russian tanks have provided new teeth to India's strike formations in the plains and corrected the imbalance that had resulted from Pakistan's acquisition of T-80 UD from Ukraine and the Al Khalid tanks jointly designed with China. Hence, armour modernization is proceeding apace but cannot yet be classified as a success story.

Generating firepower asymmetries

In a future conventional war that will be fought under the nuclear shadow, manoeuvre will be extremely limited. This restriction will lead to much greater emphasis being placed on firepower to achieve the laid down military aim. Hence, it is imperative that artillery modernization is undertaken with alacrity so as to generate firepower asymmetries on the future battlefield. After a long spell of keeping the powder dry, action on modernization of the Indian Artillery is livening up once again.

Beginning in January 2008, the MOD issued three global tenders for 155 mm guns and howitzers for the mountains, the plains and self-propelled guns for the deserts. Summer and winter trials were expected to be held over the next one year and it was anticipated that contracts would be awarded as early as in the first half of 2010. However, none of the manufacturers have as yet been invited for trials. It is a well-established fact that potent artillery firepower had turned the tide and eventually paved the way for victory during the Kargil conflict. Despite the lessons learnt in Kargil, modernization of the artillery has continued to lag behind. The last major acquisition of towed gunhowitzers was that of about 400 pieces of 39-calibre 155 mm FH-77B howitzers with a range of 30 km from Bofors of Sweden in the mid-1980s.

This gun had proved its mettle in the Kargil conflict. After two decades of neglect during which the 100 mm and 122 mm field guns of Russian origin and the indigenously developed and manufactured 75/24 Indian Mountain Gun joined the long list of equipment bordering on obsolescence but still in service with the army, tenders were floated and trials were held for a 52-calibre 155 mm gun to replace all field and medium guns. Just when a contract for 120 tracked and 180 wheeled self-propelled (SP) 155 mm guns was about to be concluded after years of protracted trials, South African arms manufacturer Denel, a leading contender for the contract, was alleged to have been involved in a corruption scam in an earlier deal for antimaterial rifles (AMRs).

The other two howitzers in contention, from Soltam of Israel and BAE (Bofors) of Sweden reportedly did not meet the laid down criteria and Army HQ recommended fresh trials, setting the programme back at least three to four years. Another bone of contention was that the howitzers that had been offered were technology demonstration models and not guns that were in actual service with the home country armies.

10

Developing Strategic Leaders for the 21st Century

STRATEGIC LEADERSHIP: FRAMEWORK FOR A 21ST CENTURY NATIONAL SECURITY STRATEGY

The next president of the United States must forge a new national security strategy in a world marked by enormous tumult and change and at a time when America's international standing and strategic position are at an historic nadir. Many of our allies question our motives and methods; our enemies doubt American rhetoric and resolve. Now, more than at any time since the late 1940s, it is vital to chart a new direction for America's global role.

Our core goals today are the same ones envisaged by our founding fathers: the resolute pursuit of security, liberty, and prosperity both for our own people and as the basis for a just and stable inter-national order. The challenge is to advance these goals in a new global landscape. The 21st century is an era of deep interconnectedness, creating unparalleled opportunities but also great dangers from which no nation can be immune. It is also an era of increasingly diffuse power, spreading to many different states and from states to non-state actors of many different kinds. America is well equipped by geography, demography, and national temperament and values to flourish in this environment. But to do so will require a new kind of American leadership: strategic leadership.

Strategic leadership requires making wise and deliberate choices about how, when, and with whom to lead. While America remains the single most powerful country in the world today, it cannot take global leadership for granted, nor can it revert to what worked in previous eras. Both the scope and the limits of American power must be taken into account. Moreover, leadership is not an entitlement; it has to be earned and sustained. Leadership that serves common goals is the best way to inspire the many different peoples of the world to make shared commitments.

The United States must lead primarily when our interests most warrant it and when we are most able to achieve the objectives at hand. Despite the prevalent presumption that America must always be in charge, effective leadership is not always centered in Washington. At times, our interests are best served when others lead with us, or even take our place at the helm. Climate change could be an example of shared leadership; regional peacekeeping efforts will likely offer opportunities for other nations to lead. A doctrine of strategic leadership seeks effective action rather than American leadership for its own sake. It exercises judgment as much as resolve.

America's longstanding allies will continue to be our most valued partners, along with key global and regional institutions. On many issues, however, the United States must be pragmatic and flexible enough to work with a wide variety of states on different issues. Whether they are old allies or new potential partners, we should engage with others, seeking to surface differences of opinion and new insights before views have hardened. And while being clear on its own red lines, Washington should be willing to adapt its positions to gain the consensus ultimately needed for constructive policy making and implementation.

Operationally, strategic leadership has five principal requisites: exercising strong state-craft, ensuring 21st century military strength, enhancing prosperity and development, encouraging democracy and human rights, and energizing

America at home. It also means setting priorities. From the first day the next administration takes office, it will be pressured from many directions on many different issues. Given the press of events and the breadth of the agenda, three principal criteria should guide initial priorities: the urgency of the issue; its importance to American security and to the world at large; and the transformational potential of successful policy outcomes. Applying these criteria yields five initial strategic priorities:

- COUNTERTERRORISM: The United States must revamp its counterterrorism strategy to place highest priority on preventing catastrophic terrorism, including a comprehensive review of homeland security policy and organization. It must integrate military, diplomatic, political, economic and other instruments of power and influence; adapt military strategy to better fit counterterrorism missions; and ensure consistency with the rule of law and fundamental American principles.
- NUCLEAR NONPROLIFERATION: The United States must reaffirm the vision of a world free of nuclear weapons and take practical steps to reduce the salience of these weapons. We should start by reducing nuclear force levels to 1,000 weapons, provided Russia does likewise.
- CLIMATE CHANGE AND OIL DEPENDENCE: The United States must envision a low-carbon world and persuade other nations to join in deciding on and taking early actions that will make it a reality. Climate change affects the security of every person and nation on the planet, which is why we must work with others to dramatically reduce greenhouse gas emissions and change current patterns of energy consumption. At the same time, we must spark innovation across a wide array of new technologies, spurring competitiveness and progressively reducing oil dependence at home.
- THE MIDDLE EAST: The United States must develop a comprehensive, integrated regional strategy that includes drawing down militarily and building up

diplomatically in Iraq; pursuing dual-track deterrence and engagement with Iran; taking a high-level and sustained role in Israeli Palestinian peace efforts; and promoting regional security cooperation and democratic reform.

- EAST ASIA: The United States must renew its commitment to comprehensive engagement in Asia. We must maximize the prospects that China and India will rise as open, vibrant markets and stable rights-regarding governments, while also reassuring long-standing friends and allies of U.S. security commitments and willingness to cooperate on issues of concern throughout the region.

Our founders believed that they were creating a nation that would secure life, liberty, and prosperity for all Americans. At the same time, our nation would also stand together with all other people against tyranny, inequality, and injustice. At its best, America has pursued its interests in ways that further those global human interests. It has sought partners and helped build institutions to strengthen the ability of all nations to tackle common problems. And it has been willing to strengthen other nations and help them regain their power and prosperity as members of a spreading zone of liberty and peace.

America can and must do so again. Strategic leadership provides a framework for a national security strategy that meets the demands and needs of our current century. Such leadership recognizes that in an interconnected world the best way to secure our own interests is to understand and help secure the interests of others. It understands that in a world in which power has diffused, leadership can mean convening, listening and brokering agreements as well as seizing the initiative and expecting others to follow.

Strategic Leadership: Framework for a 21st Century National Security Strategy provides an intellectual and policy blueprint for the next administration. This paper focuses on four foundational components of strategic leadership: the security environment in which the next administration will operate, the core goals it should seek to achieve, the overarching doctrine of strategic leadership, and a set of initial policy priorities for its first year in office. This is not a document of domination, denial, or disengagement, but rather a program of action meant to marshal the best practices and ideas of the progressive tradition in American foreign policy and adapt them to a rapidly changing world.

A LEADER DEVELOPMENT STRATEGY FOR A 21ST CENTURY ARMY

The Army Leader Development Strategy (ALDS) builds on our Army's experiences since the end of the Cold War including the past eight years of war in Iraq and Afghanistan and on our assessment that the future operational environment will be even more uncertain, complex, and competitive as hybrid threats challenge us across the full spectrum of operations.

Our enemies – regular and irregular – will be well armed, well trained, well equipped, and often ideologically inspired. We must overmatch their training with our training and with the development of our leaders. We must counter their ideologies with our history and with a sustained commitment to our values. They will be patient, and they will adapt. We must learn faster, understand better, and adapt more rapidly. Our enemies will decentralize, partner, and network to form syndicates of threats against us. We must form our network by partnering with our Joint, Interagency, Intergovernmental, Multinational (JIIM) teammates to defeat their networks. We are developing our leaders in a competitive learning environment, and it is in this environment above all others where we must prevail.

This Army Leader Development Strategy for a 21st Century Army responds to this competitive learning environment and is the outcome of a campaign of learning over the past year. It has been produced by an extensive enterprise of stakeholders both inside and outside the Army. It is informed by comprehensive lessons learned from our on going conflicts, assessments of the future operational environment, the Army

Capstone Concept, the CSA's Green Book article "The Army of the 21st Century," and our doctrine especially FM 3.0 (Operations). It articulates the characteristics we desire in our Army leaders as they progress through their careers (ends). It establishes eight imperatives for the integration of policies, programs, and initiatives to produce Army leaders (ways). It provides guidance for career long development of Army leaders through education, training, and experience (means). Implementing annexes for officer, noncommissioned officer, warrant officer, and DA civilian describe how we will make certain that our Army's most important core competency—leader development—will produce confident, competent, versatile leaders for our 21st Century Army.

It is well known that over the past several years we have become an Army out of balance. It is less well known but increasingly evident that we are out of balance in developing our leaders. We are out of balance in preparing our leaders for full spectrum operations. We are out of balance in building a bench of leaders not only through operational experience but also through professional military education and assignment in broadening experiences. We are out of balance in setting objectives and providing resources for our leaders to train their units at home station, at the Combat Training Centers, and while deployed. This leader development strategy seeks to restore balance and prepare for a future of full spectrum operations by introducing a series of imperatives which will become the "touchstone" for policies, processes, and resources to support our leader development programs.

It is one of the enduring strengths of our Army that throughout our nation's history we have developed leaders capable of meeting both current and future national security challenges. Yet, we must not take our past success in developing leaders for granted. Our leaders are performing superbly in combat in Iraq and Afghanistan today, but we must review and revise our leader development strategy to prepare the next generation of leaders for the complexities of the future operational environment waged across the spectrum of conflict. This requires continual adaptation.

In this leader development strategy we will discuss how our institution will adapt the way in which we develop our leaders. We will describe the challenges of the operational environment, the implications of the operational environment on leader development, and the mission, framework, characteristics, and imperatives of our strategy. Finally, we will discuss how we intend to implement this strategy.

IMPLICATIONS OF THE OPERATIONAL ENVIRONMENT ON OUR LEADER DEVELOPMENT STRATEGY

The increasing competitiveness of the future security environment suggests that we may not be able to dominate everywhere and within and across all dimensions of the spectrum of conflict as we have for the past quarter century. However, we must remain capable of dominating at times and in places of our choosing. Moreover, this increasing competiveness exists in an environment of increasing complexity requiring leaders who are confident, versatile, adaptive, and innovative. They must also function in a variety of situations against myriad threats and with a diverse set of national, allied and indigenous partners.

Such an environment demands that we develop leaders who *understand* the context of the factors influencing the military situation, *act* within that understanding, continually *assess and adapt* those actions based on the interactions and circumstances of the enemy and environment, *consolidate* tactical and operational opportunities into strategic aims, and be able to effectively *transition* from one form of operations to another. We seek to develop leaders who will thrive in this environment.

The Army and its leaders must be capable of Full Spectrum Operations (FSO) in this operational environment. We have identified three paradigm shifts in this environment that must be addressed in our leader development strategy:

The effect of complexity and time. The Army is our nation's campaign quality force. Therefore, we must prepare leaders to execute missions in extended campaigns – campaigns mean time, time means change, and change requires leaders who can anticipate change, create opportunities, and manage transitions. We must prepare our leaders for increasing "complexity" and for the challenges of operating over "extended time."

The effect of decentralization. Our adversaries will decentralize, network, and operate among the people to overcome our advantages. We are also decentralizing. As a result, at increasingly lower echelons, leaders must be able to string actions and activities together with their JIIM partners into campaigns. As we continue to modularize our force and to decentralize decision making, we must adapt our strategy to develop leaders for this increased responsibility.

The need to frame ill structured problems. In response to increasing complexity and to the shifting balance of tactical to operational art, we require leaders who are proficient in understanding and framing difficult and complex problems. We will introduce Design to complement the Military Decision Making Process (MDMP). Design provides the cognitive tools for commanders to understand and frame the ill structured problems they will encounter in this complex environment.

THE EFFECT OF INCREASING COMPLEXITY AND TIME

We have traditionally developed leaders by challenging them with "mass" and with "compressed time." Simulations were attrition based, training scenarios were designed against an enemy predictably arrayed on the battlefield, and leaders had to master the factors of time and distance. To "raise the bar" on the leader in training, we added another enemy formation or we compressed time. This was effective in developing a leader to operate in the context of well defined problems against an enemy confronting us with a single threat – generally traditional combat in attack or defend scenarios.

Now, we must develop leaders who are effective in the context of ill defined problems against an enemy likely to present us with a variety of threats. We must develop leaders by challenging them with "complexity" and "extended time." We "raise the bar" on the leader in training and education by adding the complexities of societal, religious, tribal, and economic factors – and occasionally by adding mass – and we develop leaders who can anticipate the adaptations and transitions an enemy will make during the course of an extended campaign. That is, over extended time. If, as conventional wisdom suggests, necessity is the mother of invention, then, in our terms, complexity is the mother of innovation. The task, then, is to replicate the challenges of complexity and extended time in the training environment – at schools, training centers, and home station.

It's important to note that an operational environment characterized by complexity and extended time challenges military leaders and civilian leaders alike. Institutional policies and processes optimized for a world of mass and rapid decisive campaigns against predictable peer competitors must adapt to the new norm of uncertainty and protracted conflict.

THE EFFECT OF DECENTRALIZATION

An emerging insight from our on going operations reinforced by observations in recent wargames is that the operational environment requires greater decentralization of capability and decision making authority. Stated another way, leaders at lower levels of command will assume greater responsibility for the accomplishment of the joint force commander's campaign objectives. Through modularity, we have significantly decentralized our organizational structures in response to this emerging insight. Our preparation of leaders to operate in this environment and to lead these decentralized organizations has not kept pace.

The responsibilities of the empowered and enabled leader in a decentralized environment clearly increase. As always, military leaders will be responsible for delivering military capability. However, in the operational environment we have described in this strategy, the most important insights into mission accomplishment often come from bottom up, not top down. The decentralized leader has a much greater and much more important role in assisting echelons of leaders above them to understand the "context" of their operations. Therefore, we have to decentralize, but we also have to be able to aggregate the "wisdom" of those leaders at lower echelons whom we have empowered and enabled. Moreover, our leaders must become teammates with the Joint, Interagency, Intergovernmental, and Multinational (JIIM) partners operating in the complex environment with us.

Here, too, the shifting nature of the operational environment affects development of our military and civilian leaders alike. Our Army is hierarchical by nature, but we must match tactical agility with institutional agility, and we must develop military and civilian leaders who can create an environment of collaboration and trust to promote adaptation and innovation.

Simply stated, this paradigm shift requires us to increase our commitment to leader development.

THE NEED TO FRAME ILL STRUCTURED PROBLEMS

We have learned many lessons from our eight years of wartime experience. Few would dispute the assertion that the challenges we will continue to face in this era of persistent conflict will be ill defined and multifaceted. Concurrent with this Leader Development Strategy, we will introduce the concept of Design into our doctrine (FM 5 0: The Operations Process). Design is a methodology that provides leaders with the cognitive tools to understand a problem and appreciate its complexities before seeking to solve it. Design complements the Military Decision Making Process (MDMP) and will be incorporated into leader education and training. Design will not only assist our leaders in the initial stages of campaign development but also in anticipating change, creating opportunities, and managing transitions during the course of a campaign. The creative thinking accessible to us through an appreciation of Design will be a cornerstone of our leader development strategy for both military and civilian leaders.

11

New Principles and Strategies of War

GENERAL PRINCIPLES OF WAR

The theory of warfare tries to discover how we may gain a preponderance of physical forces and material advantages at the decisive point. As this is not always possible, theory also teaches us to calculate moral factors: the likely mistakes of the enemy, the impression created by a daring action,... yes, even our own desperation. None of these things lie outside the realm of the theory and art of war, which is nothing but the result of reasonable reflection on all the possible situations encountered during a war. We should think very frequently of the most dangerous of these situations and familiarize ourselves with it. Only thus shall we reach heroic decisions based on reason, which no critic can ever shake. Any person who may present this matter differently to Your Royal Highness is a pedant, whose views will only be harmful to you. In the decisive moments of your life, in the turmoil of battle, you will some day feel that this view alone can help where help is needed most, and where a dry pedantry of figures will forsake you.

Whether counting on physical or moral advantages, we should always try, in time of war, to have the probability of victory on our side. But this is not always possible. Often we must act AGAINST this probability, SHOULD THERE BE NOTHING BETTER TO DO. Were we to despair here, we would abandon the use of reason just when it becomes most necessary, when everything seems to be conspiring against us. Therefore, even when the likelihood of success is against us, we must not think of our undertaking as unreasonable or impossible; for it is always reasonable, if we do not know of anything better to do, and if we make the best use of the few means at our disposal.

We must never lack calmness and firmness, which are so hard to preserve in time of war. Without them the most brilliant qualities of mind are wasted. We must therefore familiarize ourselves with the thought of an honorable defeat. We must always nourish this thought within ourselves, and we must get completely used to it. Be convinced, Most Gracious Master, that without this firm resolution no great results can be achieved in the most successful war, let alone in the most unsuccessful.

Certainly this thought frequently occupied the mind of Frederick II during his first Silesian wars. Because he was familiar with it he undertook his attack near Leuthen, on that memorable fifth of December, and not because he believed that his oblique formation would very likely beat the Austrians.

In any specific action, in any measure we may undertake, we always have the choice between the most audacious and the most careful solution. Some people think that the theory of war always advises the latter. That assumption is false. If the theory does advise anything, it is the nature of war to advise the most decisive, that is, the most audacious. Theory leaves it to the military leader, however, to act according to his own courage, according to his spirit of enterprise, and his selfconfidence. Make your choice, therefore, according to this inner force; but never forget that no military leader has ever become great without audacity.

TACTICS OR THE THEORY OF COMBAT

War is a combination of many distinct engagements. Such a combination may or may not be reasonable, and success depends very much on this. Yet the engagement itself is for the moment more important. For only a combination of successful engagements can lead to good results. The most important thing in war will always be the art of defeating our opponent in combat. To this matter Your Royal Highness can never turn enough attention and thought. I think the following principles the most important:

General Principles For Defense

1. To keep our troops covered as long as possible. Since we are always open to attack, except when we ourselves are attacking, we must at every instant be on the defensive and thus should place our forces as much under cover as possible.
2. Not to bring all our troops into combat immediately. With such action all wisdom in conducting a battle disappears. It is only with troops left at our disposal that we can turn the tide of battle.
3. To be little or not at all concerned about the extent of our front. This in itself is unimportant, and an extension of the front limits the depth of our formation (that is, the number of units which are lined up one behind the other). Troops which are kept in the rear are always available. We can use them either to renew combat at the same point, or to carry the fight to other neighboring points. This principle is a corollary of the previous one.
4. The enemy, while attacking one section of the front, often seeks to outflank and envelop us at the same time. The units which are kept in the background can meet this attempt and thus make up for the support usually derived from obstacles in the terrain. They are better suited for this than if they were standing in line and extending the front. For in this case the enemy could easily outflank them. This principle again is a closer definition of the second.
5. If we have many troops to hold in reserve, only part of them should stand directly behind the front. The rest we should put obliquely behind. From this position they in turn can attack the flank of the enemy columns which are seeking to envelop us.

6. A fundamental principle is never to remain completely passive, but to attack the enemy frontally and from the flanks, even while he is attacking us. We should, therefore, defend ourselves on a given front merely to induce the enemy to deploy his forces in an attack on this front. Then we in turn attack with those of our troops which we have kept back. The art of entrenchment, as Your Royal Highness expressed so excellently at one time, shall serve the defender not to defend himself more securely behind a rampart, but to attack the enemy more successfully. This idea should be applied to any passive defense. Such defense is nothing more than a means by which to attack the enemy most advantageously, in a terrain chosen in advance, where we have drawn up our troops and have arranged things to our advantage.
7. This attack from a defensive position can take place the moment the enemy actually attacks, or while he is still on the march. I can also, at the moment the attack is about to be delivered, withdraw my troops, luring the enemy into unknown territory and attacking him from all sides. The formation in depth i.e., the formation in which only twothirds or half or still less of the army is drawnup in front and the rest directly or obliquely behind and hidden, if possibleis very suitable for all these moves. This type of formation is, therefore, of immense importance.
8. If, for example, I had two divisions, I would prefer to keep one in the rear. If I had three, I would keep at least one in the rear, and if four probably two. If I had five, I should hold at least two in reserve and in many cases even three, etc.
9. At those points where we remain passive we must make use of the art of fortification. This should be done with many independent works, completely closed and with very strong profiles.
10. In our plan of battle we must set this great aim: the attack on a large enemy column and its complete

destruction. If our aim is low, while that of the enemy is high, we will naturally get the worst of it. We are pennywise and poundfoolish.

11. Having set a high goal in our plan of defense (the annihilation of an enemy column, etc.), we must pursue this goal with the greatest energy and with the last ounce of our strength. In most cases the aggressor will pursue his own aim at some other point. While we fall upon his right wing, for example, he will try to win decisive advantages with his left. Consequently, if we should slacken before the enemy does, if we should pursue our aim with less energy than he does, he will gain his advantage completely, while we shall only half gain ours. He will thus achieve preponderance of power; the victory will be his, and we shall have to give up even our partly gained advantages. If Your Royal Highness will read with attention the history of the battles of Ratisbon and Wagram, all this will seem true and important. In both these battles the Emperor Napoleon attacked with his right wing and tried to hold out with his left. The Archduke Charles did exactly the same. But, while the former acted with great determination and energy, the latter was wavering and always stopped halfway. That is why the advantages which Charles gained with the victorious part of his army were without consequence, while those which Napoleon gained at the opposite end were decisive.
12. Let me sum up once more the last two principles. Their combination gives us a maxim which should take first place among all causes of victory in the modern art of war: "Pursue one great decisive aim with force and determination."
13. If we follow this and fail, the danger will be even greater, it is true. But to increase caution at the expense of the final goal is no military art. It is the wrong kind of caution, which, as I have said already in my "General Principles," is contrary to the nature of war. For great aims we must dare great things. When we are engaged

> in a daring enterprise, the right caution consists in not neglecting out of laziness, indolence, or carelessness those measures which help us to gain our aim. Such was the case of Napoleon, who never pursued great aims in a timid or halfhearted way out of caution.

If you remember, Most Gracious Master, the few defensive battles that have ever been won, you will find that the best of them have been conducted in the spirit of the principles voiced here. For it is the study of the history of war which has given us these principles. At Minden, Duke Ferdinand suddenly appeared where the enemy did not expect him and took the offensive, while at Tannhausen he defended himself passively behind earthworks. At Rossbach, Frederick II threw himself against the enemy at an unexpected point and an unexpected moment. At Liegnitz, the Austrians found the King at night in a position very different from that in which they had seen him the previous day. He fell with his whole army upon one enemy column and defeated it before the others could start fighting.

At Hohenlinden, Moreau had five divisions in his front line and four directly behind and on his flanks. He outflanked the enemy and fell upon his right wing before it could attack.

At Ratisbon, Marshal Davout defended himself passively, while Napoleon attacked the fifth and sixth armycorps with his right wing and beat them completely.

Though the Austrians were the real defenders at Wagram, they did attack the emperor on the second day with the greater part of their forces. Therefore Napoleon can also be considered a defender. With his right wing he attacked, outflanked and defeated the Austrian left wing. At the same time he paid little attention to his weak left wing (consisting of a single division), which was resting on the Danube. Yet through strong reserves (i.e., formation in depth), he prevented the victory of the Austrian right wing from having any influence on his own victory gained on the Rossbach. He used these reserves to retake Aderklaa.

Not all the principles mentioned earlier are clearly contained in each of these battles, but all are examples of active defense.

The mobility of the Prussian army under Frederick II was a means towards victory on which we can no longer count, since the other armies are at least as mobile as we are.

On the other hand, outflanking was less common at that time and formation in depth, therefore, less imperative.

General Principles For Offense

1. We must select for our attack one point of the enemy's position (i.e., one section of his troopsa division, a corps) and attack it with great superiority, leaving the rest of his army in uncertainty but keeping it occupied. This is the only way that we can use an equal or smaller force to fight with advantage and thus with a chance of success. The weaker we are, the fewer troops we should use to keep the enemy occupied at unimportant points, in order to be as strong as possible at the decisive point. Frederick II doubtlessly won the battle of Leuthen only because he massed his small army together in one place and thus was very concentrated, as compared to the enemy.
2. We should direct our main thrust against an enemy wing by attacking it from the front and from the flank, or by turning it completely and attacking it from the rear. Only when we cut off the enemy's line of retreat are we assured of great success in victory.
3. Even though we are strong, we should still direct our main attack against one point only. In that way we shall gain more strength at this point. For to surround an army completely is possible only in rare cases and requires tremendous physical or moral superiority. It is possible, however, to cut off the enemy's line of retreat at one point of his flank and thereby already gain great success.
4. Generally speaking, the chief aim is the certainty (high probability) of victory, that is, the certainty of driving the enemy from the field of battle. The plan of battle must be directed towards this end. For it is easy to

change an indecisive victory into a decisive one through energetic pursuit of the enemy.

5. Let us assume that the enemy has troops enough on one wing to make a front in all directions. Our main force should try to attack the wing concentrically, so his troops find themselves assailed from all sides. Under these circumstances his troops will get discouraged much more quickly; they suffer more, get disorderedin short, we can hope to turn them to flight much more easily.
6. This encirclement of the enemy necessitates a greater deployment of forces in the front line for the aggressor than for the defender.

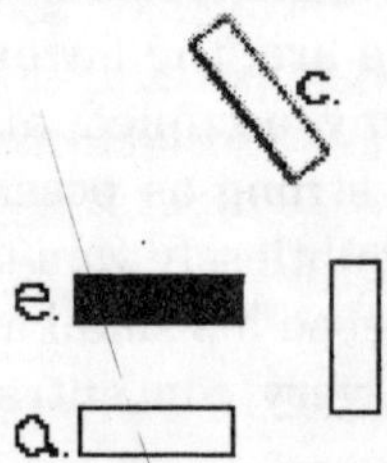

If the corps a b c should make a concentric attack on the section e of the enemy army, they should, of course, be next to each other. But we should never have so many forces in the front line that we have none in reserve. That would be a very great error which would lead to defeat, should the enemy be in the least prepared for an encirclement.

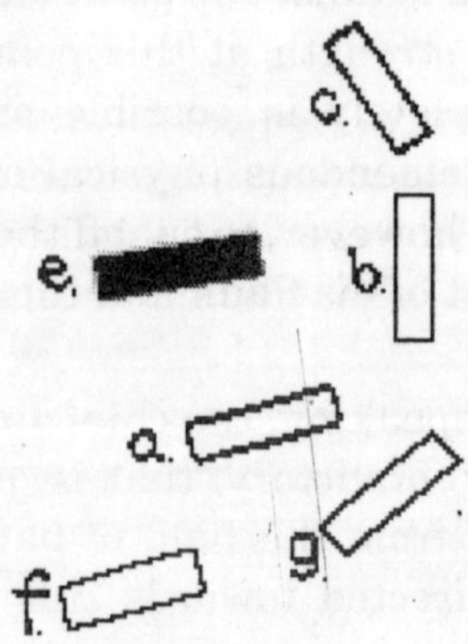

If a b c are the corps which are to attack section e, the corps f and g must be held in reserve. With this formation in depth we are able to harass the same point continuously. And in case our troops should be beaten at the opposite end of the line, we do not need to give up immediately our attack at this end, since we still have reserves with which to oppose the enemy. The French did this in the battle of Wagram. Their left wing, which opposed the Austrian right wing resting on the Danube, was extremely weak and was completely defeated. Even their center at Aderklaa was not very strong and was forced by the Austrians to retreat on the first day of battle. But all this did not matter because Napoleon had such depth on his right wing, with which he attacked the Austrian left from the front and side. He advanced against the Austrians at Aderklaa with a tremendous column of cavalry and horseartillery and, though he could not beat them, he at least was able to hold them there.

7. Just as on the defensive, we should choose as the object of our offensive that section of the enemy's army whose defeat will give us decisive advantages.
8. As in defense, as long as any resources are left, we must not give up until our purpose has been reached. Should the defender likewise be active, should he attack us at other points, we shall be able to gain victory only if we surpass him in energy and boldness. On the other hand, should he be passive, we really run no great danger.
9. Long and unbroken lines of troops should be avoided completely. They would lead only to parallel attacks, which today are no longer feasible.

   Each division makes its attack separately, though according to the directions of a higher command and thus in agreement with each other. Yet one division (8,000 to 10,000 men) is never formed into one single line, but into two, three, or even four. From this it follows that a long unbroken line is no longer possible.

10. The concerted attacks of the divisions and army corps should not be obtained by trying to direct them from a central point, so that they maintain contact and even align themselves on each other, though they may be far apart or even separated by the enemy. This is a faulty method of bringing about cooperation, open to a thousand mischances. Nothing great can be achieved with it and we are certain to be thoroughly beaten by a strong opponent.

    The true method consists in giving each commander of an army corps or a division the main direction of his march, and in pointing out the enemy as the objective and victory as the goal.

    Each commander of a column, therefore, has the order to attack the enemy wherever he may find him and to do so with all his strength. He must not be made responsible for the success of his attack, for that would lead to indecision. But he is responsible for seeing that his corps will take part in battle with all its energy and with a spirit of selfsacrifice.

11. A wellorganized, independent corps can withstand the best attack for some time (several hours) and thus can not be annihilated in a moment. Thus, even if it engaged the enemy prematurely and was defeated, its fight will not have been in vain. The enemy will unfold and expend his strength against this one corps, offering the rest a good chance for an attack.

    The way in which a corps should be organized for this purpose will be treated later.

    We therefore assure the cooperation of all forces by giving each corps a certain amount of independence, but seeing to it that each seeks out the enemy and attacks him with all possible selfsacrifice.

12. One of the strongest weapons of offensive warfare is the surprise attack. The closer we come to it, the more fortunate we shall be. The unexpected element which the defender creates through secret preparations and

through the concealed disposition of his troops, can be counterbalanced on the part of the aggressor only by a surprise attack.

Such action, however, has been very rare in recent wars, partly because of the more advanced precautionary measures, partly because of the rapid conduct of campaigns. There seldom arises a long suspension of activities, which lulls one side into security and thus gives the other an opportunity to attack unexpectedly. Under these circumstancesexcept for nightly assaults which are always possible (as at Hochkirch) we can surprise our opponent only by marching to the side or to the rear and then suddenly advancing again. Or, should we be far from the enemy, we can through unusual energy and activity arrive faster than he expects us.

13. The regular surprise attack (by night as at Hochkirch) is the best way to get the most out of a very small army. But the aggressor, who is not as well acquainted with the terrain as the defender, is open to many risks. The less well one knows the terrain and the preparations of the enemy, the greater these risks become. In many instances, therefore, these attacks must be considered only as desperate means.
14. This kind of attack demands simpler preparations and a greater concentration of our troops than in the daytime.

FUNDAMENTALS OF MILITARY STRATEGY

Strategy and tactics are closely related. Both deal with distance, time and force but strategy is large scale while tactics are small scale. Originally strategy was understood to govern the prelude to a battle while tactics controlled its execution. However, in the world wars of the 20th century, the distinction between maneuver and battle, strategy and tactics, became blurred. Tactics that were once the province of a company of cavalry would be applied to a panzer army. It is often said that the art of strategies defines the goals to achieve in a military campaign, while tactics defines the methods to achieve these goals. Strategic goals could be "We want to conquer area X", or "We want to stop country Y's expansion in world trade in commodity Z"; while tactical decisions range from "We're going to do this by a naval invasion of the North of country X", "We're going to blockade the ports of country Y", all the way down to "C Platoon will attack while D platoon provides fire cover".

In its purest form, strategy dealt solely with military issues. In earlier societies, a king or political leader was often the same person as the military leader. If he was not, the distance of communication between the political and the military leader was small. But as the need of a professional army grew, the bounds between the politicians and the military came to be recognized. In many cases, it was decided that there was a need for a separation. As French statesman Georges Clemenceau said, "war is too important a business to be left to soldiers." This gave rise to the concept of the grand strategy which encompasses the management of the resources of an entire nation in the conduct of warfare.

In the environment of the grand strategy, the military component is largely reduced to operational strategythe planning and control of large military units such as corps and divisions. As the size and number of the armies grew and the technology to communicate and control improved, the difference between "military strategy" and "grand strategy" shrank.

Fundamental to grand strategy is the diplomacy through which a nation might forge alliances or pressure another nation into compliance, thereby achieving victory without resorting to combat. Another element of grand strategy is the management of the postwar peace. As Clausewitz stated, a successful military strategy may be a means to an end, but it is not an end in itself. There are numerous examples in history where victory on the battlefield has not translated into long term peace, security or tranquility.

PRINCIPLES OF MILITARY STRATEGY

Many military strategists have attempted to encapsulate a successful strategy in a set of principles. Sun Tzu defined 13 principles in his The Art of War while Napoleon listed 115 maxims. American Civil War General Nathan Bedford Forrest required only one: "to git thar furst with the most men". The fundamental concepts common to most lists of principles are:

1. The Objective
2. Offense
3. Cooperation
4. Concentration (Mass)
5. Economy
6. Manoeuvre
7. Surprise
8. Security
9. Simplicity

Which are reflected in the United States Army's United States Army Field Manual (FM3) of Military Operations (sections 432 to 439) as:

1. Objective (Direct every military operation towards a clearly defined, decisive, and attainable objective)
2. Offensive (Seize, retain, and exploit the initiative)
3. Mass (Concentrate combat power at the decisive place and time)
4. Economy of Force (Allocate minimum essential combat power to secondary efforts)
5. Maneuver (Place the enemy in a disadvantageous position through the flexible application of combat power)
6. Unity of Command (For every objective, ensure unity of effort under one responsible commander)
7. Security (Never permit the enemy to acquire an unexpected advantage)
8. Surprise (Strike the enemy at a time, at a place, or in a manner for which he is unprepared)
9. Simplicity (Prepare clear, uncomplicated plans and clear, concise orders to ensure thorough understanding)

Some strategists assert that adhering to the fundamental principles guarantees victory while others claim war is unpredictable and the general must be flexible in formulating a strategy. Field Marshal Count Helmuth von Moltke expressed strategy as a system of "ad hoc expedients" by which a general must take action while under pressure. These underlying principles of strategy have survived relatively unscathed as the technology of warfare has developed.

Strategy (and tactics) must constantly evolve in response to technological advances. A successful strategy from one era tends to remain in favor long after new developments in military weaponry and matériel have rendered it obsolete. World War I, and to a great extent the American Civil War, saw Napoleonic tactics of "offense at all costs" pitted against the defensive power of the trench, machine gun and barbed wire. As a reaction to her WWI experience, France entered World War II with a purely defensive doctrine, epitomized by the "impregnable" Maginot Line, but only to be completely circumvented by the German blitzkrieg.

STRATEGIES FOR WAR

The 20th century has seen veritable successive 'revolutions' in warfare, starting with the advent of air power in World War I, and cemented by aircraft carriers further extending this reach across the oceans by World War II. This was followed by the introduction of nuclear weapons, development of nuclear warfighting doctrines, growth of missile and electronic warfare, and a move towards increasing coordination and jointness between the single Services. In the last two decades, technological advances have provided near realtime situational awareness and minimal sensorshooter cycle, even as the reach, accuracy and lethality of modern weapons have attained unprecedented levels. Over this period, the 'ways and means' of war have undergone constant transformation. The ends for which war was waged have also expanded, from territorial ambitions to increasing geostrategic spheres of influence, to pursuit of religiousideological conflicts, and again a reversion towards safeguarding of territorial and socioeconomic interests. The nature of war, as seen through its ways, means and ends, has probably traversed its largest arc of change in the last 100 years.

The evolutionary trends of war led to several assessments, even before 9/11, of the emerging nature of 21st century warfare.

This was appreciated as being more diverse and divisive, with the ways, means and ends of war continuing to change, along with traditional rationale and actors, and expectations of a transmutation of conflict, from total to limited war, from interstate to intrastate war, and from regular, structured warfare to irregular warfare. Wars of choice were assessed to more likely dominate the 21st century, with significant effort required to keep them limited amidst a danger of cascading effect upon wider areas in the world.

The tragic events of 9/11 and the ensuing wars against (and by) terrorism have exemplified these earlier estimates and the wider spectrum of modern war.

In the constant evolution of the nature of war, it is reasonable to expect that changes would be reflected in revision of not only the doctrines of warfighting, but also the underlying Principles of War (PoW). However, whilst warfighting doctrines have undergone significant changes in the last two decades, there has been little debate on the corresponding evolution of the PoW, which provide the (conceptual) foundation for building these warfighting doctrines. A review of the prevailing PoW, in the light of the current nature and spectrum of war, would reveal significant deficiencies and point out the revisions necessary for the principles to have continued relevance in the 21st century.

The PoW have been codified from the time of Sun Tzu, and evolved/refined by Napoleon, Clausewitz, J.F.C. Fuller, and thence given institutionalised definition and interpretation by various nations and militaries. The fact that there is still no consensus on a single list of PoW underscores the complexities in addressing war across time and space.

Fair degree of commonality in the list and understanding of the PoW amongst the various nations, though some emphases and nuances would naturally vary. In the modern spectrum of war, however, some of these principles appear excessively focussed on conventional, unlimited, war, and do not adequately cover the imperatives of other forms of war, such as limited conventional war and subconventional war, which are both more widespread and more likely in the postCold War geostrategic environment. Conventional limited wars are restricted in aim, scope and methods, and may require a broader canvas and interpretation of the PoW to meet their specific requirements. Subconventional war, where at least one actor is a nonstate and the war is characterised by an irregular and covert fabric such as for terrorism, militancy, insurgency, proxy war and civil war, may also need a more flexible interpretation of the PoW, especially since such warfare may take place in own territory and impose limitations on the applicability of the PoW.

However, even this would be more relevant for fighting against subconventional forces, rather than in the waging of such form of warfare, since the latter is the domain of mostly nonstate actors who do not follow established norms and laws of war. Hence, full application of the PoW to them would remain tenous. Some of the existing PoW, with slight amendments, would retain their validity in this context, even whilst others may be seen to suffer from limitations in addressing the wider spectrum of modern war.

The principle of Selection and Maintenance of Aim is the primary PoW, which entails that the desired 'endstate' must be clearly defined and selection of the attainable aim done after careful costbenefit analysis, keeping in mind the resources available. More often than not, this principle has been interpreted in purely military terms (since it is, after all, a principle of 'war'). But, accepting the Clausewitzian precept that war is an extension of politics by other means, the issue of politics can never be separated from the military objective. Military aims would have to be situated in the political purpose for the use of force. In the era of 'total wars,' the selection and maintenance of aim/objective was relatively simpler, with full national resources being devoted to the war and all costs deemed acceptable, since the purpose was survival on one side and 'unconditional surrender' or annihilation on the other. But the nature of war itself has been changing, with total, unlimited war becoming a considerably lesser viable option.

In an increasingly globalised and interdependent world, political restraints (including those of domestic pressures) would have a major influence in the way war can be waged, and what sort of endstate can be achieved. This is even more critical for countries that possess nuclear weapons. It can be argued that 'asymmetric warfare' has emerged primarily because of the politicomilitary restraints in an information age. The problem is that the 'endstate' is becoming less easy to define. For example, the war against global terrorism might seek to rid the world of the scourge of terrorism. But it obviously remains unachievable without a major politicalideological campaign of ideas.

Nuclear weapon states, in particular, have to seriously rethink the issue of military objectives and aims. Warfighting with nuclear weapons would defeat the very logic of war as a rational instrument of policy since it would destroy the very object it seeks to gain. Similarly, even a conventional war between nuclear weapon states would require redefinition of the traditional concepts of victory and defeat. Risk of escalation to nuclear weapons use can nullify what might have been seen as a 'decisive' military victory in a nonnuclear weapon environment.

This has wideranging implications for the way wars can be fought. But, from the point of view of this examination, the critical point is that the very concept of 'victory' would need to be redefined in a war using conventional weapons and forces under a nuclear overhang. Countries placed in such situations would either have to avoid a direct war (as indeed the two superpowers did during the Cold War), or plan and fight a limited war (e.g. SinoRussian border war 1969, and IndoPak Kargil War 1999). The former, avoidance of direct war, had led to the use of proxy wars; while the latter permits only a war with limited objectives. It is not surprising, therefore, that China has adopted a military doctrine of "local, border war under hightech conditions." This, in turn, would require far greater synergy between political aims and military goals. The military aim of modern war may accordingly require refinement, with consequent shift in focus onto attaining key objective areas that signify political victory or provide the postwar political leverage for conflict resolution, rather than seeking 'decisive' military victory as defined in the past.

In the case of fighting insurgency/militancy/terrorism, the military objective may need to be similarly attuned to the political purpose, and limited to providing the modicum of security necessary for generating movement towards a politicoeconomic solution.

An excessively ambitious aim, such as "stamping out all violent opposition" or "overthrow of the state" through the use of military force is more likely to fuel that very violence, and also provide nonstate actors with an image of victory even if they merely survive or avoid total military defeat. This has been evinced in the ongoing Iraq War, where the desire to crush militant opposition has been faulted as an inappropriate and inapplicable politicomilitary aim and military strategy, and has probably instead contributed to deterioration of the security environment, rather than provide stability for attaining the political objectives.

The nature of modern warfare emphasises the need to synergise military objectives with political goals, with an inherent recognition of the fact that the latter could change frequently and demand similar readjustment of military objectives and strategy. Such continued synergy was demonstrated in the IndoPak Kargil War 1999, where Indian political desire to limit the war to the Indian side of the Line of Control (LoC) was supported by a military strategy to "containevictdeny," and included political clearance for use of air power in India's own territory.

Inversely, political goals may also be affected by the military situation, and require reorientation according to the military gains or losses in order to derive the best 'endstate' possible, as seen in the IndiaPakistan War 1971, where the capture of Dhaka was reportedly not part of the original aim.

Hence, while "Selection and Maintenance of Aim" as a PoW remains at the core of modern warfare, its application has undergone significant change with the need for maintaining greater and constant synergy with the political purpose of the war, particularly in the case of limited and subconventional wars. Accordingly, the "aim" in the earlier Principle of War needs a more comprehensive and representative interpretation to encompass both political and military aims and, most importantly, the maintenance of synergy between them. The revisions in interpretation warrant a more appropriate term, such as Maintenance of Synergy in PoliticoMilitary Aims. The principle of Offensive Action, which is often held as the chief means of achieving victory, entails control over the purpose, scope, intensity and pace of operations, and retention of initiative at all times. This places a premium on early action, even preemption. But the nature of subconventional warfare, especially terrorism, inherently provides early initiative to the nonstate actor. Preemptive action here is difficult, and may well prove counterproductive, such as in the case of faulty intelligence, or due to collateral damage in the apparent absence of adequate justification. This would push the civil populace to favour the nonstate actors, as partly experienced in the current Iraq War, and provide strategiclevel backlash for tactical actions. In such cases, a higher level of own security and rapid response capability would serve the war aims better than focus on offensive action per se. In the case of conventional limited war, with an inherently higher premium on preemption, there may be less scope for regaining the offensive or dictating fresh parameters against preemptive strike, within the limitations of time, area, scale and methods available.

This was seen in the IndoPak War in Kargil, 1999, wherein any Indian attempt to develop military offensive action beyond the tactical level purely on military logic could have escalated the war to the detriment of the war's politicostrategic objective. Hence, the view that offensive action per se is the means to attaining the initiative and freedom of action, and positive results thereby, needs adjustment. In the available technological environment, and ongoing technodoctrinal focus on rapid response capability, the requirement is not so much on maintaining offensive action, but rather on the maintenance and exploitation of Freedom of Action (FoA) by a variety of measures, since the latter would provide broader options and initiative for decisive, including offensive, action.

Freedom of Action has, accordingly, become a core principle across the spectrum of modern warfare, with the requirements extending from its attainment and maintenance for own forces, across all levels and dimensions of war, to the disruption and denial of similar freedom to the opponent. Freedom of Action would need to cover the various dimensions of war, viz. land, sea, air and information. This would also entail the exploitation of own Freedom of Action by the employment of offensive doctrines, such as attainment and utilisation of favourable situation or air superiority, sea control, command of the air/ sea, information superiority, escalation control/dominance, etc. The development and exploitation of Freedom of Action in all dimensions and theatres/battlefields would require the support of robust physical and information security, sound logistics and administration, exercise of mobility, maintenance of initiative, suitable deployment of offensive forces, etc. Each of these aspects would need to be addressed in the military doctrines flowing from the overarching PoW, of maintenance and exploitation of Freedom of Action. It stands to reason that the side losing freedom of action would thereby lose its ability to influence the conduct of the war, and be forced to constantly react to the exercise of corresponding freedom by the opponent.

The principle of Mass/Concentration of Force is viewed as the concentration of combat power at the decisive time and place, to achieve decisive results. This principle has been highly valued, from SunTzu through Napoleon to World War II, wherein it denoted the destructive power of a force. The principle of mass providing a distinct advantage is perhaps embedded in Napoleon's supposed remarks that even God is on the side of the bigger battalions! Mass, no doubt, denoted the killing power of a force, seen essentially in terms of quantity. This was the logic that gave the Roman Phalanx its distinct advantage in battle, and why modern militaries still look at a 3:1 favourable ratio of forces as a doctrinal parameter for successful offensive action. But, if viewed more closely, what we can observe is that killing power as a function of mass was true when the quantum of killing power in a unit element of force was limited. Hence, to maximise the overall impact of killing power, mass and concentration of force became a necessary principle. In substance, since the accuracy, rate of fire, and range of the manmachine combination that produced the weapon system was limited, this was sought to be compensated by concentrating combat power, so that the friendly force could kill the maximum number of enemy forces/weapon systems. In battlefields that were concentrated in space, mass also provided enhanced moral power because of the emotional psychological support derived from a greater number of friendly forces.

Generation of mass, whether by massing more soldiers or by dispensing more projectiles onto the target, remained intrinsically important because of the limitations of range, target location and acquisition, accuracy and lethality of weapons, and the friction in war (that Clausewitz talked of). This also placed limits on the quantum of combat power that could be concentrated in time and space. In reality, however, the foundations of this principle started getting eroded with the advancement of technology. For example, the carnage at Verdun in World War I demonstrated how even a single machine gun could concentrate more firepower in the hands of a single soldier than what was possible earlier. Advances in military technology have been rapidly altering the traditional aggregative relation between quantum of forces and their combat power. Nowhere has this been more obvious than in the advent of air power, which provided the means to outflank the enemy from the third dimension. This changed the battlefield completely, and rendered the surface forces vulnerable except through acquiring a counter outflanking capability with their own air power.

Even here, technological changes have determined a continuous expansion of the 'engagement zone', which itself challenges the traditional concept of concentration of force, as brought about by advances in air power. One element of this was airtoair warfare becoming allweather with beyond visual range (BVR) capability soon after the end of World War II. However, employment of air power against surface targets remained limited to what was essentially 'lineofsight' targeting till recently, when improvements in targeting technology have enabled the application of combat power by diverse and geographically separated force elements. Space capabilities are expected to further expand this envelope, and in fact have already done so in the form of surveillance and information warfare, e.g. target spotting by an unmanned aerial vehicle (UAV), its classification and targeting by a centre possibly in another continent, and prosecution by a cruise missile launched from a submarine in another theatre, more than 1,000 km away. Expansion of the battlefield along with compression of time has provided a totally different dimension to concentration of combat power in time and space compared to what the principle of mass/concentration of force conveys. In determining the nature of change in this principle, we need to revisit the purpose of concentration of force and augmentation of combat power. Simply, this was to attain a certain destructive effect, wherein the massing of force appeared to provide the best means for attaining this end.

Consequently, this assumed the status of a PoW. The impact of advanced weapon technologies in terms of range, accuracy and lethality, synergised with parallel advancements in sensor and command and control (C_2) technologies, has led to a situation wherein firepowereffect, as a derivative of cosmbat power, is no longer a summation of the mass of forces. All other things being equal, and leaving the intangibles like morale, etc. out of consideration for the time being, effective combat power could be denoted normatively by the equation:

Combat Power CP = Q x D x M

where Q is Quantity,

D is Destructive Power (a combination of range, accuracy and lethality) per unit weapon, and

M is Mobility (or manoeuvre to enable concentration in time and space)

It is obvious that if D, the destructive power of the force (weapon/soldier) is low, then Q, the quantity of force needed, would have to be high. In other words, a greater mass would be necessary to maintain the requisite combat power as constant. But, where D is higher, and M is developed, the Q quotient could be much lower, i.e. concentration of force would not be required, as the requisite combat power was being applied by the other components. The applicability of the above can be seen even in World War II, wherein the combination of German Panzer Divisions and aerial dive bombers in the Blitzkrieg in France, and Allied "thousand bomber raids" over Germany, were examples of augmenting combat power through enhancing Mobility, Destructive Power and Quantity, respectively.

The recent wars in Iraq and Afghanistan have further demonstrated the applicability of the above, wherein requisite combat power was attained with a lesser concentration of forces than would have been the case earlier, by a corresponding increase in precision strike, destructive power and mobility of the forces used. This fact has also been evident throughout military history, where lesser numbers of higher range and accuracy weapons, with higher rates of fire and speed of delivery, have habitually prevailed against larger concentration of opposing forces, due to their relatively higher concentration of firepower.

But, since the weapons and systems in most wars, including the Napoleonic and two World Wars, tended to be comparable for the opposing sides, concentration of forces was perceived as providing the decisive edge, whereas it was actually the concentration of firepower enabled by the massing of forces that was responsible for this effect. In other words, it was the Q+Q, that is (Quality +Quantity) paradigm (both of firepower and manpower) that held the key.

The distinction is important today, when advanced military technologies have led to provision of unprecedented levels of discriminate destructive power in small elements of force, which can be delivered more accurately, at longer ranges, and in smaller timeframes, upon the desired target. The source of that firepower could be naval, air or land power, which is also the central logic for joint operations. The most recent and dramatic example in support of the need to replace the existing principle of mass/concentration of force to one of concentration of firepower is to be found in the Iraq War where the United States reversed the traditionally accepted force ratios necessary for offensive action completely on their head.

Similarly, the United States employed forces widely dispersed across the globe, ranging from home bases to warships and aircraft carriers, and special forces operating with missiles, UAVs, space assets, etc. in the 200102 War in Afghanistan, so as to bring firepower concentrated on specific tactical targetseven employing B52 strategic bombers for close air support missions with the barest minimum military force deployed on land. This did not mean that the principle of concentration of force per se was ignored, but that its effect was attained through concentration of effective firepower, independent of the position and number of weapon firing platforms rather than from the aggregation of combat power platforms in time and space. Today, two B2s can provide the same effect, through accurate delivery of firepower, which required 50 B52s a decade ago, and 1,000 bombers in World War II.

Modern battlefields are expanding in space, even as they are contracting in time, due to the speed and reach of modern firepower. Hence, there will continue to be greater dispersion of forces, especially amongst naval and air platforms. This would seem to violate the principle of concentration of force, as understood hitherto. However, there is no contradiction if the principle is viewed instead as Concentration of Firepower, with its components being the emulative effect of the Quantity, Destructive Power and Mobility paradigm.

Economy of Effort is the principle requiring forces to be judiciously employed so as to maximise the effect of available resources, including through apportionment of resources between the main and secondary efforts. This has been seen as an adjunct to the principle of Concentration of Force (or firepower, as suggested above), and the focus is on the availability of forces. The core, however, relies on attaining the maximum effect for available resources, which also provides the conceptual foundation for the modern doctrine of "EffectsBased Operations." Hence, it may be more appropriate to view this principle instead as the Attainment of Effect, i.e. expand the current understanding from merely fullest use of available forces, to production of the desired effect through best employment of these resources, including by development of different strategies/tactics. For example, guerrilla warfare was developed in response to the adversary's superior force and firepower, wherein it neutralised own inferiority by exploiting potential strengths in relation to the prevailing environment (jungles, mountains, and now also urban areas). This, and also terrorist methods of waging war, such as 9/11 or the Madrid bombings, are not adequately covered under the principle of Economy of Force/Effort, but would be well supported by a shift in focus on production of effect using available resources. The relation between "Effect" and 'Force" may be considered as an equation:

E = F x S

Where E is Effect,

F is Force/Firepower, and

S is Strategy

Thus, while the old principle of Economy of Effort sought to maximise the effect for a given force, it inherently accepted that this maximum effect need not correspond to what was required. This was in consonance with wars being 'total' or unlimited, where the emphasis was on maximum effective utilisation, rather than on utilisation for maximum (desired) effect. However, by shifting focus on attaining the desired effect, rather than on economising the effort, we emphasise the goal more than the means.

Thus, the earlier 'economy' of effort would correspond to the component of strategy in the above equation, as a means to attaining the goal. However, strategy would also have other components, and not just judicious employment of forces. Effect could also be achieved by enhancing the firepower and other strategy quotients. Hence, attainment of effect would provide a more useful principle. The principle of Flexibility has been replaced by Manoeuvre, Initiative and/or Mobility by some countries. The principle is looked at in both active and reactive manner, leading to different interpretations and terms used by various nations. For example the US definition of manoeuvre is more active, in that it entails placing the enemy at disadvantage through the flexible application of own combat power at the strategic, operational and tactical levels of war. The Indian Army Doctrine is, however, somewhat reactive, in that it deems flexibility as the capability to react appropriately to changing situations.

The Indian Maritime Doctrine is a mix of both, and views flexibility as the capacity to cope with a rapidly changing situation and seize fleeting opportunities, wherein it entails both physical mobility and reaction capability, with the latter accruing from planning, staffwork and the commander's mental outlook.

In the various definitions/interpretations, we can see two themes: first, the ability to respond to change and, second, the ability to impose change. In essence, the principle of Flexibility/ Manoeuvre/Initiative/Mobility all look at the Management of Change, both in imposition upon the enemy, by the use of manoeuvre and 'flexible' application of combat power, and in reacting to change that is imposed by the enemy or that occurs otherwise.

The purpose, in both cases, is to derive advantage from a change in situation that could occur or be created by either side. The change may occur in the various dimensions of war, i.e. through forces arrayed on land, sea or air, and also at the various levels of warfare, viz. tactical, operational or strategic.

Thus, change may be introduced by the application or redeployment of physical forces in the three dimensions, by the timing of executing change, and also by the very rate of change. In fact, the rate of change or pace/tempo of battle is increasingly being recognised as a key factor in introducing and exploiting vulnerabilities in the enemy's Information Decision Action (IDA) Cycle, also leading to suggestions of time becoming an independent dimension of war.

The 'manoeuvrist' concept of warfare, espoused in the UK Joint Warfare Doctrine, also envisages application of multiple lines of operation, in physical dimensions, at a higher speed and tempo, so as to overwhelm the enemy's mental and moral capability to cope/respond.

DEVELOPMENT OF MILITARY STRATEGY

Early Military Strategy

The principles of military strategy can be found as far back as 500 BC in the works of Sun Tzu and Chanakya. The campaigns of Alexander the Great, Chandragupta Maurya, Hannibal, Qin Shi Huang, Julius Cæsar, Zhuge Liang, and Khalid ibn alWalid demonstrate strategic planning and movement. Mahan describes in the preface to The Influence of Sea Power upon History how the Romans used their sea power to effectively block the sea lines of communication of Hannibal with Carthage; and so via a maritime strategy achieved Hannibal's removal from Italy, despite never beating him there with their legions.

In 1520 Niccolò Machiavelli's Dell'arte della guerra (Art of War) dealt with the relationship between civil and military matters and the formation of the grand strategy. In the Thirty Years' War, Gustavus Adolphus of Sweden demonstrated advanced operational strategy that led to victories in Holy Roman Empire area.

It was not until the 18th century that military strategy was subjected to serious study. In the Seven Years' War (17561763), Frederick the Great improvised a "strategy of exhaustion" to hold off his opponents and conserve his Prussian forces. Assailed from all sides by France, Austria, Russia and Sweden, Frederick exploited his central position which enabled him to move his army along interior lines and concentrate against one opponent at a time. Unable to achieve victory, he was able to stave off defeat until a diplomatic solution was reached. Frederick's "victory" led to great significance being placed on "geometric strategy" which emphasized lines of manoeuvre, awareness of terrain and possession of critical strongpoints.

Genghis Khan and the Mongols

As a counterpoint to European developments in the strategic art, the Mongol Emperor Genghis Khan provides a useful example. Genghis' successes, and those of his successors, were based upon manoeuvre and terror. The point of Genghis' strategic assault was nothing less than the psychology of the opposing population. By a steady and meticulous implementation of this strategy, Genghis and his descendants were able to conquer most of Eurasia.

The building blocks of Genghis' army and his strategy were his tribal levies of mounted archers and (just as important) the vast horseherds of Mongolia. Each archer had at least one extra horse; (it was an average five horses per man) thus the entire army could move with incredible rapidity. Moreover since horse milk and horse blood were the staples of the Mongolian diet, Genghis' horseherds functioned not just as his means of movement but also as his logistical tail. All other necessities could be foraged and plundered. It was not until well into the 20th century that any army was able to match the rapidity of deployment of Genghis' armies. Compared to the armies of Genghis, all other armies were heavy and comparatively immobile. Through manoeuver and continuous assault, Chinese, Persian, Arab and Eastern European armies could be stressed until they broke, and then annihilated in pursuit.

When confronted with a fortified city, the Mongol imperatives of manoeuver and speed required that it be quickly subdued. Here the fear engendered by the awful reputation of the Mongolians helped. So too did primitive biological warfare. A trebuchet or other type of ballista weapon would be used to launch dead animals and corpses into a barricaded city, spreading disease and death among the inhabitants. If a particular town or city displeased the Mongolian Khan, everyone in the city would be killed to set an example for all other cities. This could be called a form of psychological warfare.

Note that of the above list of strategic terms, even this elementary summary indicates that the Mongols strategy was directed towards an objective (that schwerpunkt (main focus) being nothing less than the psychology of the opposing population) achieved through the offensive; the offensive was characterized by concentration of forces, manoeuvre, surprise and simplicity.

Napoleonic Strategy

The French Revolution and the Napoleonic Wars that followed revolutionized military strategy. The impact of this period was still to be felt in the American Civil War and the early phases of World War I. With the advent of cheap small arms and the rise of the drafted citizen soldier, armies grew rapidly in size to become massed formations. This necessitated dividing the army first into divisions and later into corps. Along with divisions came divisional artillery; lightweight, mobile and with great range and firepower. The rigid formations of pikemen and musketeers firing massed volleys gave way to light infantry fighting in skirmish lines.

Napoleon I of France took advantage of these developments to pursue a brutally effective "strategy of annihilation" that cared little for the mathematical perfection of the geometric strategy. Napoleon invariably sought to achieve decision in battle, with the sole aim of utterly destroying his opponent, usually achieving success through superior manouevre. As ruler and general he dealt with the grand strategy as well as the operational strategy, making use of political and economic measures.

While not the originator of the methods he used, Napoleon very effectively combined the maneuver and battle stages into one event. Before this, General Officer had considered the approach to battle a separate event. However, Napoleon used the maneuver to battle to dictate how and where the battle would progress. The Battle of Austerlitz was a perfect example of this maneuver. Napoleon withdrew from a strong position to draw his opponent forward and tempt him into a flank attack, weakening his center. This allowed the French army to split the allied army and gain victory.

Napoleon used two primary strategies for the approach to battle. His "Maneuver De Derrière" was intended to place the French Army across the enemy's lines of communications. This forced the opponent to either march to battle with Napoleon or attempt to find an escape route around the army. By placing his army into the rear, his opponents supplies and communications would be cut. This had a negative effect on enemy morale. Once joined, the battle would be one in which his opponent could not afford defeat. This also allowed Napoleon to select multiple march routes into a battle site. Initially, the lack of force concentration helped with foraging for food and sought to confuse the enemy as to his real location and intentions. This strategy, along with the use of forced marches created a morale bonus that played heavily in his favor.

The "indirect" approach into battle also allowed Napoleon to disrupt the linear formations used by the allied armies. As the battle progressed enemy committed their reserves to stabilize the situation, Napoleon would suddenly release the flanking formation to attack the enemy. His opponents, being suddenly confronted with a new threat and with little reserves, had no choice but to weaken the area closest to the flanking formation and draw up a battle line at a right angle in an attempt to stop this new threat. Once this had occurred, Napoleon would mass his reserves at the hinge of that right angle and launch a heavy attack to break the lines. The rupture in the enemy lines allowed Napoleon's cavalry to flank both lines and roll them up leaving his opponent no choice but to surrender or flee.

The second strategy used by Napoleon I of France when confronted with two or more enemy armies was the use of the central position. This allowed Napoleon to drive a wedge to separate the enemy armies. He would then use part of his force to mask one army while the larger portion overwhelmed and defeated the second army quickly. He would then march on the second army leaving a portion to pursue the first army and repeat the operations. This was designed to achieve the highest concentration of men into the primary battle while limiting the enemy's ability to reinforce the critical battle. The central position had a weakness in that the full power of the pursuit of the enemy could not be achieved because the second army needed attention. So overall the preferred method of attack was the flank march to cross the enemies logistics. Napoleon used the central position strategy during the Battle of Waterloo Hundred Days. Napoleon masked Arthur Wellesley, 1st Duke of Wellington and massed against the Prussian army, and then after the Ligny battle was won, Napoleon attempted to do the same to the Allied/English army located just to the south of Waterloo. His subordinate was unable to mask the defeated Prussian army, who reinforced the Waterloo battle in time to defeat Napoleon and end his domination of Europe. It can be said that the Prussian Army under Gebhard Leberecht von Blücher used the "maneuver de derrière" against Napoleon who was suddenly placed in a position of reacting to a new enemy threat.

Napoleon's practical strategic triumphs, repeatedly leading smaller forces to defeat larger ones, inspired a whole new field of study into military strategy. In particular, his opponents were keen to develop a body of knowledge in this area to allow them to counteract a masterful individual with a highly competent group of officers, a General Staff. The two most significant students of his work were Carl von Clausewitz, a Prussian with a background in philosophy, and AntoineHenri Jomini, who had been one of Napoleon's staff officers. Clausewitz's On War has become the bible of strategy, dealing with political, as well as military, leadership. His most famous assertion being:

> *"War is not merely a political act, but also a real political instrument, a continuation of policy carried out by other means."*

Clausewitz dismissed "geometry" as an insignificant factor in strategy, believing instead in the Napoleonic concept of victory through battle and destruction of the opposing force, at any cost. However, he also recognized that limited warfare could influence policy by wearing down the opposition through a "strategy of attrition".

In contrast to Clausewitz, AntoineHenri Jomini dealt mainly with operational strategy, planning & intelligence, the conduct of the campaign, and "generalship" rather than "statesmanship". He proposed that victory could be achieved by occupying the enemy's territory rather than destroying his army. As such, geometric considerations were prominent in his theory of strategy. Jomini's two basic principles of strategy were to concentrate against fractions of the enemy force at a time and to strike at the most decisive objective.

One notable exception to Napoleon's strategy of annihilation and a precursor to trench warfare were the Lines of Torres Vedras during the Peninsular campaign. French Armies lived off the land and when they were confronted by a line of fortifications which they could not out flank, they were unable to continue the advance and were forced to retreat once they had consumed all the provisions of the region in front of the lines.

The Peninsular campaign was notable for the development of another method of warfare which went largely unnoticed at the time, but would become far more common in the 20th century. That was the aid and encouragement the British gave to the Spanish to harass the French behind their lines which led them to squander most of the assets of their Iberian army in protecting the army's line of communications. This was a very cost effective move for the British, because it cost far less to aid Spanish insurgents than it did to equip and pay regular British army units to engage the same number of French troops. As the British army could be correspondingly smaller it was able to supply its troops by sea and land without having to live off the land as was the norm at the time. Further, because they did not have to forage they did not antagonise the locals and so did not have to garrison their lines of communications to the same extent as the French did. So the strategy of aiding their Spanish civilian allies in their guerrilla or 'small war' benefited the British in many ways, not all of which were immediately obvious.

APPLICATION OF THESE PRINCIPLES IN TIME OF WAR

The principles of the art of war are in themselves extremely simple and quite within the reach of sound common sense. Even though they require more special knowledge in tactics than in strategy, this knowledge is of such small scope, that it does not compare with any other subject in extent and variety. Extensive knowledge and deep learning are by no means necessary, nor are extraordinary intellectual faculties. If, in addition to experienced judgment, a special mental quality IS required, it would be, after all that has been said cunning or shrewdness. For a long time the contrary has been maintained, either because of false veneration for the subject or because of the vanity of the authors who have written about it. Unprejudiced reflection should convince us of this, and experience only makes this conviction stronger. As recently as the Revolutionary War we find many men who proved themselves able military leaders, yes, even military leaders of the first order, without having had any military education. In the case of Condé, Wallenstein, Suvorov, and a multitude of others it is very doubtful whether or not they had the advantage of such education.

The conduct of war itself is without doubt very difficult. But the difficulty is not that erudition and great genius are necessary to understand the basic principles of warfare. These principles are within the reach of any wellorganized mind, which is unprejudiced and not entirely unfamiliar with the subject. Even the application of these principles on maps or on paper presents no difficulty, and to have devised a good plan of operations is no great masterpiece. The great difficulty is this:

To Remain Faithful Throughout To The Principles We Have Laid Down For Ourselves.

To call attention to this difficulty is the purpose of these closing remarks, and to give Your Royal Highness a clear idea of it I consider the most important object of this essay.

The conduct of war resembles the workings of an intricate machine with tremendous friction, so that combinations which are easily planned on paper can be executed only with great effort. The free will and the mind of the military commander, therefore, find themselves constantly hampered, and one needs a remarkable strength of mind and soul to overcome this resistance. Many good ideas have perished because of this friction, and we must carry out more simply and moderately what under a more complicated form would have given greater results.

It may be impossible to enumerate exhaustively the causes of this friction; but the main ones are as follows:

1. Generally we are not nearly as well acquainted with the position and measures of the enemy as we assume in our plan of operations. The minute we begin carrying out our decision, a thousand doubts arise about the dangers which might develop if we have been seriously mistaken in our plan. A feeling of uneasiness, which often takes hold of a person about to perform something great, will take possession of us, and from this uneasiness to indecision, and from there to half measures are small, scarcely discernible steps.
2. Not only are we uncertain about the strength of the enemy, but in addition rumor (i.e., all the news which we obtain from outposts, through spies, or by accident) exaggerates his size. The majority of people are timid by nature, and that is why they constantly exaggerate danger. All influences on the military leader, therefore, combine to give him a false impression of his opponent's strength, and from this arises a new source of indecision.

   We cannot take this uncertainty too seriously, and it is important to be prepared for it from the beginning.

   After we have thought out everything carefully in advance and have sought and found without prejudice the most plausible plan, we must not be ready to abandon it at the slightest provocation. On the contrary, we must be prepared to submit the reports which reach us to careful criticism, we must compare them with each other, and send out for more. In this way false reports are very often disproved immediately, and the first reports confirmed. In both cases we gain certainty and can make our decision accordingly. Should this certainty be lacking, we must tell ourselves that nothing is accomplished in warfare without daring; that the nature of war certainly does not let us see at all times where we are going; that what is probable will always be probable though at the moment it may not seem so; and finally, that we cannot be readily ruined by a single error, if we have made reasonable preparations.

3. Our uncertainty about the situation at a given moment is not limited to the conditions of the enemy only but of our own army as well. The latter can rarely be kept together to the extent that we are able to survey all its parts at any moment, and if we are inclined to uneasiness, new doubts will arise. We shall want to wait, and a delay of our whole plan will be the inevitable result.

   We must, therefore, be confident that the general measures we have adopted will produce the results we expect. Most important in this connection is the trust which we must have in our lieutenants. Consequently, it is important to choose men on whom we can rely and to put aside all other considerations. If we have made appropriate preparations, taking into account all possible misfortunes, so that we shall not be lost immediately if they occur, we must boldly advance into the shadows of uncertainty.

4. If we wage war with all our strength, our subordinate commanders and even our troops (especially if they are not used to warfare) will frequently encounter difficulties which they declare insurmountable. They find the march

too long, the fatigue too great, the provisions impossible. If we lend our ear to all these DIFFICULTIES, as Frederick II called them, we shall soon succumb completely, and instead of acting with force and determination, we shall be reduced to weakness and inactivity.

To resist all this we must have faith in our own insight and convictions. At the time this often has the appearance of stubbornness. but in reality it is that strength of mind and character which is called firmness.

5. The results on which we count in warfare are never as precise as is imagined by someone who has not carefully observed a war and become used to it.

   Very often we miscalculate the march of a column by several hours, without being able to tell the cause of the delay. Often we encounter obstacles which were impossible to foresee. Often we intend to reach a certain place with our army and fall short of it by several hours. Often a small outpost which we have set up achieves much less than we expected, while an enemy outpost achieves much more. Often the resources of a region do not amount to as much as we expected, etc.

   We can triumph over such obstacles only with very great exertion, and to accomplish this the leader must show a severity bordering on cruelty. Only when he knows that everything possible is always being done, can he be sure that these small difficulties will not have a great influence on his operations. Only then can he be sure that he will not fall too far short of the aim which he could have reached.

6. We may be sure that an army will never be in the condition supposed by someone following its operations from an armchair. If he is sympathetic to the army he will imagine it from a third to a half stronger and better than it really is. It is quite natural that the military commander will make the same mistake in planning his first operations. Consequently, he will see his army

melt away as he never thought it would, and his cavalry and artillery become useless. What appeared possible and easy to the observer and to the commander at the opening of a campaign is often difficult and even impossible to carry out. If the military leader is filled with high ambition and if he pursues his aims with audacity and strength of will, he will reach them in spite of all obstacles; while an ordinary person would have found in the condition of his army a sufficient excuse for giving in.

Masséna proved at Genoa and in Portugal the influence of a strongwilled leader over his troops. At Genoa, the limitless exertion to which his strength of will, not to say his harshness, forced people, was crowned with success. In Portugal he at least retreated later than anyone else would have.

Most of the time the enemy army is in the same position. For example, Wallenstein and Gustavus Adolphus at Nuremberg, and Napoleon and Bennigsen after the battle of Eylau. But while we do not see the condition of the enemy, our own is right before our eyes. The latter, therefore, makes a greater impression on ordinary people than the first, since sensuous impressions are stronger for such people than the language of reason.

7. The provisioning of troops, no matter how it is done, whether through storehouses or requisitions, always presents such difficulty that it must have a decisive influence on the choice of operations. It is often contrary to the most effective combination, and forces us to search for provisions when we would like to pursue victory and brilliant success. This is the main cause for the unwieldiness of the whole war machine which keeps the results so far beneath the flight of our great plans.

A general, who with tyrannical authority demands of his troops the most extreme exertions and the greatest privations, and an army which in the course of long wars has become hardened to such sacrifices will have a tremendous advantage over their adversaries and will reach their aim much faster in spite of all obstacles. With equally good plans, what a difference of result!

8. We cannot stress the following too much: Visual impressions gained during actual combat are more vivid than those gained beforehand by mature reflection. But they give us only the outward appearance of things, which, as we know, rarely corresponds to their essence. We therefore run the risk of sacrificing mature reflection for first impression.

The natural timidity of humans, which sees only one side to everything, makes this first impression incline toward fear and exaggerated caution. Therefore we must fortify ourselves against this impression and have blind faith in the results of our own earlier reflections, in order to strengthen ourselves against the weakening impressions of the moment.

These difficulties, therefore, demand confidence and firmness of conviction. That is why the study of military history is so important, for it makes us see things as they are and as they function. The principles which we can learn from theoretical instruction are only suited to facilitate this study and to call our attention to the most important elements in the history of war. Your Royal Highness, therefore, must become acquainted with these principles in order to check them against the history of war, to see whether they are in agreement with it and to discover where they are corrected or even contradicted by the course of events. In addition, only the study of military history is capable of giving those who have no experience of their own a clear impression of what I have just called the friction of the whole machine.

Of course, we must not be satisfied with its main conclusions, and still less with the reasoning of historians, but we must penetrate as deeply as possible into the details. For the aim of historians rarely is to present the absolute truth. Usually they wish to embellish the deeds of their army or to demonstrate the concordance of events with their imaginary rules. They invent history instead of writing it. We need not study much history for the purpose we propose. The detailed knowledge of a few individual engagements is more useful than the general knowledge of a great many campaigns. It is therefore more useful to read detailed accounts and diaries than regular works of history. An example of such an account, which cannot be surpassed, is the description of the defense of Menin in 1794, in the memoirs of General von Scharnhorst. This narrative, especially the part which tells of the sortie and break through the enemy lines, gives Your Royal Highness an example of how to write military history. No battle in history has convinced me as much as this one that we must not despair of success in war until the last moment. It proves that the influence of good principles, which never manifests itself as often as we expect, can suddenly reappear, even under the most unfortunate circumstances, and when we have already given up hope of their influence.

A powerful emotion must stimulate the great ability of a military leader, whether it be ambition as in Caesar, hatred of the enemy as in Hannibal, or the pride in a glorious defeat, as in Frederick the Great. Open your heart to such emotion. Be audacious and cunning in your plans, firm and persevering in their execution, determined to find a glorious end, and fate will crown your youthful brow with a shining glory, which is the ornament of princes, and engrave your image in the hearts of your last descendants.

STRATEGY

This term means the combination of individual engagements to attain the goal of the campaign or war. If we know how to fight and how to win, little more knowledge is needed. For it is easy to combine fortunate results. It is merely a matter of experienced judgment and does not depend on special knowledge, as does the direction of battle.

The few principles, therefore, which come up in this connection, and which depend primarily on the condition of the respective states and armies, can in their essential parts be very briefly summarized:

General Principles

Warfare has three main objects:

(a) To conquer and destroy the armed power of the enemy;

(b) To take possession of his material and other sources of strength, and

(c) To gain public opinion.

To accomplish the first purpose, we should always direct our principal operation against the main body of the enemy army or at least against an important portion of his forces. For only after defeating these can we pursue the other two objects successfully.

In order to seize the enemy's material forces we should direct our operations against the places where most of these resources are concentrated: principal cities, storehouses, and large fortresses. On the way to these objectives we shall encounter the enemy's main force or at least a considerable part of it.

Public opinion is won through great victories and the occupation of the enemy's capital.

The first and most important rule to observe in order to accomplish these purposes, is to use our entire forces with the utmost energy. Any moderation shown would leave us short of our aim. Even with everything in our favor, we should be unwise not to make the greatest effort in order to make the result perfectly certain. For such effort can never produce negative results. Suppose the country suffers greatly from this, no lasting disadvantage will arise; for the greater the effort, the sooner the suffering will cease.

The moral impression created by these actions is of infinite importance. They make everyone confident of success, which is the best means for suddenly raising the nation's morale.

The second rule is to concentrate our power as much as possible against that section where the chief blows are to be delivered and to incur disadvantages elsewhere, so that our chances of success may increase at the decisive point. This will compensate for all other disadvantages.

The third rule is never to waste time. Unless important advantages are to be gained from hesitation, it is necessary to set to work at once. By this speed a hundred enemy measures are nipped in the bud, and public opinion is won most rapidly.

Surprise plays a much greater role in strategy than in tactics. It is the most important element of victory. Napoleon, Frederick II, Gustavus Adolphus, Caesar, Hannibal, and Alexander owe the brightest rays of their fame to their swiftness. Finally, the fourth rule is to follow up our successes with the utmost energy. Only pursuit of the beaten enemy gives the fruits of victory.

The first of these rules serves as a basis for the other three. If we have observed it, we can be as daring as possible with the last three, and yet not risk our all. For it provides us with the means of constantly creating new forces in our rear, and with fresh forces any misfortune can be remedied.

Therein lies the caution which deserves to be called wise, and not in taking each step forward with timidity.

Small states cannot wage wars of conquest in our times. But in defensive warfare even the means of small states are infinitely great. I am, therefore, firmly convinced that if we spare no effort to reappear again and again with new masses of troops, if we use all possible means of preparation and keep our forces concentrated at the main point, and if we, thus prepared, pursue a great aim with determination and energy, we have done all that can be done on a large scale for the strategic direction of the war. And unless we are very unfortunate in battle we are bound to be victorious to the same extent that our opponent lags behind in effort and energy.

In observing these principles little depends on the form in which the operations are carried out. I shall try, nevertheless, to make clear in a few words the most important aspects of this question.

In tactics we always seek to envelop that part of the enemy against which we direct our main attack. We do this partly because our forces are more effective in a concentric than in a parallel attack, and further because we can only thus cut off the enemy from his line of retreat. But if we apply this to the whole theater of war (and consequently to the enemy's lines of communication), the individual columns and armies, which are to envelop the enemy, are in most cases too far away from each other to participate in one and the same engagement. The opponent will find himself in the middle and will be able to turn against the corps one by one and defeat them all with a single army. Frederick II's campaigns may serve as examples, especially those of 1757 and 1758.

The individual engagement, therefore, remains the principal decisive event. Consequently, if we attack concentrically without having decisive superiority, we shall lose in battle all the advantages, which we expected from our enveloping attack on the enemy. For an attack on the lines of communication takes effect only very slowly, while victory on the field of battle bears fruit immediately.

In strategy, therefore, the side that is surrounded by the enemy is better off than the side which surrounds its opponent, especially with equal or even weaker forces.

Colonel Jomini was right in this, and if Mr. von Bülow has demonstrated the opposite with so much semblance of truth, it is only because he attributed too great an importance to the interruption of provisions and carelessly and completely denied the inevitable success of battle.

To cut the enemy's line of retreat, however, strategic envelopment or a turning movement is very effective. But we can achieve this, if necessary, through tactical envelopment. A strategic move is, therefore, advisable only if we are so superior (physically and morally) that we shall be strong enough at the principal point to dispense with the detached corps.

The Emperor Napoleon never engaged in strategic envelopment, although he was often, indeed almost always, both physically and morally superior.

Frederick II used it only once, in 1757, in his invasion of Bohemia. To be sure, the result was that the Austrians could not give battle until Prague, and what good was the conquest of Bohemia as far as Prague without a decisive victory? The battle of Kolin forced him to give up all this territory again, which proves that battles decide everything. At the same time he was obviously in danger at Prague of being attacked by the whole Austrian force, before Schwerin arrived. He would not have run this risk had he passed through Saxony with all his forces. In that case the first battle would have been fought perhaps near Budin, on the Eger, and it would have been as decisive as that of Prague. The dislocation of the Prussian army during the winter in Silesia and Saxony undoubtedly caused this concentric maneuver. It is important to notice that circumstances of this kind are generally more influential than the advantages to be gained by the form of attack. For facility of operations increases their speed, and the friction inherent in the tremendous warmachine of an armed power is so great in itself that it should not be increased unnecessarily.

Moreover, the principle of concentrating our forces as much as possible on the main point diverts us from the idea of strategic envelopment and the deployment of our forces follows automatically. I was right, therefore, in saying that the form of this deployment is of little consequence. There is, however, one case in which a strategic move against the enemy's flank will lead to great successes similar to those of a battle: if in a poor country the enemy has accumulated with great effort stores of supplies, on whose preservation his operations absolutely depend. In this case it may be advisable not to march our main forces against those of the enemy, but to attack his base of supply. For this, however, two conditions are essential:

(a) The enemy must be so far from his base that our threat will force him into a considerable retreat, and

(b) We must be able to obstruct his advance in the direction followed by his principal force with only a few troops (thanks to natural and artificial obstacles), so that he cannot make conquests somewhere else which will compensate for the loss of his base.

The provisioning of troops is a necessary condition of warfare and thus has great influence on the operations, especially since it permits only a limited concentration of troops and since it helps to determine the theater of war through the choice of a line of operations.

The provisioning of troops is carried on, if a region possibly permits it, through requisitions at the expense of the region.

In the modern method of war armies take up considerably more territory than before. The creation of distinct, independent corps has made this possible, without putting ourselves at a disadvantage before an adversary who follows the old method of concentration at a single point (with from 70,000 to 100,000 men). For an independent corps, organized as they now are, can withstand for some time an enemy two or three times its superior. Then the others will arrive and, even if the first corps has already been beaten, it has not fought in vain, as we have had occasion to remark. Today, therefore, the divisions and corps move into battle independently, marching side by side or behind each other and only close enough to take part in the same battle, if they belong to the same army.

This makes possible immediate provisioning without storehouses. The very organization of the corps with their General Staff and their Commissariat facilitates this. If there are no MORE decisive motives (as for example the location of the enemy's main army), we choose the most fertile provinces for our operations; for facility of provisioning increases the speed of our actions. Only the situation of the enemy's main force which we are seeking out, only the location of his capital and the place of arms which we wish to conquer are more important than provisioning. All other considerations, such as the advantageous disposition of our forces, of which we have already spoken, are as a rule much less important.

In spite of these new methods of provisioning, it is quite impossible to do without any depots whatever. Therefore, even when the resources of the region are quite sufficient, a wise military leader does not fail to establish depots in his rear for unexpected emergencies and in order to be able to concentrate his forces at certain points. This precaution is of the sort which are not taken at the expense of the final goal.

Defensive

Politically speaking defensive war is a war which we wage for our independence. Strategically it is the kind of campaign in which we limit ourselves to fighting the enemy in a theater of war which we have prepared for this purpose. Whether the battles which we wage in this theater of war are offensive or defensive, makes no difference. We adopt a strategic defensive mainly when the enemy is superior. Fortresses and entrenched camps, which constitute the chief preparations for a theater of war, afford, of course, great advantages, to which may be added the knowledge of the terrain and the possession of good maps. A smaller army, or an army which is based on a smaller state and more limited resources, will be better able to withstand the enemy WITH these advantages than without them.

In addition there are the following two reasons which can lead us to choose a defensive war.

First, when the regions surrounding the theater of war render operations extremely difficult because of lack of provisions. In this case we avoid a disadvantage which the enemy is forced to undergo. This is the case now (1812) with the Russian army. Second, when the enemy is superior in warfare. In a theater of war which we have prepared, which we know, and in which all minor conditions are in our favor, war is easier to conduct, and we commit fewer mistakes. When lack of trust in our troops and generals forces us to wage defensive war, we often like to combine tactical with strategic defensive. In that case we fight battles in prepared positions because we are thus again exposed to fewer mistakes.

In defensive just as in offensive warfare, it is necessary to pursue a great aim: the destruction of the enemy army, either by battle or by rendering its subsistence extremely difficult. Thus we shall disorganize it and force it into a retreat, during which it will necessarily suffer great losses. Wellington's campaign in 1810 and 1811 is a good example.

Defensive warfare, therefore, does not consist of waiting idly for things to happen. We must wait only if it brings us visible and decisive advantages. That calm before the storm, when the aggressor is gathering new forces for a great blow, is most dangerous for the defender.

If the Austrians after the battle of Aspern had increased their forces threefold, as they might have and as the Emperor Napoleon did, then and only then would they have made good use of the lull which lasted until the battle of Wagram. This they did not do, and consequently the time was lost. It would have been wiser to profit from Napoleon's disadvantageous position, and to gather the fruits of the battle of Aspern.

The purpose of fortifications is to keep a considerable part of the enemy's army occupied as siege troops, to give us an opportunity to defeat the rest of his army. Consequently, it is best to fight our battles behind our fortifications and not in front of them. But we must not stand by idly, while they are being conquered, as Bennigsen did during the siege of Danzig.

Large rivers, across which it is difficult to throw a bridge (such as the Danube below Vienna and the Lower Rhine), offer a natural line of defense. But we should not distribute our forces evenly along the river bank in order to prevent any crossing whatsoever. That would be most dangerous. On the contrary, we should watch the river and fall upon the enemy from all sides the minute he crosses, while he has not yet reassembled his forces and is still restricted to a narrow space on the river bank. The battle of Aspern offers a good illustration. At Wagram the Austrians had yielded to the French too much territory without the slightest necessity, so that the disadvantages inherent in a river crossing had disappeared.

Bibliography

Anil. C.K. : *Military and Democracy in South Asia : Challenges, Politics and Power*, Sumit Enterprises, Delhi, 2009.

Backman, Jules. *War and Defense Economics.* New York: Rinehart, 1952.

Bellamy, C.: *Knights in White Armour: The New Art of War and Peace*, London, Random House, 1997.

Benedict, Murray Reed, *Farm Policies of the United States, 1790-1950.* New York: Twentieth Century Fund, 1953.

Burnham, John. *Total War: The Economic Theory of a War Economy.* Boston: Meador Publishing Company, 1943.

Clayton, James L. *The Economic Impact of the Cold War: Sources and Readings.* New York, 1970.

Connery, Robert H. *The Navy and Industrial Mobilization in World War II.* Princeton, N.J., 1951.

Davies.A.: *Telecommunications and Politics. The Secentralised Alternative*, London, Pinter, 1994.

Digumarti Bhaskara Rao: *Military Conversion : Impact on Science and Technology*, Discovery, Delhi, 2003.

Duscha, Julius. *Arms, Money and Politics.* New York, 1965.

Ellis, John. *World War II: A Statistical Survey: The Essential Facts and Figures for all the Combatants.* New York: Facts on File, 1993.

Greider, William. *Fortress America: The American Military and the Consequences of Peace.* New York, 1998.

Grey, Jeffrey. *The Commonwealth Armies and the Korean War: An Alliance Study.* (1988).

Gunnar Myrdal: *Asian Drama; An Inquiry into the Poverty of Nations.* New York: Random House, 1968.

Huntington, S.P.: *The China Modernisation Military and the State*, N.Y., Vintage Books, 1964.

Johnston, William. *A War of Patrols: Canadian Army Operations in Korea* (2003).

Kapur, C.K. : *Chinese Military Modernisation*, Manas, Delhi, 2003.

Lamb, Alastair: *The China-India Border: The Origins of the Disputed Boundaries*. L. Oxford University Press, 1964.

Lens, Sidney, *Military-Industrial Complex*. Philadelphia: Prigrim Press, 1970.

Mary, W.: *Asian Power and Politics: the Cultural Dimensions of Authority*, Cambridge, Belknap Press, 1985.

Melman, Seymour. *Pentagon Capitalism: The Political Economy of War*. New York, 1970.

Milward, Alan S. *War, Economy and Society, 1939-1945*. Berkeley: University of California Press, 1977.

Moulton, Harold Glenn. *Fundamental Economic Issues in National Defense*. Washington, DC: Brookings Institution, 1941.

Posen, B.R.: *The Sources of Military Doctrine*, Ithaca, 1984, Cornell Univ. Press.

Raj Kumar: *Weapons and Military Technology*, Sumit Enterprises, Delhi, 2009.

Ramesh, J.: *Making Sense of Chindia: Reflections on China and India*. New Delhi, India Research Press, 2005.

Roll, Eric. *Combined Food Board: A Study in Wartime International Planning*. Stanford: Stanford University Press, 1956.

Rosen, P.: *Societies and Military Power: India and its Armies*, Ithaca, Cornell University Press, 1996.

Rowland, J.: *A History of Sino-Indian Relations: Hostile Co-existence*. London, D. Van Nostrand Company, 1967.

Singh, R.S.N. : *Asian Strategic and Military Perspective*, Lancer, Delhi, 2005.

Strahan, Jerry E. *Andrew Jackson Higgins and the Boats That Won World War II*. Baton Rouge: Louisiana State University Press, 1994.

Thayer, George. *The War Business: The International Trade in Armaments*. New York, 1969.

Vatter, Harold G. *U.S. Economy in World War II*. New York: Columbia University Press, 1985.

Index

□□□